Tokyo

Tokyo

Memory, Imagination, and the City

Edited by
Barbara E. Thornbury
Evelyn Schulz

LEXINGTON BOOKS
Lanham • Boulder • New York • London

Published by Lexington Books
An imprint of The Rowman & Littlefield Publishing Group, Inc.
4501 Forbes Boulevard, Suite 200, Lanham, Maryland 20706
www.rowman.com

Unit A, Whitacre Mews, 26-34 Stannary Street, London SE11 4AB

Copyright © 2018 by Lexington Books

All rights reserved. No part of this book may be reproduced in any form or by any electronic or mechanical means, including information storage and retrieval systems, without written permission from the publisher, except by a reviewer who may quote passages in a review.

British Library Cataloguing in Publication Information Available

Library of Congress Cataloging-in-Publication Data Available

ISBN 978-1-4985-2367-7 (cloth : alk. paper)
ISBN 978-1-4985-2368-4 (electronic)

∞™ The paper used in this publication meets the minimum requirements of American National Standard for Information Sciences Permanence of Paper for Printed Library Materials, ANSI/NISO Z39.48-1992.

Printed in the United States of America

Contents

Introduction   vii
    Barbara E. Thornbury and Evelyn Schulz

1. Pulling the Thorns of Suffering: Remembering Sugamo in Itō Hiromi's "The Thorn-Puller"   1
    Jeffrey Angles

2. Pavane for a Dead Princess, or Exploring Geographies of the City, the Mind, and the Social: Fujita Yoshinaga's *Tenten* and Miki Satoshi's *Adrift in Tokyo*   25
    Kristina Iwata-Weickgenannt

3. On Möbius Strips, Ruins, and Memory: The Intertwining of Places and Times in Hino Keizō's Tokyo   45
    Mark Pendleton

4. Mapping Environments of Memory, Nostalgia, and Emotions in "Tokyo Spatial (Auto)biographies"   69
    Evelyn Schulz

5. Held Hostage to History: Okuda Hideo's "Olympic Ransom"   97
    Bruce Suttmeier

6. The Tokyo Cityscape, Sites of Memory, and Hou Hsiao-Hsien's *Café Lumière*   117
    Barbara E. Thornbury

7. Remaking Tayama Katai's *Futon* in Nakajima Kyōko's *FUTON*: Remembrance and Renewal of Urban Space through the Art of Rewriting   137
    Angela Yiu

8 The Child of Memory: Cityscapes in Tsushima Yūko's Short
   Fiction of the 1980s 159
   Eve Zimmerman

Index 179

About the Editors and Contributors 187

Introduction

Barbara E. Thornbury and Evelyn Schulz

The Meiji Restoration in 1868 brought an end to the Tokugawa shoguns' two-and-a-half-century hegemony and marked the formation of Japan as a modern nation-state with Tokyo as its capital. Known as Edo until the Restoration, the city has consolidated its role as the central locus where multiple discourses on Japanese national identity and history are generated and interact. Tokyo as it is experienced today is mapped with numerous mnemonic sites that represent its multilayered past. They are locations where critical narratives of nation-building, modernity, and globalization continue to take shape—and deleted or buried narratives of the city and its people are being resuscitated. A maze of spatial memory archives, Tokyo embodies places of identity as well as alterity.

Tokyo: Memory, Imagination, and the City is a collection of eight essays written by scholars of Japanese studies based in England, Germany, Japan, and the United States. By looking at Tokyo urban space from the perspective of memory in works of the imagination—novels, short stories, poetry, essays, and films—we hope to open up new ways of thinking about the city. The book's focus is on texts produced in Japan since the 1980s. The closing years of the Shōwa period (1926–1989) were a watershed decade of spatial transformation in Tokyo. It was also a time (in Japan, as elsewhere) when conversations about the nature of memory—historical, cultural, collective, and individual—intensified. The contributors to the volume share the view that works of the imagination are constitutive elements of how cities are experienced and perceived. Each of the essays responds to the growing interest in (and, we think, helps fill the need for) studies on Tokyo with a literary-cultural orientation.

MEMORY AND THE CITY

In his introduction to *Urban Memory: History and Amnesia in the Modern City*, Mark Crinson captures what we, too, mean by "urban memory" as it relates to Tokyo: "Urban memory can be an anthropomorphism (the city having a memory) but more commonly it indicates the city as a physical landscape and collection of objects and practices that enable recollections of the past and that embody the past through traces of the city's sequential building and rebuilding" (2005, xii). Twice massively destroyed (by earthquake and war) and rebuilt during the twentieth century—and, for decades now, willingly tearing down and rebuilding in the name of progress—Tokyo today is a place where objects of recollection are perhaps fewer and harder to recognize than those of other major cities. "Whatever vestiges of Edo had survived the Restoration," James White points out, "vanished" after the 1923 Great Kantō Earthquake (2011, 16). Some decades later, Tokyo, like other Japanese cities, Carola Hein notes, rose "from the utter destruction of the Second World War with astounding speed" leaving behind "few direct reminders of the war" (2003, 1)—and, it can be added, few direct reminders of the city as it existed prior to that time. Tokyo, as scholars repeatedly point out, "is notably bereft of physical monuments. Collective memories, yes; monuments, no" (White 2011, 21). Tokyo is even notably bereft of the not-so-monumental structures (such as historic buildings) that symbolize and make visible the city's past. What Tokyo does have in abundance is works of the imagination that are both the product of and the embodiment of memory—and can be counted among the "practices that enable recollections of the past" that are a key part of Crinson's definition of urban memory. In spatial terms, such texts probe deeply into every corner of Tokyo to find and reveal the city's sites of memory, to borrow historian Pierre Nora's suggestive phrase *lieux de mémoire* (1996–1998 [1984–1992])—and, by doing so, themselves become metaphorical sites of memory.

In its subject matter and theoretical approach, "Memory and City: Port B and the Tokyo Olympics," a chapter in Peter Eckersall's book *Performativity and Event in 1960s Japan: City, Body, Memory*, provided a model for our project. In it, Eckersall reveals ways in which the theatre director and actor Takayama Akira (b. 1969) and his Tokyo-based troupe Port B "explores how the layers of history remain in the present as a kind of substratum that can be made visible and be critically evaluated through the medium of contemporary arts" (2013, 134). Looking specifically at Takayama's 2007 performance piece *Tōkyō/Orinpikku* (trans. *Tokyo/Olympics*), Eckersall writes that it "reactivates a sense of historical awareness among audiences and cuts a swathe through the socio-political terrain of the city of Tokyo" (Ibid., 139). *Tokyo/Olympics* was structured as an actual tour of 1964 Tokyo Olympics-related sites, "taking audiences [by bus] to places where memories of the past and the archeology of the present might be found in a kind of dialogue about the city then and now" (Ibid., 146).

The texts on which our chapters focus have an analogous effect, taking people—through words printed in books and images recorded on film—to different parts of the city where dialogues between the past and present take place. In Tokyo, which is now preparing to host the 2020 Olympics, the 1964 Olympic games "have long been a subject of complicated acts of memory" (Ibid., 150)—which is also the topic of a chapter in this volume that looks at Okuda Hideo's 2008 novel *Orinpikku no minoshirokin* ("Olympic Ransom"). Again, to quote Eckersall:

> *Tokyo/Olympics* figures our sense of temporality to give a sense of the past sitting alongside and in immediate contrast with the globalizing present-day world. By placing bodies into local spaces and emphasizing the contrast between the global postmodern city and the broken fragments of a city *living in the past*, *Tokyo/Olympics* works against the inevitability of a globalizing flattening out of history and culture . . . [and] can be read as a corporeal recuperation of the disconnected threads of history. . . . In *Tokyo/Olympics*, place and time become more blended and, perhaps contradictorily, more interrupted. Something other than what one normally expects is produced from this cracking open of history. Small moments . . . glossed over by the intensity of the past are revived in the present. The point is not to measure everything but to make it visible to the imagination. . . . *Tokyo/Olympics* can be understood as a work particularizing daily experiences of space and history. (Ibid., 158)

As the following chapters show, Tokyo is replete with all sorts of memories. The memories are individual, calling forth and shaping stories about lives spent in the city. And, they are collective, drawing their lifeblood from historical events that took place in or affected the culture of the city—perhaps not directly experienced by the writers and directors whose work is discussed, but nevertheless remembered by them in different ways. Within the chapters there are references, for example, to Tokyo's Edo past, the 1923 earthquake, the wartime air raids, Japan's colonization of Taiwan, the postwar Occupation, the 1964 Olympics, and the bubble- and post-bubble eras. All of us as contributors to this project proceed from the assumption that "[m]emory is not a simple record of events but a dynamic process that always transforms what it dredges up from its depths" (Obrist 2014, 57).

TOKYO SINCE THE EIGHTIES

The chapters in this book look at work that emerged against the backdrop of "world city Tokyo"—which is to say, Tokyo of the 1980s and the years that have since followed. The bursting of the asset bubble in the early nineties temporarily slowed, but did not stop, the spatial remaking of Tokyo—in response to which numerous writers and artists have felt, and continue to feel, the need to foreground memory in their work.[1] "The transformation of Japanese cities in the last thirty years—and more especially over the last fifteen years—has been dramatic," Paul Waley wrote in an article published in 2013. The observation applies most notably to Tokyo.

> Not only have skyscrapers come to predominate in city center areas, but high-rise residential buildings now pepper the previously low-rise suburbs. This change has been effected principally through creeping, and often less-than-transparent easing of regulations on building heights, but it has been accompanied by a powerful rhetoric establishing the advantages of high-rise cities set within the framework of a weak public realm, strong private property rights, and a growing culture of business-led urban restructuring. (46)

The economic and social processes implied by the terms modernization and globalization are the wellspring feeding the rapid changes to Tokyo's urban fabric. White amalgamates the wording of several scholars when he says that "Tokyo is a city of 'plasticity and fluidity,' 'never finished,' 'always in flux,' 'in a permanent state of construction'" (2011, 29).[2] Proof abounds in buildings and developments across the city, including skyline-altering structures such as the Skytree communication tower, which was completed in 2012, and Mori Tower, the centerpiece of the Roppongi Hills residential-hotel-retail-office complex that opened in 2003.[3] Manifestations of history and memory are continually erased by progress-driven urban planning—as they were, to be sure, by the catastrophic 1923 earthquake and the firebombing that took many lives and destroyed much of the city in the last two years of the Second World War.

The bursting of Japan's economic bubble in the early 1990s marks a significant turning point in the perception and depiction of Tokyo. Dystopian images of growing inequality and precariousness have arisen to challenge postwar visions of economic growth and their promise of prosperity for everyone. Economists not only speak of the "lost decade" of the 1990s but of a lost two-and-a-half decades, during which Japan has failed to find sustainable solutions for its social and economic problems. In Tokyo, there is growing interest in making the city more livable and homelike. There is a palpable longing for the temporal and spatial situatedness implied by the Japanese word *furusato*—with its sense of belonging, permanence, and home. As seen in television shows, films, and all manner of publications, nostalgic appreciation of the urban culture of the Edo (or Tokugawa) period (1603–1868) and of the everyday culture of the Shōwa era is a well-established trend. Certain Tokyo neighborhoods (one thinks immediately of Yanaka, for instance) are prized as places where "old Tokyo" still survives. Such relatively quiet neighborhoods, to which visitors flock in search of picturesque, old-fashioned wooden houses and small, locally owned shops and restaurants, are counterweights to the accelerated rhythms of urban life. They suggest a belongingness that thwarts the dominant image of Tokyo as a monumental megacity of speed, alienation, and amnesia. They are considered places of resistance to the rapid growth of Tokyo and its efficient chronopolitics (Radović, Jager, and Beyerle 2008; Schulz 2013).

ADMINISTRATIVE AND GEOGRAPHIC TOKYO

At 13.5 million people, the population of the Tokyo Metropolis is equivalent to 11% of Japan's total. One of Japan's forty-seven prefectures, the metropolis comprises the twenty-three wards (more precisely, "special wards" [*tokubetsu ku*]) of central Tokyo; the twenty-six cities, three towns, and one village of the "suburban" Tama area that stretches west of the city center; and the Izu and Ogasawara island chains in the Pacific Ocean at a distance from the rest of the prefecture. Around 9.24 million people live in the ward area, 4.22 million in Tama, and just 26,000 in the islands. Tokyo's neighbors are Saitama Prefecture to the north, Chiba Prefecture to the east, Kanagawa Prefecture to the south, and Yamanashi Prefecture to the west. What is officially called the Tokyo Megalopolis Region (also referred to as Greater Tokyo), which includes the Tokyo Metropolis and Saitama, Chiba, and Kanagawa Prefectures, takes in 30% of Japan's total population—some thirty-eight million people (Tokyo Metropolitan Government 2017).[4]

The chapters in this volume focus almost exclusively on locations within the central part of Tokyo. In 1943, "Tokyo City" (today's twenty-three-ward area) was merged into the Tokyo Metropolis. The offices of the Tokyo Metropolitan Government (which administers the entire metropolis) are in Shinjuku Ward, housed in buildings that include the instantly recognizable, forty-eight-floor, doubled-towered high-rise designed by architect Tange Kenzō (1913–2005). Tokyo's wards today refer to themselves as "cities"—an outgrowth of a measure enacted in 2000 by Japan's legislature—the National Diet—that declared the wards city-like in their administration. Although "ku" is still used in the Japanese name of each ward, as in Shibuya-ku, when using English on their websites and in printed material, the wards now call themselves "city"—as in Shibuya City.[5] Scholars, for the most part, continue to use the word ward for these administrative divisions, which is the practice we employ in the chapters here.

While the day-to-day lives of central-Tokyo residents are affected by the policies of the ward in which they live when it comes to matters ranging from residency, healthcare, and education to taxes, disaster preparedness, and trash collection, Tokyo is normally thought of less in terms of wards per se than in terms of its distinctive neighborhoods. This can be seen just by taking a quick look at any one of the many Tokyo guidebooks published for the domestic tourism market. *Tōkyō besuto supotto* ("Tokyo's Best Spots"), for example, enumerates the thirteen "best areas" in the city. They are, according to the editors of the guidebook, Tokyo Skytree Town (the dining, shopping, and entertainment complex built in conjunction with Skytree tower and its observation decks); Harajuku and Omotesandō; Asakusa; Ginza; Odaiba; Tokyo Station and Marunouchi; Roppongi; Shibuya; Shinjuku; Ikebukuro; Tsukiji and Tsukishima; Akihabara; and Ueno (Shōbunsha Tōkyō Gaidobukku 2016, 6–7). Even though Shibuya and Shinjuku also happen to be the names of wards (the only two on the list), the guidebook is specifically pointing visitors to the intensively developed and lively areas around Shibuya and Shinjuku Stations. Looking at Tokyo in terms of its distinctive neighborhoods is also reflected in English-language scholarship—a sampling of places and related studies includes Akasaka and Inarichō (Heine 2012), Akihabara (Morikawa 2012), Roppongi (Cybriwsky 2011), San'ya (Fowler 1996; Thornbury 2014), Shibuya (Yoshimi 2011), Shinjuku (Cassegard 2013), the Tsukiji fish market (Bestor 2004), and "Yanesen" (Yanaka, Nezu, and Sendagi) (Sand 2013).[6] A large number of locations across Tokyo—large and small, in plain sight and hidden (including one that could be real, but is in fact imagined)—are the subject matter of our book.

Yamanote and Shitamachi are two fundamental concepts that inevitably come up when talking about Tokyo. The nomenclature is a carryover from the Edo period, when the Tokugawa shoguns ruled Japan from their Edo castle stronghold. Edward Seidensticker firmly established the English-language terms "high city" (for Yamanote) and "low city" (for Shitamachi) with the publication in 1983 of his book *Low City, High City: Tokyo from Edo to the Earthquake*. The terms harbor much complexity. Retaining the original Japanese words, Waley offers a concise summary:

> Shitamachi and Yamanote are central to urban discourse on Tokyo. They are the main street-level, vox-pop. divisions of the city and they are also spatial metaphors for the kind of people who live there, for differing approaches to life. The terms apply, in the case of Shitamachi, to the flatlands in the east of the city and, in that of Yamanote, to the hilly west. . . . Shitamachi and Yamanote have no administration nor borders and, having no borders, the ground they are conventionally thought to cover (to the extent that any such claim can be made) has shifted. Shitamachi has moved east from the city center, which itself has shifted westwards, while Yamanote has shifted even further west. For much of the 20th century, Shitamachi was slowly marginalized but, more recently, as it has attenuated in its spatial and social significance, it has been reinvented, both through a process of internalization and through one of celebration. (2002, 1533)

Yamanote—the topographically higher part of the city where those who held power during the Edo period had their estates—still denotes a sense of privilege (Heine 2012, 4). Similarly, Shitamachi—the topographically lower, crowded, and bustling "commoner" sector of Edo—continues to resonate with a kind of "old Tokyo" authenticity. Even so, as Waley notes, it is impossible to demarcate exactly where Yamanote and Shitamachi are. Maps of Tokyo give few clues: there is a Yamanote Avenue (a major road on central Tokyo's west side), although Yamanote is best known as the name of Tokyo's main train line, which runs in a loop that, roughly speaking, encloses the central, "Yamanote" part of the city. Asked to name a place-specific reference to Shitamachi, most people can cite only the Shitamachi Museum, which houses a collection of Edo/Tokyo memorabilia in a building near Ueno Station. Nevertheless, the terms remain potent elements in discourse about Tokyo, as their frequent occurrence in our chapters suggests.

The quest to conceptualize Tokyo in spatial terms goes beyond wards and neighborhoods, Shitamachi and Yamanote. For example, in his much-quoted *Tokyo: A Spatial Anthropology*, urban historian and anthropologist Jinnai Hidenobu points to Tokyo's shift since the Meiji Restoration from "a city of water" to "a city of land" (1995 [1985]). Edo's transportation system was built on a network of canals and rivers. As the city modernized, its downtown waterways were filled in and replaced with railway lines and streets. In time, elevated highways were built, too. The shift to a city on land also extends to the use of landfill to expand buildable acreage into and around Tokyo Bay.[7] The changes to the cityscape are continuous—and are integral to the narratives of Tokyo in works of the imagination.

THE CHAPTERS: TOKYO IN WORKS OF THE IMAGINATION

The eight chapters in this volume draw attention to a tiny fraction of the extremely large and diverse body of texts, both fiction and non-fiction, that are involved in the struggle to express Tokyo's eventful history. Within them, the city can be read as a place dense with sites of memory—from neighborhoods and their intertwining streets to manmade islands, landscape gardens, temples, used-book stores, and even sports stadiums. They are evidence that Tokyo, like all cities, "is a repository of memories—some purposely kept alive, some stifled, some lively and some moribund" (White 2011, 21).

Jeffrey Angles looks at *Togenuki: Shin Sugamo Jizō engi* ("The Thorn-Puller: New Tales of the Sugamo Jizō," 2007) by poet/novelist Itō Hiromi (b. 1955). Blurring the boundaries between poetry and prose, "The Thorn Puller" portrays the lives of multiple generations of women. Along with personal and family stories, the first-person narrative is laced with quotations from myths and folklore—especially tales relating to the statue of Jizō that stands in the grounds of Kōganji, a famous Buddhist temple in the historically working-class Toshima Ward neighborhood of Sugamo in north-central Tokyo. Today, Sugamo is mainly known for the temple and the bustling shopping area that grew up around it, but Kōganji was originally established in 1596, a few years prior to the start of the Tokugawa period, in what is now Tokyo's Kanda district. Just over a half century later, the temple moved to a location close to what is now Ueno Park, before settling in 1891—during the Meiji period (1868–1912)—in its current location. Destroyed in the firebombing of 1945, the temple was reconstructed in its current form in 1957.

While the reconstruction of buildings and other structures is a significant act of urban remembering, the trope of reconstruction and remembrance is also inherent in Itō's narrative strategy, which employs elements of magical realism. In "The Thorn-Puller," things as small as an amulet and as intangible as particular ways of speech form links between memory and place. Itō's work reminds readers that a city cannot be reduced merely to the physical: it is an intertextual collection of memories, stories, myths, and tales out of which the complex fabric of cultural knowledge is woven.

Kristina Iwata-Weickgenannt's focus is on the novel *Tenten* ("From Here to There," 1999) by Fujita Yoshinaga (b. 1950) and the eponymous 2007 film adaptation (released worldwide under the English-language title *Adrift in Tokyo*) directed by Miki Satoshi (b. 1961). Both works range widely across Tokyo, following two men as they walk a meandering path. They set off from Inokashira Park, a former Imperial estate in the city's western suburbs that has been in the public domain since 1913, and conclude their journey in front of the headquarters of Tokyo's Metropolitan Police Department—which is situated among the government buildings that occupy tracts of land near the Imperial Palace in the center of the city.

The protagonists of the novel and film are Fukuhara Aiichirō, a middle-aged loan shark who, as it happens, recently killed his wife, and Takemura Fumiya, a not-so-young indebted university student. Fukuhara offers Fumiya a deal he cannot not refuse: a reward of one million yen to accompany him on a walk across Tokyo. Recasting the men's memoryscapes as geographical space, the journey spirals around the Imperial Palace, the symbolic center of Japan. It also takes Fukuhara and Fumiya to the margins of Japan's post-bubble society, into a world of cosplayers, freeters, sex workers, and others living on the economic fringe. A few of the stopping-off places along the way in the novel or the film (or both), all of which relate to unresolved issues in the men's past, include Nishi Ogikubo (actually represented on film by Asagaya) in Suginami Ward, the east side of Shinjuku Station, an area near Nakano Station, the Ikebukuro neighborhood in Toshima Ward, and the Kōrakuen amusement park near Suidōbashi Station. In Fujita's novel and Miki's film, the vast expanse of Tokyo unfolds piece by piece in a way that underscores the fragmented and associative nature of memory.

Mark Pendleton analyzes the novel *Yume no shima* (1985, trans. *Isle of Dreams*, 2010) by Hino Keizō (1929–2002) as a "memory text"—one that intervenes in Japan's postwar memory politics. The novel depicts a grieving widower's encounters with a strange humanoid figure in the dystopian space of the real-life Yumenoshima, a reclaimed island in Tokyo Bay, in scenes filled with rotting corpses and deteriorating buildings. Appearing at the peak of the bubble era and using the geographical peculiarity of Yumenoshima, *Isle of Dreams* speaks to both a sense of cultural decay and memory loss associated with the historical moment when Japan's postwar vision of economic growth and prosperity had reached its apex. It also presages the material manifestation of ruin in the economic and social collapses of post-bubble Japan.

Sakai Shōzō, the protagonist of Hino's novel, works for a construction company. The glittery facades of Tokyo's modern high-rise buildings, which Sakai admires, stand in stark contrast to the austerity and liminality he experiences on Yumenoshima. The novel moves around and through Tokyo, from the Ginza shopping district that spatially represented the ethos of limitless consumption during the bubble era, to the controlled chaos of the Tsukiji market (the world's largest fish and seafood market), and locales such as Tsukishima and Harumi that are being transformed along Tokyo Bay. Pendleton demonstrates how Hino deploys the metaphor of the Möbius strip to express the intertwining of place, history, and memory in Tokyo, a city constructed in cycles of creation and destruction.

In her chapter, Evelyn Schulz introduces the term "spatial (auto)biography" to draw attention to a genre of writings that link changes that have taken place within Tokyo urban space to a writer's memories about her or his life there. Such writings retell Tokyo's history and document the continually changing cityscape from an individual's point of view. They are based on literal and figurative peripatetic wanderings through Tokyo's back alleys and neighborhoods. Offering narratives of Tokyo's history and commentary on how the city has internalized modernity, they highlight the transformations—from reconstruction and development to destruction and erasure—that are inscribed in the places the writers visit. Refracted by memory, feelings of nostalgia, and melancholy, the (auto)biographies shed light on each author's place in the history of Tokyo.

Spatial (auto)biographies are nearly unknown outside Japan. Schulz analyzes three examples by way of giving a representative overview of the genre. The first is a Tokyo tetralogy by Kobayashi Nobuhiko (b. 1932), comprising *Shisetsu Tōkyō hanjōki* ("An Account of Tokyo's Prosperity: A Personal Interpretation," 1984), *Shisetsu Tōkyō hōrōki* ("Wandering through Tokyo: A Personal Account," 1992), *Shōwa no Tōkyō, Heisei no Tōkyō* ("Tokyo in the Shōwa Period, Tokyo in the Heisei Period," 2002), and *Watashi no Tōkyō chizu* ("My Tokyo Map," 2013). The second example is *Tōkyō no ryūgi: Zeitaku-na machiaruki* ("Tokyo Style: Lavish Neighborhood Walks," 2008) by Fukuda Kazuya (b. 1960), and the third is *Yoshimoto Takaaki no Tōkyō* ("Yoshimoto Takaaki's Tokyo," 2005) by Ishizeki Zenjirō (b. 1945).

Kobayashi's tetralogy covers the period from the 1960s until 2013. Its focus is on the Shitamachi area, with chapters concentrating on districts such as Asakusa, Nihonbashi, and Tsukudajima. By the 1980s, these sites were frequently being used to evoke Tokyo's vernacular past and its local character. (Areas such as Shinjuku, Harajuku, and Roppongi, in contrast, represent Tokyo's transformation into a consumption-oriented, fast-paced, modern and global high-rise megacity.) Fukuda's work looks at Tokyo from the perspective of real or imagined walking tours through Shitamachi neighborhoods, and investigates their culinary associations with the past. His walks are "lavish" insofar as they provide an escape from bustling, global Tokyo with its towers of glass and steel. Ishizeki looks at Tokyo through the biography of Yoshimoto Takaaki (1924–2012), a celebrated philosopher and writer who addressed key issues and concerns relating to the impact of Western modernity on Japan and the social, political, and cultural contradictions and conflicts of the postwar period. Yoshimoto's life and work are deeply intertwined with Tokyo. Ishizeki pays particular attention to Tsukishima, Yoshimoto's birthplace and a part of Tokyo that well illustrates the city's rapid twentieth- and twenty-first-century metamorphosis.

Bruce Suttmeier's subject is *Orinpikku no minoshirokin* ("Olympic Ransom," 2008), a thriller by Okuda Hideo (b. 1956) that revolves around a terrorist plot to disrupt the opening ceremony of the 1964 Olympics (officially known as the Games of the XVIII Olympiad) that took place in Tokyo. The action centers on a character named Shimazaki Kunio, a graduate of the elite University of Tokyo, who vows revenge upon learning that his older brother died of a heroin overdose after years of backbreaking construction work on Olympic sites. Shimazaki's plan is to detonate dynamite at the opening ceremony in National Stadium—an event attended by tens of thousands of spectators and watched worldwide on television. In the final scene, the lone figure of the bomber furtively approaches the Olympic flame with explosives in hand, but is stopped just in time by a police bullet.

"Olympic Ransom" cuts a wide path across Tokyo, from the centrally located Olympic sites in Yoyogi and Shinjuku to laborer camps in San'ya and Ueno in the city's northeast quadrant. For a while, Shimazaki avoids capture by hiding out on Yumenoshima in Tokyo Bay. Because the island was undeveloped at the time and considered uninhabitable, the police did not think to search for him there. However, unlike Hino's dystopian Yumenoshima two decades later, Okuda's provides temporary shelter for Shimazaki—a depiction that accords well with the novel's focus on the potential of the counter-factual to challenge and enrich understandings of history and memory.

Okuda's novel offers a detailed portrait of mid-sixties Tokyo, a city that tore down and reconstructed enormous parts of itself in an effort to make the best possible impression on the world as host of the first games to be held in an Asian country. In novels and other media, the late 1950s and early 1960s often serve as a kind of pre-history to contemporary Tokyo, a "simpler" time before skyscrapers, elevated highways, and other markers of global capitalism. However, Okuda's narrative eschews the nostalgia-tinged ethos of such depictions. Rather than mine the past for sites of memory, "Olympic Ransom" animates the city itself as a profoundly destabilizing actor in the story it tells. Suttmeier's chapter looks at the novel's articulation of space, interrogating the contemporary world's desire for memory as an end in itself and examining how Tokyo's postwar history invites and resists the dramatization of urban space.

Barbara Thornbury interprets the Tokyo of director Hou Hsiao-Hsien's (b. 1947) film *Kōhī jikō* (2003, trans. *Café Lumière*) as an interlocking set of *lieux de mémoire*. Presented from the point of view of Yōko, a young freelance writer, the sites of memory resonate individually and collectively, culturally and historically. In specific geographic terms, they include the aging north-central Tokyo neighborhoods whose residents, Yōko among them, are served by the slow-moving, quaintly antiquated Toden Arakawa streetcar line that traces an arc between Waseda Station in Shinjuku Ward and Minowabashi Station in Arakawa Ward. Another site of memory—and the center point of Yōko's networked Tokyo life—is found among the used-book stores and quiet cafés of Jinbōchō in Chiyoda Ward. There is also the Ginza (a part of Chūō Ward known worldwide for high-end shopping and dining)—where Yōko, in the course of doing research on the life of composer Jiang Wenye (1910–1983), seeks traces of a past that evoke the human dimension of Japan's half century of colonial occupation of Taiwan. Her search for details relating to Jiang's Tokyo biography embraces two other sites of memory—the environs of Senzoku-ike Park in Ōta Ward and the Kōenji neighborhood in Suginami Ward.

With the aim of situating Hou's film within the broader context of cinematic representations of Tokyo urban space viewed from the perspective of memory, Thornbury also brings into her discussion Kitano Takeshi's (b. 1947) film *Kikujirō no natsu* (1999, trans. *Kikujiro*). The *lieu de mémoire* cityscape of *Kikujiro* is bounded by the Asakusa neighborhood—which, more than any other single locale today, embodies the real and figurative old downtown (Shitamachi) area that is a primary defining element of Tokyo urban memory. Both *Café Lumière* and *Kikujiro* visualize Tokyo as a setting where new kinds of dynamic and compassionate relationships can arise from fragments of memories made whole.

Adaptation as a creative process rooted in memory goes to heart of Angela Yiu's chapter on the 2003 novel *FUTON* by Nakajima Kyōko (b. 1964). *FUTON* draws on two works by Tayama Katai (1872–1930)—its namesake *Futon* (1907, trans. *The Quilt*, 1981) and *Tōkyō no sanjūnen* (1917, trans. *Literary Life in Tokyo 1885–1915: Tayama Katai's Memoirs ("Thirty Years in Tōkyō")*, 1987). Another source is the novella *Hakuchi* (trans. "The Idiot," 1985) by Sakaguchi Ango (1906–1955). In writing *FUTON*, her debut novel, Nakajima exposes multiple temporal and spatial dimensions of Tokyo. She focuses on three major time frames, each of which is linked to specific locations within the city. The publication of Katai's *Futon* in 1907 is associated with the Yamanote, the firebombings of 1945 are related to the Shitamachi, and Tokyo in 2001 references both the Shitamachi and the Odaiba waterfront development (built on an island in Tokyo Bay made from reclaimed land).

In its intertextual engagement with *Futon*, Nakajima's *FUTON* directs the reader's attention to Katai's nuanced portrayal of Tokyo. *FUTON* adds an expanded cast of characters from various geographic, historical, social, cultural, and linguistic dimensions by way of exposing layers of Tokyo through time, space, memory, history, race, gender, and literary forms. The cast of characters includes, among others, an American professor of Japanese literature named Dave Macqualie, his student and lover Emi, an exchange student named Yūki (with whom Emi becomes involved), Emi's grandfather Tatsuzō, and Tatsuzō's caretaker Izumi. By taking an old text (*Futon*) and remaking it in new, up-to-date language, as Yiu notes, Nakajima engages in simultaneous acts of destruction, remembering, and renewal—just as the continually remade urban landscape can both bury and resuscitate vestiges of the past.

The cityscape of *FUTON*, as in other works by Nakajima, is a composite of multiple time frames. Tokyo in Nakajima's hands never "stops" at a single point in time—in, say, 1907, 1945, or 2001. It is, rather, a space in which different time frames co-exist and intersect. The past speaks to the present and future, which, in turn, respond to and absorb knowledge from the past. *FUTON* exemplifies two ideas that are basic to an understanding of Nakajima's urban narratives. One is the need for memory of the past, especially memory of wartime Japan, to be part of contemporary consciousness, and the other is that the stories that make up a great city such as Tokyo arise not from heroes and those in power but from the memories, hopes, and reflections of the ordinary people who live their lives there.

Eve Zimmerman explores three stories written by Tsushima Yūko (1947–2016) in the early- to mid-1980s (and all published in book form in 1984). In "Maboroshi" ("Phantom"), "Danmari-ichi" (trans. "The Silent Traders"), and "Fusehime" ("Princess Fuse"), Tsushima's protagonists reach back into their repressed memories, dreams, and forgotten maps of childhood in an effort to find an anchor for their lives. These are characters who as adults firmly hold onto their childhood pasts even as they witness firsthand the city's past seemingly being erased in the rush to build a new Tokyo.

Geographic reference points in "Phantom," "The Silent Traders," and "Princess Fuse" range from a location in Meguro Ward to Hon-komagome, a neighborhood in Bunkyō Ward where Tsushima spent part of her childhood. Against the backdrop of the construction taking place in the visible world of Tokyo, Tsushima interrogates the national myth of success that gripped the Japanese psyche in the 1980s. Eschewing a preservationist stance and expressions of cultural nostalgia, she offers her readers finely wrought observations about Tokyo that constitute a record of loss refracted through the lens of personal memory.

A NOTE ON LITERARY PRIZES AND TRANSLATION

Literary prizes are indicators of distinction for most of the writers whose work is the focus of the chapters in this volume. Such accolades serve to confer "cultural legitimacy and prestige," situating Japanese literature "within a constellation of national literatures, assuring everyone that Japan possesse[s] this marker of advanced-nation status" (Mack 2016, 670). To have prizes is to have a "national literature." Moreover, prizes memorialize the writers for whom they are named and, metaphorically, create their own sites of memory—visible in the expanding historical records listing the names of those to whom the prizes have been awarded.

During his career, Hino Keizō garnered the Akutagawa Prize, the Hirabayashi Taiko Literature Prize, the Tanizaki Jun'ichirō Prize, and the Japanese government's Arts Award (Geijutsu Senshō). Fujita Yoshinaga, Nakajima Kyōko, and Okuda Hideo are winners of the Naoki Prize. Itō Hiromi's literary awards include the Hagiwara Sakutarō Prize and the Murasaki Shikibu Prize. Fukuda Kazuya was awarded the Mishima Yukio Prize. During her lifetime, Tsushima Yūko won numerous prizes, including the Kawabata Yasunari Prize, Izumi Kyōka Prize, Noma Hiroshi Prize, Osaragi Jirō Prize, Tanizaki Jun'ichirō Prize, and Yomiuri Prize.[8] In the field of film, director Miki Satoshi is a Fantasia International Film Festival awardee. Directors Kitano Takeshi and Hou Hsiao-Hsien count prizes at the Venice Film Festival among their accolades—which, for Hou, also include a Cannes Film Festival award.

The texts discussed in this volume were originally published (or, in the case of the films, produced and released) in Japan. Their language is Japanese. All three films—Miki's *Tenten*, Hou's *Kōhī jikō*, and Kitano's *Kikujirō no natsu*—have been subtitled in English and distributed outside of Japan either through streaming services or on DVD. Hino's novel *Yume no shima* has been translated into English, as has Tsushima's story "Danmari-ichi." Jeffrey Angles has published sections of Itō's *Togenuki: Shin Sugamo Jizō engi* in translation, and is in the process of translating the complete work. Although Katai's *Futon*, the main source text for Nakajima's *FUTON* has been translated into English, Nakajima's novel—along with Okuda's *Orinpikku no minoshirokin*, Fujita's *Tenten*, Kobayashi's tetralogy (*Shisetsu Tōkyō hanjōki*; *Shisetsu Tōkyō hōrōki*; *Shōwa no Tōkyō, Heisei no Tōkyō;* and *Watashi no Tōkyō chizu*), Fukuda's *Tōkyō no ryūgi: Zeitaku na machiaruki*, Ishizeki's *Yoshimoto Takaaki no Tōkyō*, and Tsushima's "Maboroshi" and "Fuse-hime"—are currently untranslated. An aim of the chapters that follow is to broaden the scope of Japanese literary and cultural studies through engagement with all of these subtitled, translated, and yet-to-be-translated works.

* * *

"Tokyo makes us think about what it means to live in cities now," Paul Waley has written. It is a place that "forces us to question our preconceptions about modernity and about urban life." In recent years Tokyo has been the focus of an increasing number of scholarly books and journal articles written in English. However, to a degree Tokyo remains in a state of "epistemological isolation," as Waley puts it, given that "it does not fit so easily into many of the ready-made urban narratives" (2012, 331). Looking at Tokyo from the perspective of memory in works of the imagination, as we do in the chapters that follow, helps solidify the city's claim to a place within the mainstream of these urban narratives—and, at the same time, opens pathways to the creation of new ones.

NOTES

1. Scholars trace the "memory boom" back at least to the late 1970s and "the decline of utopian visions [that] supposedly redirected our gaze to collective pasts" (Olick, Vinitzky-Seroussi, and Levy 2011, 3).

2. Murakami Haruki (b. 1949) captures Tokyo's spatial transformation in his 1992 novel *Kokkyō no minami, taiyō no nishi* (trans. *South of the Border, West of the Sun*, 1998) in words said to the protagonist, Hajime, by his father-in-law as they gaze out of the window of the older man's construction company headquarters on the seventh floor of a Yotsuya high-rise:

> Look out at Tokyo here. See all the empty lots around? . . . There used to be old houses and buildings on those lots, but they've been torn down. The price of land has shot up so much old buildings aren't profitable anymore. You can't charge high rent, and it's hard to find tenants. That's why they need newer, bigger buildings. And private homes in the city—well, people can't afford their property taxes or inheritance taxes. So they sell out and move to the suburbs. And professional real estate developers buy up the old houses, put 'em to the wrecking ball, and construct brand-new, more functional buildings. So before long all those empty lots will have

new buildings on them. In a couple of years you won't recognize Tokyo. There's no shortage of capital. The Japanese economy's booming, stocks are up. And banks are bursting at the seams with cash. If you have land as collateral, the banks'll lend you as much as you possibly could want. That's why all these buildings are going up one after another. And guess who builds them? Guys like me. (1998 [1992], 127–28)

3. Such is the prominence of Skytree tower that it has been referred to as "the new symbol of Tokyo" (Jinnai 2017, 185).
4. The population figures are current as of October 1, 2015.
5. See, for example, http://www.city.shibuya.tokyo.jp/index.html.
6. *City Life in Japan: A Study of a Tokyo Ward* is Ronald P. Dore's classic 1958 study of a Tokyo neighborhood. Despite the word "ward" in the title, the book looks at the fictitiously named neighborhood Shitayama-chō. To be sure, especially given the large amounts of official statistical data generated by and about wards, studies of Tokyo often focus on wards. Tajima Kayo, for instance, has written about the large migration of people from throughout Japan to the Tokyo area during the period of Japan's rapid economic growth from the late sixties until the late eighties. He shows that the residential population of the "urban core"—the part of Tokyo that abuts Tokyo Bay in Chūō, Minato, and Shinagawa Wards ("Tokyo's central business area")—experienced a notable increase starting in the late seventies with the development of high-rise condominium buildings on land once used for industrial purposes and on newly reclaimed land. He also points out that the first decade of the twenty-first century saw young people moving to Shinjuku, Toshima, Nakano, and Bunkyō Wards—areas that "share easy access to public transit and a large stock of small rental housing units" (2014, 57–59, 61).
7. An important step towards the spatial exploitation of the bay was Tange Kenzō's utopia-like 1960 master plan "Tokyo Megalopolis." Although Tange's plan was not realized, the artificial island of Odaiba can be considered an impressive implementation of the architect's vision.
8. The individuals for whom the prizes are named are—with the exception of *Tale of Genji* author Murasaki Shikibu (ca. 978–ca. 1013)—among the most prominent Japanese novelists, poets, and short story writers of the twentieth century. They are Akutagawa Ryūnosuke (1892–1927), Hagiwara Sakutarō (1886–1942), Hirabayashi Taiko (1905–1972), Izumi Kyōka (1873–1939), Nobel Prize-winner Kawabata Yasunari (1899–1972), Mishima Yukio (1925–1970), Naoki Sanjūgo (1891–1934), Noma Hiroshi (1915–1991), Osaragi Jirō (1897–1973), and Tanizaki Jun'ichirō (1886–1965).

WORKS CITED

Bestor, Theodore. 2004. *Tsukiji: The Fish Market at the Center of the World*. Berkeley: University of California Press.
Cassegard, Carl. 2013. "Activism Beyond the Pleasure Principle? Homelessness and Art in the Shinjuku Underground." *Third Text* 27 (5): 620–33.
Crinson, Mark. 2005. "Urban Memory—An Introduction." In *Urban Memory: History and Amnesia in the Modern City*, edited by Mark Crinson, xi–xxiii. New York: Routledge.
Cybriwsky, Roman Adrian. 2011. *Roppongi Crossing: The Demise of a Tokyo Nightclub District and the Reshaping of a Global City*. Athens: University of Georgia Press.
Eckersall, Peter. 2013. *Performativity and Event in 1960s Japan: City, Body, Memory*. New York: Palgrave Macmillan.
Fowler, Edward. 1996. *San'ya Blues: Laboring Life in Contemporary Tokyo*. Ithaca: Cornell University Press.
Hein, Carola. 2003. "Rebuilding Japanese Cities after 1945." In *Rebuilding Urban Japan after 1945*, edited by Carola Hein, Jeffry M. Diefendorf, and Ishida Yorifusa, 1–16. New York: Palgrave Macmillan.
Heine, Steven. 2012. *Sacred High City, Sacred Low City: A Tale of Religious Sites in Two Tokyo Neighborhoods*. New York: Oxford University Press.

Jinnai Hidenobu. 1995 [1985]. *Tokyo: A Spatial Anthropology* (*Tōkyō no kūkan jinruigaku*). Translated by Kimiko Nishimura. Berkeley: University of California Press.

———. 2017. "The Landscape of Tokyo as a City on the Water—Past and Present." In *Waterfronts Revisited: European Ports in a Historic and Global Perspective*, edited by Heleni Porfyriou and Marichela Sepe, 177–88. New York: Routledge.

Mack, Edward. 2016. "Canonization and Popularization: Anthologies and Literary Prizes." In *The Cambridge History of Japanese Literature*, edited by Haruo Shirane and Tomi Suzuki with David Lurie, 669–671. New York: Cambridge University Press.

Morikawa, Kaichiro. 2012. "Otaku and the City: The Rebirth of Akihabara." In *Fandom Unbound: Otaku Culture in a Connected World*, edited by Mizuko Ito, Daisuke Okabe, and Izumi Tsuji, 133–57. New Haven: Yale University Press.

Murakami Haruki. 1998 [1992]. *South of the Border, West of the Sun* (*Kokkyō no minami, taiyō no nishi*). Translated by Philip Gabriel. New York: Vintage International.

Nora, Pierre (under the direction of). 1996–1998 [1984–1992]. *Realms of Memory: Rethinking the French Past* (*Les Lieux de Mémoire*), edited by Lawrence D. Kritzman. Translated by Arthur Goldhammer. 3 volumes. New York: Columbia University Press.

Obrist, Hans Ulrich, with Asad Raza. 2014. *Ways of Curating*. New York: Faber and Faber.

Olick, Jeffrey K., Vered Vinitzky-Seroussi, and Daniel Levy. 2011. "Introduction." *The Collective Memory Reader*, edited by Jeffrey K. Olick, Vered Vinitzky-Seroussi, and Daniel Levy, 3–62. New York: Oxford University Press.

Radović, Darko, Heide Jager, and Ammon Beyerle. 2008. *Another Tokyo: Nezu and Yanaka, Places and Practices of Urban Resistance*. Tokyo: Center for Sustainable Urban Regeneration, University of Tokyo.

Sand, Jordan. 2013. *Tokyo Vernacular: Common Spaces, Local Histories, Found Objects*. Berkeley: University of California Press.

Schulz, Evelyn. 2013. "Beyond Modernism." In *Future Living: Collective Housing in Japan*, edited by Claudia Hildner, 11–26. Basel: Birkhäuser.

Seidensticker, Edward. 1983. *Low City, High City: Tokyo from Edo to the Earthquake*. New York: Alfred A. Knopf.

Shōbunsha Tōkyō Gaidobukku, ed. 2016. *Tōkyō besuto supotto* ("Tokyo's Best Spots"). Tokyo: Shōbunsha.

Tajima Kayo. 2014. "Dissecting the Re-urbanization Trend in the Tokyo Metropolitan Area in 2005–2010." *Global Urban Studies* 7: 57–67.

Thornbury, Barbara. 2014. "Mapping Tokyo's 'Empty Center' in Oyama's *A Man with No Talents*." In *Literary Cartographies: Spatiality, Representation, and Narrative*, edited by Robert T. Tally Jr., 165–77. New York: Palgrave Macmillan.

Tokyo Metropolitan Government. 2017. "Tokyo's History, Geography, and Population." Accessed 17 July 2017. http://www.metro.tokyo.jp/ENGLISH/ABOUT/HISTORY/history02.htm.

Waley, Paul. 2002. "Moving the Margins of Tokyo." *Urban Studies* 39 (9): 1533–50.

———. 2012. "Placing Tokyo in Time and Space." *Journal of Urban History* 39 (2): 331–35.

———. 2013. "Pencilling Tokyo into the Map of Neoliberal Urbanism." *Cities* 32: 43–50.

White, James W. 2011. *Mirrors of Memory: Culture, Politics, and Time in Paris and Tokyo*. Charlottesville: University of Virginia Press.

Yoshimi, Shun'ya. 2011. "The Market of Ruins, or the Destruction of the Cultural City." Translated by Jo Lumley. *Japan Forum* 23 (2): 287–300.

Chapter One

Pulling the Thorns of Suffering

Remembering Sugamo in Itō Hiromi's "The Thorn-Puller"

Jeffrey Angles

From February 2006 to April 2007, Japan's most prominent contemporary feminist poet Itō Hiromi (b. 1955) serialized an inventive first-person "novel in verse" entitled *Togenuki: Shin Sugamo Jizō engi* ("The Thorn-Puller: New Tales of the Sugamo Jizō") in the important and long-running literary journal *Gunzō*. This work, which blurs the boundaries of poetry and prose, is based in large part on Itō's own experiences with her parents, her partner, the British-born artist Harold Cohen (1928–2016), and her daughters, although Itō exaggerated or fictionalized many of the details for artistic effect. One could argue that "The Thorn-Puller" is a contemporary take on the "I-novel" *(shishōsetsu)*—the type of self-confessional novel that emerged in Japan in the early twentieth century as authors seeking to explore the effects of environment on the individual mined their own lives and psychological experiences for material. However, unlike many earlier I-novels, which tend to be ponderous and dull, "The Thorn-Puller" features a narrator who is loquacious, argumentative, bawdy, funny, and even humorously self-deprecating. In addition, Itō worked numerous extended quotations from folklore, modern novels, short stories, myths, poems, popular songs, and classical texts into the work.[1] As a result, readers in the know frequently find themselves laughing out loud when they encounter already familiar turns of phrase in a radically new context. Although "The Thorn-Puller" shares a high degree of biographical self-referentiality with other forms of life writing, it is also a highly inventive, polyvocal, entertaining pastiche.

This playful style helped propel "The Thorn-Puller" into the spotlight. When *Gunzō* finished serializing the work, the publishing company Kōdansha released it in hardcover in 2007, and it quickly won two of Japan's most important literary prizes—the 2007 Hagiwara Sakutarō Prize, which is given each year by the city of Maebashi to an inventive and important work of contemporary poetry, and the 2008 Murasaki Shikibu Prize, awarded annually by the city of Uji to an outstanding piece of literature written by a woman. (Maebashi was the birthplace and home of Hagiwara Sakutarō [1886–1942], who is sometimes considered one of the fathers of contemporary modern Japanese poetry, and Uji is a city with a deep connection to Murasaki Shikibu [ca. 978–ca. 1013], the author of the classic novel *Genji monogatari* [trans. *The Tale of Genji*]. As a way of celebrating their contributions to literary history, both cities created major literary prizes in the name of their famous former inhabitants.) "The Thorn-Puller" appeared in paperback in 2011, and it has continued to sell well ever since.[2]

While the playful style is one of the main unifying features of the text, another is the motif introduced in the first chapter of the book, namely that of the miraculous "thorn-pulling" Jizō located in Kōganji, a Buddhist temple in the Sugamo neighborhood of Toshima Ward in north-central Tokyo. Sugamo is located in what was historically a fairly plebian, working-class, Shitamachi part of the city, but today it is known largely for the famous Buddhist temple located there and the bustling shopping area that grew up around it. This chapter will describe the temple's history in greater detail below but, for many years, worshippers have believed that the bodhisattva Jizō located there would alleviate their suffering, thus helping them find peace and comfort. The word *bodhisattva* comes from Sanskrit (the corresponding word in Japanese is *bosatsu*) and refers to a being who has achieved enlightenment but who, rather than renouncing the world completely, helps humanity escape suffering, see spiritual truth, and achieve a higher level of spiritual attainment. Buddhism has many bodhisattvas, which are worshipped like deities, but one of the most popular is Jizō (*Kṣitigarbha* in Sanskrit), who is known for guiding lost souls. In Japan, he is most often depicted as a monk with a shaven head and a walking stick as he traverses vast distances trying to help people in distress. The Jizō located at Kōganji in Sugamo became famous in the eighteenth century for its ability to remove "the thorns" of suffering that afflict the bodies of worshippers, and, therefore, it is popularly known as the "Thorn-Pulling Jizō" (*Togenuki Jizō*).

For over a century, worshippers flocked to Kōganji Temple on a specified pilgrimage date once a month to seek Jizō's help in removing the "thorns" of whatever bodily afflictions might be troubling them. Then, in 1897, Komi Michio, the twenty-fourth abbot in the temple's history, tripled the number of days on which the temple welcomed visitors, receiving them on the fourth, the fourteenth, and the twenty-fourth days of the month (Amano 2001, 52).

As a result of this increased accessibility, the popularity of the temple grew until now thousands upon thousands of worshippers pour into the streets of Sugamo three times per month to visit the temple and seek Jizō's divine help in healing their afflictions. In the shopping arcades that developed around the temple, pilgrims also converse, eat, have tea, shop with friends, and stroll the neighborhood. By the mid-twentieth century, the shop-lined streets near the temple had become a bustling area geared toward the flock of pilgrims who come from all over the Tokyo metropolitan area and elsewhere in the nation as well. As a result, Sugamo has earned the popular sobriquet "Harujuku for grannies" (obāchan no Harajuku)—a term that indicates that it has become an epicenter for fashions and shopping that might appeal to senior citizens, much as Harajuku in Tokyo has become an epicenter for youth fashion and culture (Asagawa 2001, 83–112; Takagi 2001, 113–40).

Itō moved from Tokyo to Kumamoto in southwestern Japan with her husband when he became a professor at Kumamoto University. After they parted ways, she left Kumamoto and established a second residence in the United States. To this day, she maintains homes in both cities and divides her time between the two. Much of the action of "The Thorn-Puller" takes place in the two places where Itō lives, namely Encinitas, California, and Kumamoto. Although much of the action takes place outside of Tokyo, the neighborhood of Sugamo and the famous Jizō temple located there serve a pivotal role in the book, and both the neighborhood and temple appear in numerous flashbacks. Itō grew up in Motohasunuma, about six kilometers away in Itabashi Ward in north-central Tokyo. Because her grandparents lived just a short walk from Sugamo in a neighborhood called Iwanosaka, the temple influenced her young imagination and played an important role in the spiritual life of her family. In the novel, as the narrator tends to the physical and emotional needs of her rapidly aging parents, her thoughts turn with increasing frequency to Sugamo's Jizō temple, which she hopes will help her and her loved ones find solace. We see in the book that these spiritual memories infiltrate the thoughts, hopes, religious practices, and prayers of many members of her family; in fact, the Jizō legend from Sugamo provides a metaphor for hope that extends across time and space, shaping the lives even of people who live far from Tokyo.

Sugamo, with its boisterous pilgrimage days three times per month and its potpourri of stands, shops, and eateries that fill the neighborhood and serve temple-goers, also provides a model for the narrator's mode of interacting with the world. As the narrator of "The Thorn-Puller" travels between her two homes on either side of the Pacific, encounters the countless people who appear as characters in the work, and wanders back through her own childhood memories, she documents the sights and sounds around her. In many ways, the carnivalesque, polyvocal style in which the work is written recalls the chaotic jumble that one finds in Sugamo's streets, which play such an important role in the work. By using the busy, eclectic city streets of Sugamo as a central motif for the narrator's mode of engagement with the world, Itō reminds us that a city is never merely a simple, inert, static place that can be reduced merely to the physical. The city also provides a mode of being and engaging with the world.

SITUATING "THE THORN-PULLER"

Itō Hiromi is one of Japan's most prominent women writers. She is a fiercely independent poet and novelist who has consistently written about motherhood, childbirth, the female body, sexuality, international migration, and mythology in dramatic and powerful language. The poet Kido Shuri (b. 1959) has described Itō's position in contemporary Japanese letters in this way: "The appearance of Itō Hiromi, a figure one might best call a 'shamaness of poetry' (*shi no miko*), was an enormous event in post-postwar poetry. Her psychological sensitivity and writing style, which cannot be captured within any existing framework, became the igniting force behind the subsequent flourishing of women's poetry, just as Hagiwara Sakutarō had revolutionized modern poetry with his morbid sensitivity and colloquial style" (Nomura and Kido 2001, 230). The comparison between Itō and Hagiwara Sakutarō, one of the most important early modern Japanese poets, suggests the colossal importance of Itō's contribution to contemporary letters. Indeed, many younger female poets, including Arai Takako (b. 1966), Minashita Kiriu (b. 1970), and Ōsaki Sayaka (b. 1982) have in private conversations described Itō's writing as a gale-wind force that swept into their lives and showed them radically new ways to write about their own experiences.[3]

Itō's work is strikingly original in both style and content. Since her early twenties, she has embarked upon a lifelong battle against the relatively circumscribed and artfully worded language that typified twentieth-century Japanese poetry, a field that was dominated by male poets. Women, she felt, had a responsibility to subvert the staid language of the male poetry establishment so that they could find their own unique voices and begin to talk about their own experiences on their own terms. As a result, Itō rejected the terse, careful, artful wording of the male poetry establishment and began writing in extended, sometimes even unwieldy, passages of text. The aspect that makes her work so different from that of other writers is not just her rejection of classical metrical patterns and terse style. She also draws inspiration from registers of diction that have been excluded from the poetic mainstream, such as childish vocabulary, honorific language, women's speech, and non-native turns of phrase. When drawing upon these "non-poetic" registers of language, she does not limit herself to small poems that might trivialize or even contain the power of that language. She evokes it on an unusually large scale, bringing it alive through the dramatic deployment of repetition and rhythm. For instance, her masterpiece *Kawara arekusa* (2005, trans. *Wild Grass on the Riverbank*, 2015) is a book-length narrative poem which describes the life of a family hurtling back and forth across the Pacific, told from the point of view of an adolescent female narrator. In it, Itō borrows lyrics of pop songs, children's jump-rope songs, passages from books on plants, as well as the run-on sentences, idiosyncratic turns of phrase, and Anglicisms heard in the speech of her own bilingual children. Because it is filled with extended quotations from various texts, stories, and songs, "The Thorn-Puller," which she started serializing the year after finishing *Wild Grass on the Riverbank*, represents another large-scale attempt to mobilize the dynamic power of real, lived language in contemporary letters.

In the late 1980s, Itō's relationship with her husband Nishi Masahiko (b. 1955), a prominent scholar of European and postcolonial literature who was then teaching at Kumamoto University, was failing, and she decided to go to the United States to start anew. One reason Itō chose the United States in particular was her growing passion for Native American poetry, which she had encountered in the influential collection *Mahō toshite no kotoba: Amerika Indian no kōshōshi* ("Words as Magic: The Oral Poetry of the American Indians," 1988), edited and translated by Kanaseki Hisao (1918–1996). The narrativity of these poems, along with their eagerness to use language in magical, even mystical ways, suggested to her a radically new approach to writing. She found in Native American writing, which deployed language in shamanistic ways to convey the voices of ancestors, spirits, and gods, the tools she needed to rebel against the inward-looking, intensely personal writing of many other Japanese poets.

Itō's interest in Native American poetry led her to the work of Jerome Rothenberg (b. 1931), the avant-garde poet who had published several key collections of Native poetry and helped make "ethnopoetics" a major force in contemporary American poetic circles. In 1990, Itō met Rothenberg when he visited Japan, and in 1991 she worked with him to get an invitation to the University of California San Diego where he was teaching. California marked a turning point in her life. She settled into life in America with her two daughters, met the artist Harold Cohen, started a relationship with him, and gave birth to her third daughter. However, her still rudimentary English meant that for some time she maintained a strong sense of being a resident alien in a foreign environment, unable to communicate fluently with the people around her. Since gaining permanent U.S. residency in 1997, Itō has continued to divide her time between California and Kumamoto. Her already prodigious output of essays has increased, and she began writing novellas as a way of exploring her experiences. The nearly three-hundred-page book "The Thorn-Puller," which uses a combination of prose and poetry to describe her life shuttling back and forth between California and Kumamoto, is the most significant product of this large-scale, international, migratory turn in her oeuvre.

A strong interest in Buddhism is another theme that runs through her work. Since the 1990s, Itō has frequently drawn inspiration from *sekkyō-bushi*, a part-poetry, part-prose, moralistic, parable-filled style of storytelling that evolved in the fifteenth and sixteenth centuries among itinerant Buddhist performers. Several of Itō's long works, notably "Watashi wa Anjuhimeko de aru" (1993, trans. "I Am Anjuhimeko," in Itō 2009) and *Wild Grass on the Riverbank* evoke *sekkyō-bushi* explicitly in their plotlines, imagery, and motifs. Other books also draw inspiration from Buddhism. *Nihon no fushigi na hanashi* ("Strange Tales from Japan," 2004), for instance, is a feminist rewriting of fourteen religious parables from a ninth-century classic collection of Buddhist tales recorded by the monk Kyōkai (8th century CE, exact dates unknown). In recent years, Itō has published *Yomitoki Han'nya shingyō* ("The Heart Sutra Explained," 2010), in which she provides essays, personal reflections, and poetic translations of several well-known Buddhist texts, including the *Heart Sutra*, a short, popular Buddhist text that expresses many of the key tenets of the religion. Because this book sold well enough to be published in a paperback edition and subsequently went through several printings, she followed it up with more books that examine different aspects of Buddhist thought and practice, including a modern translation of the thirteenth-century text *Tan'nishō* ("Lamentations of Divergences," 2012) and an examination of the ways that seated meditation might benefit one's daily life (Fujita and Itō 2016). This interest in Buddhism is one way in which Itō has been coping with the impermanency of life in recent years—a theme brought home by the death of her parents, her dogs, and her partner Harold Cohen. "The Thorn-Puller," which describes the failing health of her parents and looks at the ongoing significance of the Jizō temple in Sugamo to her family, is an important expression of these Buddhist leanings and represents a major work in in her oeuvre.

SUGAMO AS THE SITE OF FOLK MEMORY

Sugamo is one of the stops on the Japan Railways (JR) Yamanote Line, which forms a loop through central Tokyo. From Sugamo Station, groups of pedestrians, mostly senior citizens, flow toward the well-known, bustling Sugamo Jizō Shopping Street (*Sugamo Jizō Shōtengai*), which is lined with shops that have narrow storefronts but extend back from the road to maximize floor space. In the fifth chapter of "The Thorn-Puller," the narrator describes the shops that she sees as she walks through the area on an ordinary day.

As I enter the pilgrimage route, the crowds are far less than on the three monthly pilgrimage dates. There aren't as many stalls out in the street, and the ladies aren't shoving and jostling like they might on those days. Dried goods shops, plant shops, flower shops. . . .

A shop selling pharmaceuticals, a shop selling salted bean cakes, a shop selling clothing, a shop selling pickles, a shop selling *senbei* (rice crackers), a shop selling underwear, a shop selling knitted goods, a shop selling *tsukudani* (food preserved by boiling it in soy), a shop selling potato *yōkan* (sweet bean jelly), a shop selling cloth, and the shop that my mother's nurse told me about which sells honey. Then there was a shop selling kumquats, a shop selling Chinese medicine, a shop selling ginger, a shop selling wolfberry fruits, another shop selling clothing, a shop selling beads, a shop selling lamprey eels, a shop selling buckwheat noodles, a shop selling sweets, another shop selling *senbei*.

A shop selling wooden clogs, a shop selling shoes, a shop selling work clothes, a shop selling shawls, a shop selling *furoshiki* (wrapping cloths), a shop selling boards on which to dry a kimono, another shop selling clothes, another shop selling cloth, a shop specializing in acupuncture and moxabustion, a shop selling seven-spice, and here and there all over the place were vendors selling stick incense. (Itō 2011, 102–3)[4]

As this passage suggests, many of the shops specialize in traditional or old-fashioned products and services, especially food and items of clothing that elderly customers are likely to purchase on their way to or from Kōganji Temple, the social, spiritual, and economic anchor of the area.

Kōganji was founded in the year 1596 and belongs to the Sōtō Sect, one of the major branches of Zen Buddhism. At first, the temple was located in the Yushima neighborhood of Kanda, about six kilometers from its current location. In the 1650s the temple expanded its facilities and relocated to Byōbu-zaka, a spot that was home to many temples through the late nineteenth century and that is close to what is now Ueno Park in Tokyo. The temple remained there until 1891, when modern urban development and redistricting compelled it to move again, this time to its current location in Sugamo. The building constructed in Sugamo stood until 1945, when the Allied powers fighting World War II bombed Tokyo, leaving half the city a heap of ashes and charred wood. Kōganji burned in the conflagration, and it was not until 1957 that the temple was reconstructed, taking the form one sees today.

Despite these vicissitudes, the temple's legendary Jizō has been well known since the early eighteenth century, when the temple was located in Byōbu-zaka. Much of what we know about the early history of the bodhisattva comes from a document written in 1728 by a man named Tatsuke Matashirō, whose son had come down with a serious gastrointestinal disease fifteen years previously. The boy had suffered from alternating bouts of diarrhea, constipation, and severe bloating, growing "thin as a stalk of bam-

Sugamo Jizō shopping street. *Jeffrey Angles.*

boo" (Kōganji 2000, 2). Everyone in the family, including the boy, resigned himself to fate, suspecting a malevolent spirit was afflicting him. This belief led the parents to pray to the bodhisattva Jizō, the protector of children, in the hopes that he might save their son. One day, Matashirō nodded off while praying, and dreamed that a high-ranking priest appeared to him. The priest was standing at his son's bedside wrapped in a black, scented cloth. He told Matashirō to produce an image of him 1.3 *sun* (approximately 4 cm) high and float it in water. When the father protested that he could not do such a thing so quickly, the priest said, "Then I'll give something you can use to stamp out an image." When the father woke, he found what looked like a tree branch by the pillow. On one of its flat surfaces he saw what appeared to be a shadow in the shape of the bodhisattva Jizō. Realizing that this was what the priest had told him about, he inked the stick and made impressions from it, all the while reciting a mantra with each impression. After he had made ten thousand impressions on slips of paper, he took them to the Ryōgoku Bridge and placed them in the Sumida River with a dedicatory prayer. Later that night, a strange thump woke the sick boy. He said a young man of around twenty-four or twenty-five had been standing by his pillow holding a walking staff. Out of nowhere, another man wearing a black, scented priest's robe appeared, but the young man gave the priest-like man a thump with his staff and told him to leave. The following day, the boy's illness began to improve, and by the end of the year, he was entirely healthy again.

Two years later, Matashirō told this story to a priest named Nishiwaki, who asked if he could have some of the miraculous healing impressions. Matashirō gave him two he had in his pocket. Nishiwaki had been attending to a young maid who had accidentally swallowed a needle that she had been holding in her mouth while sewing. The needle lodged first in her throat, then in her stomach, causing her great pain. Hoping that Jizō would help her too, Nishiwaki put a printed image of Jizō in water and told her to drink it. A short time later, she vomited up the water and, with it, the image of Jizō. Sticking through the image was the needle that had caused her problems. Nishiwaki returned to Matashirō and told him that the image of Jizō was indeed a magical healing agent. Matashirō kept his healing stamp a secret until 1728, when the main hall of Kōganji was undergoing reconstruction. It was at that point that Matashirō gave the miraculous stamp to the temple so it might benefit visitors.

The story of the printed Jizō image removing the thorn-like needle from the suffering maid's gastrointestinal tract is what gave the "thorn-pulling Jizō" its name. Of course, "thorn" might be extended metaphorically to represent almost any other kind of suffering or ailment, either physical or mental. This miraculous tale provided a source of revenue for the temple. Even today, the temple offers for sale a series of different amulets with woodblock-style prints of the bodhisattva Jizō printed on tiny slips of paper, thin slices of wood, or scrolls. Of these, the most popular is the *mikage* or "portrait" amulet, which contains a portrait of Jizō modeled after the seventeenth-century stamped images of him and which sells for one hundred yen each (as of 2016). Folk belief has it that those who are seeking relief from external pain can affix the image to the outside of their bodies, and those seeking relief from gastrointestinal or other internal problems can dissolve the image in water, roll it up in a ball to swallow, or even swallow it whole. Another popular amulet for sale at the temple is the 300-yen *migawari* ("scapegoat") amulet, which people believe will help transfer their burdens and suffering to Jizō.

While the sale of these products might seem to some as nothing more than the crass commodification of religious belief, "The Thorn-Puller" (as well as the many blog entries on the web that describe people's experiences using these products) shows that the amulets are a way in which people have incorporated folk beliefs into the fabric of their everyday lives. In the amulets, premodern memories remain alive, connecting contemporary people with the beliefs of generations past. At one point in the novel, when the narrator's ailing mother discovers that the narrator will be visiting Sugamo, the following exchange takes place.

Protective amulets on sale inside Kōganji Temple. *Jeffrey Angles*.

> I said to my mother, I'm going to be going to Sugamo before long. I'm going to do the Jizō pilgrimage, I'm going to ask him to remove our thorns.
> My mother said, if you do, buy an amulet for me. They sell them as soon as you go in the gate, the one they call the *migawari* is the most effective, she said, they've got another one called a *mikage* amulet too, but the *migawari* is the best. (Itō 2011, 97)

The narrator's mother explains that the wooden *migawari* amulet is not something that one should just carry. For the charm to work to its fullest effect, one should burn it and consume the ashes little by little, or grind it down into powder to swallow. Although the narrator purchases a *migawari* amulet for her mother, before she can give it to her, she spends some time with her close friend Oguri in Yamaguchi City, far from Tokyo in southwestern Japan. Oguri has several growths under his arm, which he fears might be cancer. As the narrator gives him the amulet which she had bought for her mother, she tells him, "This isn't just any ordinary amulet, it is a thorn-pulling Jizō, which has divine powers, this is the one they say is the most effective of any of them, a *migawari* 'scapegoat' amulet, I'm giving it to you so you've got it, put your faith in it" (2011, 120). A short time later, she finds out that the amulet worked and he will survive. Even though all of the characters are far from the Tokyo Metropolis, the spiritual geography and grass-roots folk beliefs associated with Tokyo remain deeply imprinted upon them; in fact, their belief in the Sugamo Jizō is so strong that it is one thing on which the characters can consistently rely—perhaps even more than modern medicine.

FINDING SOLACE IN SUGAMO

The main focus of "The Thorn-Puller" is the problems of caring for one's family at the dawn of the twenty-first century. Japan has both the longest life expectancy in the world and one of the lowest birth rates among industrialized nations—a combination that means that there are more and more senior citizens but fewer young people to take care of them. A study conducted by the United Nations Department of Economic and Social Affairs just a few years before Itō wrote her book found that the percentage of citizens over sixty years old in Japan grew from 7.7% in 1950 to 11.7% in 1975, and to 23.2% in 2000. The percentage of senior citizens is expected to continue to grow to 35.1% in 2025 and 42.3% in 2050, with the median age rising from 41.2 in 2000 to the strikingly high age of 53.1 by 2050 (United Nations, DESA, Population Division 2001). Another study conducted by the Japanese government in 2013 predicted that the percentage of the total population over the age of sixty-five would be 26.8% in 2015 and could reach as high as 33.4% in 2035 (Sōmushō Tōkeikyoku 2013).

Given the top-heavy demographic and low birthrate, Japan has already reached a tipping point. The 2015 census confirmed for the first time that the Japanese population started to shrink, losing 0.7% of its total population between 2010, when it had 128.1 million people, and 2015, when it had diminished to 127.1 million (Associated Press 2016). Aging children, including many who still work full-time, are increasingly finding themselves in the position of serving as caregivers, even though they may not necessarily be young or energetic themselves. It is already clear that children alone are unable to shoulder the burden of eldercare. Numerous government studies have pointed to the fact that there is a crisis in nursing. By the year 2025 the nation will likely have a shortage of 300,000 professional caregivers (Murai 2015).

These demographic realities form the background for "The Thorn-Puller." Early in the book, the narrator is in California speaking on the phone with her elderly mother, who lives in Kumamoto. Readers quickly learn that the narrator's parents, especially her ailing mother, are almost entirely dependent on her, needing her help with almost all aspects of their own healthcare and day-to-day life. When the narrator returns to Japan, she finds her mother suffering from a whole host of issues, including depression, severe circulation problems, an increasing inability to walk, and lack of mobility in her fingers and toes resulting from what appears to have been a stroke. The narrator begins a pilgrimage of sorts, taking her mother from one doctor to another, getting referrals to another hospital or clinic, then going there only to encounter new doctors who make further referrals. The narrator quickly finds herself trapped in the labyrinthine maze of the healthcare system, but none of the doctors seems prepared to give her mother the overarching, holistic care she requires. The narrator describes this dire situation with humor, bringing levity to what in real life would no doubt be a harrowing experience. These problems are only complicated by others: a new laptop that she cannot figure out, a daughter who whines, a typhoon predicted to hit Kumamoto, arrangements for her daughter to attend public school in Kumamoto, bills that continue to mount, and so on. To further complicate matters, her partner back in California suddenly requires emergency bypass surgery, so she finds herself with no choice but to negotiate over the phone with her partner and helpful neighbors in California about the best way to handle the crisis.

This tangle of problems is closely based on the pressures that Itō experienced toward the end of her mother's life. Although both of her parents were born and raised in Tokyo, they had moved to Kumamoto to be with Itō and her husband while he was working at Kumamoto University. Several years later, even after Itō and Nishi split up and Itō relocated to California, Itō's parents elected to stay in their newly adopted city. Not having family or roots in the area meant that they continued to rely heavily on their daughter for many things, even though in the 1990s she started spending more than half the year on the other side of the Pacific.

As a result of this situation, the main characters in "The Thorn-Puller" all feel deracinated, living in places that are far from the structures of support and meaning that have guided their lives. At several points in the novel, when the narrator visits Tokyo, even she feels that she no longer entirely belongs to the city where she grew up. She notes, "My memories of Tokyo have completely faded. So many subway lines have been created since I left. New places have been erected. I don't know a thing about them. I simply say that I'm 'going' to Tokyo. I don't say I'm 'going *home*' to Tokyo" (Itō 2011, 111). Even though the narrator was born and grew up in the city, the fact that she has lived away from it for so many years leads to disorientation and loss. In several passages, she seems to be wandering half-lost among the ever-changing streets and multiplying subway lines.

In the midst of all this change, however, the temple in Sugamo remains a place of connection. As mentioned above, Itō's grandparents had lived just a brief walk from Sugamo in a neighborhood called Iwanosaka, and worshipping Jizō on the pilgrimage days was an important part of her family's spiritual beliefs. As a result, members of the family find their thoughts turning to the temple when times grow tough. For instance, early in "The Thorn-Puller," the narrator is in Kumamoto when she receives a telephone call from the nurse she has hired to take care of her ailing mother. She rushes to her mother's residence to find her weeping in bed, and the mother recounts that she has had a dream. In it, she has a chest wound when she sees Jizō in front of her: "I saw Jizō's face with thousands of needles sticking out of it. I thought, oh, my goodness, and I tried stroking his face, but then the needles started coming out where I stroked. I thought, oh, my goodness. I bared my chest and found the wound in my chest had healed" (Itō 2011, 47; Itō 2015a, 55). In this dream, the roles of the two figures are reversed. The wounded mother reaches out to help Jizō, who is covered with thorn-like needles of suffering. By performing this act of reverence, she ends up helping herself, healing the chest wound in her dream. Faith and reverence, the dream seems to be suggesting, do not just benefit the object of worship; they also provide solace to the worshipper as well, helping her to ease her own suffering.

It is no coincidence that, as her mother excitedly recounts this dream about the Sugamo Jizō, she slips back into the local, working-class dialect of Tokyo, even though she has been living for many years in Kumamoto, hundreds of kilometers away. Earlier in the same chapter, the narrator had noted that, during her youth, her parents and grandparents spoke in the accent typical of the working-class, older Shitamachi sections of Tokyo. She notes that her family, like other working-class Tokyoites, tended to replace the sound *hi* with the sound *shi*. In fact, the narrator jokes that, as a result of her family's pronunciation, she spent years as a child believing that her name was "Shiromi" instead of "Hiromi" (Itō 2011, 34; Itō 2015a, 47). Although the mother's dialect is not a prominent feature of the other conversations recorded elsewhere in the novel, her Tokyo dialect returns as she talks excitedly about her dream, and she replaces the word *hiraku* (meaning "open" or "bare") with the Shitamachi pronunciation *shiraku*. This is a subtle point, but, to the attentive reader, it immediately becomes clear that, in thinking about the Sugamo Jizō, the mother is slipping back into old habits, remembering her former identity as a resident of the bustling Shitamachi parts of the city. The Jizō is so closely linked to her memories of those parts of the city that the associations manifest in her linguistic habits.

Numerous passages in the book suggest that the Jizō and, more particularly, the temple in Sugamo represent a source of solace and belonging for Tokyoites, even when they are far from home. In an important passage in the first chapter, the narrator is in Kumamoto helping her mother, who can no longer walk or even use the toilet alone. As she washes her mother's bottom clean, she realizes that her own hand has begun to stink, and she begins to pray silently to herself, "may this stink be taken from me" (Itō 2011, 32; Itō 2016b, 156). Until this point, the text has been arranged like prose on the page, but suddenly, the text turns into what seems like poetry.

At such times I think of Lord Jizō.
The Jizō at the end of the bustling pilgrimage route where I used to walk.
At the temple with the big iron cauldrons for burning incense.
Breathe in the smoke of the incense, let it permeate her body.
Through mother's fingers, mother's toes.
Through the nerves running to the ends of her limbs.
Pull out the thorns stabbing deep, deep into her.
Take away the scent of shit that has sunk into my hands.
As I pour clear water.
Onto your small stone chest and stomach.
Let me scrub away.
Scrub away all our suffering.
(Itō 2011, 32–33; Itō 2016b, 156–57)

For the narrator, Kōganji, the famous Jizō temple in Sugamo, represents a place where one can go in search of solace and comfort, a place that offers relief from pain and that may restore a sense of belonging in the world. It does not necessarily matter to the narrator that there are countless other Jizō statues throughout the country. In fact, there are several other temples also dedicated to Jizō in neighboring temples in Sugamo. The point is that, for her, this particular place has come to represent something fundamental in her mode of being in the world—a place of tradition and history where one engages in simple acts of worship to remove suffering. A pilgrimage to Sugamo is more than a trip through a bustling part of Tokyo; it becomes part of a spiritual quest.

SUGAMO AS SPACE AND PLACE

In his influential study of geographical belonging, *Space and Place: The Perspective of Experience*, Yi-Fu Tuan (b. 1930) distinguishes between a "place"—a location to which people feel attached and that provides them with a sense of belonging—and a "space" which represents a location where people engage in activities to support their lives (2001, 3–7). Tuan points out, however, that certain locations can be both "places" and "spaces"—in other words, locations that provide a sense of belonging and a location for action. This is how the narrator of "The Thorn-Puller" experiences Sugamo. To her, Sugamo is both a "place" full of associations that helps her mother feel a sense of tradition and belonging, and, at the same time, it is also a "space" where the narrator can act in a way that she hopes will shape her life in a positive way. Tuan points out that, when it comes to a location like Sugamo that has a religious significance, people experience it as a kind of "hazy 'mythical' space that surrounds the field of pragmatic activity, to which we do not consciously attend and which is yet necessary to our sense of orientation—of being securely in the world" (Ibid., 86). As an example, Tuan notes that knowing the direction of Mecca helps to give a sense of orientation in the world to Muslims, who rely upon that knowledge in creating an overall worldview that benefits them wherever they might be living. Similarly, in "The Thorn-Puller," the concrete "place" of Sugamo transforms into a hazy mythical "space" that exists beyond the immediate boundaries of one's daily life, but that still gives one a general sense of overall orientation in the world. Sugamo helps to ground the characters' worldview and cosmology, even when they are living quite far from it.

In an important passage in "The Thorn-Puller" when the narrator is visiting Sugamo, she realizes the extent to which the old spiritual practices and folk traditions of the place remain with her, even though she ordinarily lives far away and her thoughts do not necessarily turn to Sugamo on a daily basis. Revisiting the temple, she comments to herself,

> It was strange.
> I hadn't come to worship there in ages, but I still remembered what worshippers are supposed to do.
> You wash your hands to purify them.
> Then you toss some sticks of incense into the gigantic incense burner.
> You'll get pushed, you can't pay those people any heed, you'll remain stuck and won't be able to get close to the incense burner unless you push your way toward it through the crowds, once you get there you fan the smoke toward you with your hand, you fan it toward yourself, then you rub it on the part of your body that ails you, head, face, shoulders, chest, hands, throat, then you go to the main hall of the temple, you throw some change into the collection box, then pray.
> Then you get in the line for the Washing Kannon and wait your turn, but that day, we decided to forgo that because of the lines. (Itō 2011, 104)

The places that Itō mentions in this passage are all sights that pilgrims to Kōganji Temple are likely to see. The large incense burner mentioned in this passage is an enormous metal cauldron that stands just off the Sugamo Jizō Shopping Street as one approaches the temple. Covered with a roof to protect the incense and ashes inside from rain, the cauldron smolders with smoke rising from the constant offerings of incense from pilgrims and passers-by.

To the left-hand side of the cauldron is the statue of the "Washing Kannon" (*Arai-Kannon*) mentioned at the end of the passage cited above. Kannon is the Japanese name of the Buddhist bodhisattva who is believed to be a perfect embodiment of the virtues of compassion and mercy. Kannon is not the main deity worshipped at Kōganji, but the Kannon statue that stands at the side of the temple grounds has, like Jizō, grown popular among temple-goers seeking an end to their own suffering. The story of the statue dates back to the year 1657, when a large swath of the city of Edo burned in an enormous, two-day fire known as the Meireki conflagration (*Meireki no taiga*). It is estimated that thirty thousand people died, and legend has it that one of them was the wife of a temple-goer at Kōganji. Mourning her loss, the widower donated a stone statue of Kannon to the temple. For reasons that have been lost to history, a belief emerged over time that, if one were to pour water over the statue and scrub the affected part of one's own body with a scrub brush, any affliction that one had in the same spot would go away (Sugamo Jizō-dōri Shōtengai Shinkō Kumiai 1999; Kōganji 2000, 32). In some ways, the "Washing Kannon" statue fulfills a function similar to the miraculous sixteenth-century Jizō image in that washing the statue of Kannon at Kōganji and consuming an image of Jizō (either through plastering it on the outside of the body or swallowing it) serve as ways for people to rid themselves of bodily ailments. One might argue that the "Washing Kannon," which stands outside year round, serves as a public, easily accessible substitute for the temple's miraculous stick used to print images of Jizō, which is too small and fragile for the temple to place on display. Over the course of centuries, the face of the "Washing Kannon" was worn nearly flat by worshippers. In 1992 priests replaced the old statue with a new one that still stands outside in the grounds of the temple today. For the sake of preservation, priests have also forbidden the use of scrub brushes. Instead, they request that people use cloths and sponges to clean the statue. In front of the statue are buckets filled with water, holders for flowers, and railings to keep order among the long lines of worshipers who congregate and wait to wash the statue on the temple's three monthly pilgrimage days.

REMEMBERING SUGAMO ACROSS GENERATIONS OF WOMEN

In several passages of the "The Thorn-Puller," the narrator recounts some of the details of her family's history, and it becomes increasingly clear what a large role the Jizō and Kannon statues located there played in their lives. In the second chapter, for instance, there is an extended passage that describes the life of the narrator's grandparents in the nearby neighborhood of Iwanosaka. As the narrator notes, Iwanosaka is a former post town where, in the Edo period, travelers could find lodgings as they travelled north along the Nakasendō Highway out of Edo. As Japan entered the modern era, it became a neighborhood where poor and working-class families came to live. "Through the beginning of the twentieth century, there were still a number of wooden apartments and cheap row houses close to the station. All sorts of people congregated there: beggars, hobos, vendors selling incense for the Jizō in Sugamo, and men who hung around on the street but were willing to push carts full of luggage for spare change" (Itō 2011, 35; Itō 2015a, 47–48).

The narrator notes that there were so many indigent people in the neighborhood that people began to adopt unwanted children, knowing that, when a

Worshippers at Kōganji scrubbing the "Washing Kannon." *Jeffrey Angles.*

child was sent out for adoption, they would arrive with money and clothing from their former family. Although the book does not give much in the way of historical background, in early modern Japan, if a family had more children than they could support, the parents might send one or more of the children to other families for adoption, hoping that they could find a better life elsewhere. Children and adolescents sent out to live with other families might work with their adoptive families as laborers, shop clerks, apprentices, entertainers, or, in some unfortunate situations, perhaps even as sex workers. The narrator of "The Thorn-Puller" notes that each time a new child arrived in Iwanosaka there would be feasting and celebration in the community. Soon afterward, however, many of the children met with unexpected deaths. "When the deaths came to light, it became apparent that the crime wasn't the work of one or two rogues; the entire neighborhood had been involved.... Sometimes the community would raise the child and put it to work. Sometimes they would simply kill it. They killed dozens of infants simply because they were too young to be of any use" (Itō 2011, 35–36; Itō 2015a, 48).

The narrator offers this story about the Iwanosaka child murders as background information to show how difficult life was for her grandparents' generation in the Shitamachi neighborhoods of Tokyo and the extraordinary lengths to which residents would go to get their hands on even a little cash. Like many families at the time, her grandparents had numerous children, and so her grandfather left his family and went off to the island of Sado in the Sea of Japan to earn some money. While working there, he suffered a stroke and became half-paralyzed, leaving her grandmother Toyoko to fend for the entire family. The narrator notes, "She did anything and everything she could think of to make money. Anything and everything. She worked her fingers to the bone. She sewed, she sang, she worked like mad trying to provide for her children and husband" (Itō 2011, 36; Itō 2015a, 49). For some time, Toyoko began to be possessed by spirits who would speak through her, make predictions, and answer people's questions. She tried to monetize her spiritual gift by selling her services as a shamaness to the community. However, as soon as she did, the spirits stopped coming to her, and she was thrown into even greater despair and desperation than before. It was then, the narrator tells us, that Toyoko heard for the first time about the miraculous Jizō at Kōganji, and she went there to pray. After she did so, the situation finally began to stabilize somewhat for the family.

It was another working-class woman who lived in the neighborhood—a woman who sold incense on the streets in front of Kōganji—who told the narrator's grandmother Toyoko how effective the temple's statues were in helping to alleviate suffering. In mentioning this detail, Itō makes it clear that sharing the healing graces of the miraculous deities of Sugamo has been one method that troubled women have used for generations to help one another. This is enacted most dramatically in subsequent chapters when the narrator goes to Sugamo to get a protective amulet for her mother in Kumamoto as her health fails. As mentioned above, the narrator ends up sharing that amulet with her friend who appears to have cancer. Later she returns to get a second amulet, which brings great joy to her mother. As a dedicated feminist, Itō is interested in the kinds of connections women forge with each other and the methods they use to provide one another with aid. In this context, the miraculous statues of Jizō and Kannon at Kōganji in Sugamo take on a special significance. Although Jizō and Kannon are accessible to all people, regardless of gender, the overwhelming majority of the people who put their faith in them in the novel are women, especially troubled and indigent women who feel that they have few other resources. Itō seems to be suggesting that spiritual faith is an especially strong aid to women. Throughout the book, the narrator's thoughts turn to the Sugamo Jizō when things go badly with her own parents, children, and husband. In her repeated discussions of the temple at Sugamo, Itō demonstrates that seeking refuge and succor at the temple has helped women across generations deal with and perhaps even gain some small sense of agency.

In connection with the influence of Sugamo on the lives of multiple generations of women, there is one particularly relevant conversation in the book in which the narrator talks with her ailing mother about her memories of Sugamo. The conversation takes place immediately after the dream in which the narrator's mother imagines wiping away the thorns in Jizō's face and immediately receiving his help. Since the dream has excited the mother so much, the narrator changes the subject and begins asking her mother what she and her grandmother did when they went to worship at Kōganji.

> So what did you do when you'd get to Sugamo?
> We'd go to the temple, of course. They've got that big pot full of burning incense, and we'd rub the smoke on the parts of my body that were giving us trouble. Then we'd wash it, of course.
> Wash what?
> The Jizō, with his clothes off.
> Are you sure it was Jizō you washed? People usually wash the statue of Kannon...
> Nope. (Mother's response is emphatic.) The statue didn't have the face of a Kannon. It had the face of a Jizō. There was a scrub brush there, and if you scrubbed the part of the statue that was giving you trouble, then Jizō would take the thorns away.
> Are you sure you're not talking about the statue of Kannon that people wash?
> Nope. (Once again, mother fires back without hesitation.) I'm telling you, the Jizō had the face of a young child. Kannon doesn't look like that. (Itō 2011, 47–8; modified from Itō 2015a, 56)

The mother is clearly confusing the two miraculous statues of Kōganji: the Jizō, which helps worshippers rid themselves of the thorns of suffering but is rarely if ever on display, and the Kannon, which stands out in the open in front of the temple and which worshippers wash as a means of healing the parts of their body that are giving them trouble. This conversation suggests that the mother is growing increasingly confused with age and perhaps even developing the first signs of dementia, but the message that comes across is that it almost does not matter who the deities were. What is important is that the temple in Sugamo is itself a site of refuge, and the acts of faith performed there were what is important to both her and her grandmother before her.

The narrator wants to find out more about her mother's and grandmother's habits when going to worship at Sugamo. When she asks what her grandmother wore on those visits, her mother's confusion begins to show through, producing a humorous exchange in which her mother does not seem to be tracking too well.

> What do you call that kind of clothing Grandma wore when she went to see the statue?
> Those? Another relative named Tokiyo took them all away.
> No, Mom. I'm not asking you who took them away.
> I've still got one left, so if you want to wear it, I've got one for you. You'd have to look in the chest of drawers though.
> No, Mom. I'm not asking 'cause I want to wear it. I was just wondering what you call the clothing Grandma used to wear.
> It's an *akashi*. In June, you'd wear an *akashi*. There was also something called a *jōfu*. I've forgotten. Back in the old days, you'd wear certain things during certain months. In June a such-and-such, in July a such-and-such, and so on. And then in July, you'd wear a kimono of silk gauze.
> The kind I'm talking about is a single-layered kimono. It's light grey and has a small, intricate pattern.
> Oh, that one. I've got one of those at my place.
> Mom, I'm trying to ask you what that kind of kimono is called. (I want to be able to write about the kind of kimono that she wore. Whenever I think of my grandmother, that's how I remember her.)
> You think I'd remember something like that? (Itō 2011, 48–49; Itō 2015a, 56–57).

As the conversation progresses, it gets so mixed up that the narrator's mother (who we learn in this passage is named Māko) begins to confuse experiences that she had in Sugamo with her own mother (Toyoko) with experiences that she had at Sugamo with her own daughter, the narrator (Hiromi). Itō seems to have included this humorous exchange in order to provide a bit of levity, but it also shows us that worshipping at Sugamo was an experience shared by multiple generations of the same family. The narrator's mother comments,

> And if anything happened to Mother, she'd immediately go to the Jizō. Anything difficult or trying, she'd set off right away.
> You mean she'd go on the special days set aside for worship?
> That's right. On the fourteenth.
> Isn't the twenty-fourth the usual day to worship Jizō?
> Yep, that's right.

> But just now, you said you'd go on the fourteenth.
> Oh, I did? Well then, I guess I was right, maybe we did go on the fourteenth. I wonder why I went on the fourteenth. Maybe because it was empty? If my daughter was with me, then I'd have to hold her hand, so I suppose it was easier when the place was empty. She was weak and always, always sick. She cost us so much at the doctor's that it became a real issue. Your grandmother and I prayed, we even gave up drinking tea so Jizō would be more likely to lend us his ear. We went to pray and wash Jizō every month.
> Which daughter are you talking about?
> Māko. No, wait. I'm Māko. It couldn't have been Aiko, so who was it? Oh, I'm thinking of Shiromi. Shiromi was the one with the weak constitution. (Itō 2011, 49–50; Itō 2015a, 57)

In her confusion, the mother switches the topic of conversation from her mother's trips to Sugamo to her own trips to Sugamo. Then, in the final lines quoted above, she seems to forget whom she is talking about and to whom she is speaking. The daughter she is describing is, in fact, the person who is sitting right in front of her asking questions—Hiromi, whose name appears here as "Shiromi," pronounced in the Tokyo fashion. The important point is that the mother (Māko) has mapped the relationship that the grandmother (Toyoko) and mother (Māko) had with Sugamo onto the relationship that the mother (Māko) and the narrator (Hiromi) had with Sugamo. In the process, Sugamo quite literally becomes a shared experience that links together three different generations of women in the family.

The mother's memories have become muddled, but there is no question that her faith remains unshaken and that, for her, as well as her mother before her and her daughter afterward, Sugamo represents a site that allowed her to gain a sense of purpose and mastery over the difficulties in her life. To return to the formulation presented by Tuan, the mystical "space" of Sugamo in which people perform their acts of ritual becomes a "place" that allows them to feel a sense of belonging and purpose. The fact that Sugamo operates as both a real "space" of ritual and a "place" of belonging helps to give worshippers a sense of orientation in the world, even when they are far away from Sugamo physically. In passages such as this, Itō seems to be reminding us, her readers, that cities and neighborhoods are not just physical locations. They are also intertextual, polyvocal collections of beliefs, memories, stories, myths, and tales that weave together to create a complex fabric of cultural knowledge and memory that goes beyond statues, buildings, streets, and individual generations. "The Thorn-Puller" is much more than an amusing story of a narrator trying to find humor in her life as she cares for her rapidly aging parents, argumentative husband, and needy children. It is a reminder that the city streets of Tokyo are alive with stories, mapped through the operations of memory which unfold and play out across multiple generations.

NOTES

1. The narrator of *The Thorn-Puller* is, like the author herself, a middle-aged woman named "Itō." Because Itō Hiromi has exaggerated and shaped her own experiences in writing the book, readers should not assume a complete equivalency between Itō and the protagonist. I will use Itō's name when writing about her own experiences, but I will refer to the "narrator" when talking about the main figure in the novel.
2. I have published several chapters of the book in English with the eventual goal of completing a translation of the entire work. See Itō 2015a, Itō 2016a, Itō 2016b, and Itō 2017. I have included references to both the original, complete Japanese novel as well as the partial English translation for the convenience of both Japanese and Anglophone readers.
3. Itō's writing shaped an entire generation of younger poets, first by broadening the types of subject matter that poets could write about, and second, by trying to capture and record the unique rhythms and qualities of spoken language in her writing. One sees these trends in the following works: Arai 2007, Arai 2013, Minashita 2005, Minashita 2008, and Ōsaki 2014. For English translations of Arai Takako, Minashita Kiriu, and Ōsaki Sayaka, see Angles 2016; Arai 2010; Itō, Hirata, and Arai 2016; and Minashita, Park, Sekiguchi, and Arai 2006.
4. "The Thorn-Puller" often does not use traditional punctuation, such as quotations around quoted speech. Itō also frequently uses sentence fragments or long sentences with clauses loosely connected by commas. The translations provided in this chapter reflect some of those non-standard writing practices.

WORKS CITED

Amano Tōru. 2001. "Jizō-dōri kūkan no hensen ("Changes in the Space of Jizō Street")." In *Daitoshi kōreisha to sakariba: Togenuki Jizō o tsukuru hitobito* ("Senior Citizens and the Bustling Areas of the Metropolis: The People behind the Creation of the Thorn-Pulling Jizō"), Reprint, 41–82. Toshi Kenkyū Sōsho 7. Tokyo: Tōkyō Toritsu Daigaku Shuppankai.

Angles, Jeffrey, editor and translator. 2016. *These Things Here and Now: Poetic Responses to the March 11, 2011 Disasters*. Tokyo: Josai University Educational Corporation University Press.

Arai Takako. 2007. *Tamashii dansu* ("Soul Dance"). Tokyo: Michitani.

———. 2010. *Soul Dance*. Translated by Jeffrey Angles. Tokyo: Mi'Te Press.

———. 2013. *Betto to shoki* ("Beds and Looms"). Tokyo: Michitani.

Asagawa Tatsuto. 2001. "Togenuki Jizō e iku hito ikanai hito ("People Who Go to the Thorn-Pulling Jizō and Those Who Do Not")." In *Daitoshi kōreisha to sakariba: Togenuki Jizō o tsukuru hitobito* ("Senior Citizens and the Bustling Areas of the Metropolis: The People behind the Creation of the Thorn-Pulling Jizō"), Reprint, 83–112. Toshi Kenkyū Sōsho 7. Tokyo: Tōkyō Toritsu Daigaku Shuppankai.

Associated Press. 2016. "Census First to Confirm Shrinking of Population." *The Japan Times Online*, February 26. http://www.japantimes.co.jp/news/2016/02/26/national/census-first-to-confirm-shrinking-of-population/.

Fujita Isshō and Itō Hiromi. 2016. *Zen no kyōshitsu: Zazen de tsukamu Bukkyō no shinzui* ("The Zen Lecture Hall: The Essence of Buddhism as Grasped through Seated Meditation"). Chūō shinsho 2365. Tokyo: Chūō Kōronsha.

Ishii Tatsuhiko. 1999. "Ikizuku nikutai toshite no shi: Itō Hiromi no ars poetica ("Poetry as Living Flesh: The Ars Poetica of Itō Hiromi")." In *Gendai shi toshite no tanka* ("Tanka as Modern Poetry"), 221–33. Tokyo: Shoshi Yamada.

Itō Hiromi. 1993. *Watashi wa Anjuhimeko de aru* ("I Am Anjuhimeko"). Tokyo: Shichōsha.

———. 2004. *Nihon no fushigi na hanashi* ("Strange Tales from Japan"). Tokyo: Asahi Shinbunsha.

———. 2005. *Kawara arekusa* ("Wild Grass on the Riverbank"). Tokyo: Shichōsha.

———. 2007. *Togenuki: Shin Sugamo Jizō engi* ("The Thorn-Puller: New Tales of the Sugamo Jizō"). Tokyo: Kōdansha.

———. 2009. *Killing Kanoko: Selected Poems of Hiromi Itō*. Translated by Jeffrey Angles. Notre Dame, IN: Action Books.
———. 2010. *Yomitoki Han'nya shingyō* ("The Heart Sutra Explained"). Tokyo: Mainichi Shinbun Shuppan.
———. 2011. *Togenuki: Shin Sugamo Jizō engi* ("The Thorn-Puller: New Tales of the Sugamo Jizō"). Tokyo: Kōdansha Bunko.
———. 2012. *Tadotadoshiku koe ni dashite yomu Tan'nishō* ("Reading the *Lamentations of Divergences* Falteringly Out Loud"). Tokyo: Puneumasha.
———. 2013. *Yomitoki Han'nya shingyō* ("The Heart Sutra Explained"). Tokyo: Asahi Bunko.
———. 2015a. "Mother Leads Me from Iwanosaka toward Sugamo" (Chapter 2 of "The Thorn-Puller: New Tales of the Jizō Statue at Sugamo"). Translated by Jeffrey Angles. *Monkey Business: New Writing from Japan* 5: 47–58.
———. 2015b. *Wild Grass on the Riverbank*. Translated by Jeffrey Angles. Notre Dame, Indiana: Action Books.
———. 2016a. "Itō Crosses the Ocean and the Broad Slope of the Underworld While Throwing Peaches" (Chapter 3 of "The Thorn-Puller: New Tales of the Jizō Statue at Sugamo"). Translated by Jeffrey Angles. *Tripwire* 11: 40–51.
———. 2016b. "Itō Returns to Japan and Finds Herself in a Real Pinch" (Chapter 1 of "The Thorn-Puller: New Tales of the Jizō Statue at Sugamo"). Translated by Jeffrey Angles. *Monkey Business: New Writing from Japan* 6: 144–57.
———. 2017. "Evil Fourishes but Itō Encounters Jizō in Broad Daylight" (Chapter 5 of "The Thorn-Puller: New Tales of the Jizō Statue at Sugamo"). Translated by Jeffrey Angles. *Monkey Business: New Writing from Japan* 7: 36–47.
Itō, Hiromi, Toshiko Hirata, and Takako Arai. 2016. *Poems of Hiromi Itō, Toshiko Hirata & Takako Arai*. Translated by Jeffrey Angles. Newtown, Australia: Vagabond Press.
Kanaseki Hisao. 1988. *Mahō toshite no kotoba: Amerika Indian no kōshōshi* ("Words as Magic: The Oral Poetry of the American Indians"). Tokyo: Shichōsha.
Kōganji. 2000. *Kōganji shi: Togenuki Jizō-zon* ("A History of Kōganji Temple: The Thorn-Pulling Jizō Statue"). Tokyo: Kōganji.
Minashita Kiriu. 2005. *Onsoku heiwa* ("Sonic Peace"). Tokyo: Shichōsha.
———. 2008. *Z-kyō* ("The Scream / The Z-Border"). Tokyo: Shichōsha.
Minashita, Kiriu, Kyong-Mi Park, Ryoko Sekiguchi, and Takako Arai. 2006. *Four from Japan: Contemporary Poetry & Essays by Women*. Translated by Sawako Nakayasu. Brooklyn: Litmus Press/Belladonna Books.
Murai, Shusuke. 2015. "Government Earmarks Funds to Deal with Caregiver Shortage." *The Japan Times Online*, January 21. http://www.japantimes.co.jp/news/2015/01/21/national/facing-severe-caregiver-shortage-government-dedicates-funds-to-promoting-profession/.
Nomura Kiwao and Kido Shuri. 2001. *Sengo Meishi Sen II* ("Famous Postwar Poems II"). Gendai Shi Bunko Tokushū Han 2. Tokyo: Shichōsha.
Ōsaki Sayaka. 2014. *Yubi sasu koto ga dekinai* ("Pointing Impossible"). Tokyo: Seidosha.
Sōmushō Tōkeikyoku. 2013. "Tōkei kara mita wagakuni no kōreisha (65-sai ijō): Keirō no Hi ni chinande" ("Our Nation's Senior Citizens [65 Years and Older] as Seen through Statistics: In Conjunction with Respected for the Aged Day"). Government website. *Tōkeikyoku Hōmupēji, Heisei 25-Nen, Tōkei Topikkusu No. 72*. September 15. http://www.stat.go.jp/data/topics/topi721.htm.
Sugamo Jizō-dōri Shōtengai Shinkō Kumiai. 1999. "Togenuki Jizō-zon, Kōganji, Sugamo Jizō-Dōri Shōtengai" ("The Thorn-Pulling Jizō Statue, Kōganji Temple, and the Sugamo Jizō Shopping Street"). 2016. http://www.sugamo.or.jp/prayer_detail01.html.
Takagi Kōichi. 2001. "Sakariba toshite no Togenuki Jizō" ("The Thorn-Pulling Jizō as an Bustling Entertainment Space"). In *Daitoshi kōreisha to sakariba: Togenuki Jizō o tsukuru hitobito* ("Senior Citizens and the Bustling Areas of the Metropolis: The People behind the Creation of the Thorn-Pulling Jizō"), Reprint, 113–40. Toshi Kenkyū Sōsho 7. Tokyo: Tōkyō Toritsu Daigaku Shuppankai.
Tuan, Yi-Fu. 2001. *Space and Place: The Perspective of Experience*. 5th edition. Minneapolis: University of Minnesota Press.

United Nations, DESA, Population Division. 2001. "World Population Ageing 1950–2050 Japan." *World Population Ageing: 1950–2050 (Japan)*. http://www.un.org/esa/population/publications/worldageing19502050/pdf/119japan.pdf.

Chapter Two

Pavane for a Dead Princess, or Exploring Geographies of the City, the Mind, and the Social

Fujita Yoshinaga's Tenten *and*
Miki Satoshi's Adrift in Tokyo

Kristina Iwata-Weickgenannt

"In the rush of our daily lives," urban historian Jinnai Hidenobu laments, "and accustomed as we are to moving about by subway and automobile, we have few chances to take a leisurely walk around the city" (1995 [1985], 2)—and, as a result, we grow insensitive to Tokyo's beauty. To Jinnai, Tokyo's charm may not be immediately obvious. Rather than possessing a wealth of well-preserved historical buildings and a large number of architecturally distinctive structures or an overall consistent urban design, Jinnai observes, it is the peculiar blend of old and new elements that gives each Tokyo neighborhood—and Tokyo as a whole—its special character. Locating the city's fascination in its details, Jinnai insists that "[f]or the walker in Tokyo, the unexpected is always waiting" (Ibid.).

The literary and cinematic narratives under discussion in this chapter—the novel *Tenten* ("From Here to There," 1999) and its 2007 movie adaptation (also titled *Tenten*)—extend an invitation to explore Tokyo with the eyes of a stroller. Written by Fujita Yoshinaga (b. 1950), *Tenten* was first published by Futabasha Publishing. Paperback editions were published in 2002 by Futaba Bunko and in 2005 by Shinchō Bunko. Despite its apparent commercial success in Japan, the novel has neither been translated into any foreign language nor has it attracted much journalistic or scholarly attention. In contrast, Miki Satoshi's (b. 1961) film adaptation was released with English subtitles in 2009 as *Adrift in Tokyo*,[1] and is available through commercial streaming services in the United States and elsewhere.

Starring hugely popular Odagiri Joe (b. 1976) as Fumiya and veteran actor Miura Tomokazu (b. 1952) as Fukuhara in the lead roles, *Adrift in Tokyo* was shown at film festivals around the globe. At the 2008 Fantasia International Film Festival in Montreal, one of the largest and most influential genre-film festivals in North America, the 101-minute-long film received the Best Script Award for Miki as well as Special Mention for Miura and Odagiri. In the same year, Miura was also given the Japanese Kinema Junpō Award for the best supporting actor. Established by the cinema magazine *Kinema Junpō* in 1925, this award boasts a longer history than the U.S. Academy Awards (founded 1929) and to this day remains one of Japan's most important cinema awards.

Extensive and seemingly aimless walking is a key component of *Tenten* and *Adrift in Tokyo*, and so is the unexpected. Both stories are characterized by a series of chance encounters and unforeseen twists and turns, in the plot as well as in regard to the walking route. *Tenten* and *Adrift in Tokyo* tell the story of Takemura Fumiya, a hopelessly indebted university student, and the significantly older loan shark Fukuhara Ai'ichirō. The two men set out as opponents. Unable to pay his rent, let alone pay off his debts, Fumiya (who, in contrast to the older, more authoritative Fukuhara, is always called by his given name in both texts) is kicked out of his shabby Kichijōji apartment in the beginning of the story. Having neither relatives nor friends to rely on, he suspiciously accepts a deal proposed by the intimidating debt collector Fukuhara who offers him a reward of one million yen for accompanying him on a walk across Tokyo. Starting out in Inokashira Park, which straddles the cities of Mitaka and Musashino in Tokyo's western suburbs, they progress at a leisurely pace and without following a pre-set course, but neither are they detached observers, nor is their stroll in fact aimless; it is not even completely voluntary on both parts. The two men visit a number of places that are included in any decent guidebook, but they are not sightseeing. Neither intellectual, observant flâneurs in the sense of Walter Benjamin (1991 [1929]) nor tourists, Fukuhara and Fumiya depart on a journey with no return.

Tenten and *Adrift in Tokyo* represent an unusual kind of road novel/road movie in which the journey takes on a metaphoric meaning, if a different one for both characters. Fukuhara's final destination lies in the central district of Kasumigaseki just south of the moat-encircled Imperial Palace. Home to most of Japan's cabinet ministry offices, Kasumigaseki figuratively stands for Japan's administrative bureaucracy. In a similar way, Nagatachō, the name of the neighboring district where the Diet and the Prime Minister's Office are located, is used as metonym for the elected government. Japan's Supreme Court, too, is but a stone's throw away from Kasumigaseki and Nagatachō, and so is the Metropolitan Police Department, casually referred to as Sakuradamon after its location, where Fukuhara is headed. There, he intends to turn himself in for having accidentally killed his wife.

Fond of walking, Fukuhara and his wife had dreamed of spending their old age strolling around Tokyo. Since this is no longer possible, Fukuhara engages Fumiya in his project instead. Apart from a few notable exceptions, Tokyo urban space takes on a rather subdued, abstract meaning in Miki's film, but in Fujita's novel, the city itself takes center stage. In fact, the author's meticulous descriptions allow the reader to trace the two men's walking route in quite some detail. However, while even those familiar with Tokyo will be tempted to refer to a map or even to "follow" the two by accessing panoramic street views on the internet, Fukuhara navigates the city without ever consulting a plan. In *Tenten*, Fukuhara and Fumiya's memoryscapes are translated into geographical space—space replete with symbolic meaning. While geographically their journey spirals around the heart of Japan (its political, juridical, and symbolic center), it also takes the two protagonists to the very margins of Japanese post-bubble society, away from the shiny grand avenues, deep into the labyrinth of Tokyo's back alleys, and into the maze of their own memories.

This chapter traces and interconnects both narratives' layered geographies of the mind, the city, and the social. I show that, although differently accentuated, both texts use *walking* as a means to link the past (memories) with the present (Tokyo places). I argue that, especially in the film, this is not limited to a simple updating of already existing connections. By including vivid but fake memories of specific places, *Adrift in Tokyo* in particular stresses the constructional character of memory. Just as the old and new in the urban fabric of Tokyo are not always easy to separate or necessarily authentic, memories are shown to be (sometimes rather unreliable) products of the present.

TWO AUTEURS: FUJITA YOSHINAGA AND MIKI SATOSHI

Born in Fukui City (Fukui Prefecture), Fujita Yoshinaga dropped out of Waseda University and moved to Paris, where he spent several years working, inter alia, as a flight attendant for Air France and translating French mystery novels into Japanese. Upon his return to Japan, he began publishing essays while working as French teacher. His writing career took off in 1986 when he debuted as a writer of crime fiction with *Yabō no rabirinsu* ("Labyrinth of Ambition"), a whodunit set in Paris. In 1995, Fujita received the Mystery Writers of Japan Award (*Nihon suiri sakka kyōkai shō*) as well as a special award from the Japan Adventure Fiction Association (*Nihon bōken shōsetsu kyōkai tokubetsu shō*) for a spy novel set in 1930s Europe, *Kōtetsu no kishi* ("Steel Knight"). This novel shares its title with a popular Japan-exclusive video game in which players reenact major World War II battles, but it is not directly related in content. In 1999, Fujita received a small literary award, the Shimasen Romance Literature Prize (*Shimasen ren'ai bungaku shō*) for one of his first works in the genre, *Kyūai* ("Yearning for Love," 1999). In terms of literary prizes, Fujita reached a high point in his career in 2001 when *Ai no ryōbun* ("Territory of Love," 2011) was selected for the Naoki Prize, Japan's most prestigious literary award for popular fiction. Created by the writer Kikuchi Kan (1888–1948) in 1935, the Naoki Prize was meant to complement the Akutagawa Prize for serious literature—which Kikuchi simultaneously founded in memory of his writer friend Akutagawa Ryūnosuke (1892–1927). So far, Fujita's fame is largely limited to Japan, as his essays and novels have not yet been translated into another language.

While most of his early novels are set in Paris, Fujita's focus eventually shifted in the late 1990s to depictions of Tokyo's dark underside. Around the same time, his repertory expanded to include love stories. *Tenten* integrates elements of both genres, crime and romance, although the often exaggerated, overly stereotypical descriptions Fujita employs give the text a strong parodist touch. Fumiya, for example, was abandoned by his birth mother at age three, raised single-handedly by his father, a professional swindler who dumped him (when he was just in second grade) at an acquaintance's house in Nagano Prefecture. As if that was not enough, his first stepmother dies of a hornet sting, the second eventually disappears, and his stepfather is arrested for stealing cars. In other words, Fumiya is misfortune incarnate, and has no memories of loving or being loved. Therefore, it comes as no surprise that, among all the women in the world, he falls for the striptease dancer Misuzu who, like Fumiya, is an unloved child (although unlike him she has a wealthy old-family background). Misuzu is unable to return Fumiya's feelings and eventually resolves to become a Buddhist nun.

Miki Satoshi, the director of *Tenten*'s 2007 film adaptation, is firmly rooted in Japan's entertainment scene. Born in Yokohama, he started his career working as an assistant television writer after graduating from Keiō University. He became known nationwide as stage director for the City Boys, a comedy trio founded in 1979, whose yearly live events Miki oversaw from 1989 to 2000. In 1992, he started to occasionally write scripts for television dramas (*dorama*). He began directing *dorama* in 2002, two years after he made his debut as a film director and scriptwriter. Most of his films are comedies, with a focus on the slightly absurd and whimsical. *Adrift in Tokyo* is no exception: director-writer Miki picks up on the parodist side of Fujita's novel and expands it into a full-fledged comedy.

The film's plot is greatly streamlined and characterized by an overall shift to and expansion of Fukuhara's side of the story. The entire episode surrounding Fumiya's lover Misuzu, for instance, is left out, while several scenes are added showing the amateur investigations undertaken into the sudden disappearance of Fukuhara's wife by her co-workers. Mrs. Fukuhara herself also appears in the film, once in a flashback and twice lying dead on her bed. Although the characters are seen walking most of the time, the connection between the plot and specific locations is not as tight as in *Tenten* and it is impossible to reconstruct the walking route. Some of the locations will be easily recognized by anyone who is familiar with Tokyo, but often seemingly adjacent neighborhoods are far apart in reality. For the most part, rather than promenading along Tokyo's famous grand avenues, such as the Ginza or Omotesandō, the two protagonists are seen wandering through the city's nondescript backstreets. Many well-known landmarks, such as the novel's Igusa Hachiman Shrine (located between Kichijōji and Nishi Ogikubo), are replaced by less easily identifiable locations. In *Adrift in Tokyo*, therefore, the cityscape is used as a backdrop before which human emotions such as loneliness and alienation, but also friendship and trust, are acted out in a light and entertaining way. The city is turned into a giant stage for a walk imbued with ritual, and the unfolding of an unlikely friendship.

REPETITION WITH VARIATION: INTERTEXTUAL ECHOING IN *TENTEN* AND *ADRIFT IN TOKYO*

Before looking at discourses on time/memory, space, and the unexpected in *Tenten* and *Adrift in Tokyo* in more detail, we need to consider the relationship between the two texts. On a fundamental level, Fujita's novel and Miki's film are autonomous works that may be enjoyed and interpreted as such. Especially for "unknowing audiences" (Hutcheon 2006, 120), who do not have any knowledge of (the existence of) the respective other text, appreciating them as aesthetic statements in their own right is the only possible way to approach the version they are experiencing. However, "knowing audiences" (Ibid.) will not only recognize the relationship to the respective other work, but their appreciation is likely to be influenced by the impression left by the previously consumed text: "If we know that prior text, we always feel its presence shadowing the one we are experiencing directly" (Ibid., 6).

Although it can safely be assumed that many readers of this chapter will be unfamiliar with at least one, if not both, versions of Fumiya and Fukuhara's journey across Tokyo, the following analysis deliberately weaves together the two texts. This is not simply to avoid the danger of reinstating the long-obsolete, hierarchizing binary between an "original" and a presumably inferior "derivative." Adaptations are understood here not as attempts at faithful replication in a different media or genre, but rather as palimpsests—as necessarily involving both repetition and variation, familiarity and novelty. Linda Hutcheon describes adaptations as an "ongoing dialogue with the past" (Ibid., 116). Insofar as it recalls the work that came before, adaptation may itself be regarded as an act of memory. The joint discussion of *Tenten* and *Adrift in Tokyo* thus allows for another layer of memory to take shape, that of "intertextual echoing" (Ibid., 117).

The following analysis will focus on themes and motifs in *Tenten* and *Adrift in Tokyo*, as well as the textual interplay between the two texts. The discussion begins with the spatial and temporal dimension of Fumiya and Fukuhara's walking route, suggesting that in both works it runs contrary not only to the historical direction of urban development, but also to the characters' own histories. The implied return to origins is then examined in a section dealing with the symbolic meaning the walk takes on for each character. This is followed by an exploration of Miki's constructivist approach to memory and the way the unexpected as well as the unlikely (re-)shape the memoryscape in *Adrift in Tokyo*. The chapter closes with a discussion of the film's shift in focus away from the visceral experience of the city to an emphasis on urban interpersonal relationships. To illustrate that shift, I take a close look at Miki's use of a common trope in Japanese film and *dorama*, namely food and meals.

FROM SUBURB TO CENTER, FROM PRESENT TO PAST

Fumiya and Fukuhara's walk across Tokyo has little to do with a leisure activity. Despite all its lightness, it bears serious undertones. Unable to repay his debts of 840,000 yen, Fumiya has been hiding from loan sharks for several months—in the novel the reader learns that to get away from them he even moved from central Takadanobaba to Kichijōji, located a twenty-minute train ride away in Tokyo's western suburbs. The attempts to hide are in vain: Fukuhara sniffs him out and threatens to make him work for several months on a deep-sea fishing fleet if he does not accompany him on the walk. In addition, Fumiya is kicked out of his apartment the day before the proposed start. Thus, left with little choice, he disposes of the majority of his few belongings and sets out literally homeless, with only a small backpack in the novel and no luggage at all in the film.

Fumiya meets Fukuhara at the foot of a bridge, which underscores the symbolic transition to the new life that lies ahead of them. The bridge is located in Inokashira Park just behind Kichijōji Station, an extremely popular spot for springtime cherry blossom viewing. There is a large, picturesque lake at the center of the park. Legend has it that couples will break up if they ride one of the swan-shaped rental boats. The explanation offered cites the jealousy of Benzaiten, a Buddhist goddess who is revered in a small temple situated on a tiny island in the lake. This dark, somewhat spine-chilling side of the park's image took on an element of reality when, in 1994, park workers discovered various parts of a human body that were disposed of in plastic bags in a trash can. The gruesome case remains unsolved to this day and famously served as an inspiration for Kirino Natsuo's (b. 1951) bestselling novel *OUT* (1998, trans. *OUT*, 2004), which came out a year before *Tenten*.[2] However, in *Tenten* and *Adrift in Tokyo*, the only reference to a famous feature of the park is the Inokashira *dango*, also known as *mifuku dango*, small roasted dumplings made of pounded rice. As detailed below, especially in the film, eating takes on a symbolic meaning that goes far beyond simple food intake, and this is the first instance of Fumiya and Fukuhara sharing a meal.

While the history of *mifuku dango* remains obscure, that of the park itself is well-documented. It was opened to the public in 1917, with the abovementioned boat rental opening a few years later. The foundation of the park thus coincides with the time when Tokyo began its quick westward sprawl. During the Taishō era (1912–1926), the number of people living in cities and leading consumer lifestyles quickly increased. Especially to the west of the Yamanote and Shitamachi areas of central Tokyo, residential towns mushroomed along newly established railroad lines, many of them modeled after English garden cities (*den'en toshi*). Angela Yiu (2006) has shown how contemporary writers such as Kunikida Doppo (1871–1908) and others boosted the popularity of these architecturally "Western" areas among the urban elite. The expansion of the suburbs continued in the postwar era, and so did the association with literature. This is true in particular of the area served by Asagaya, (Nishi) Ogikubo, and Kichijōji Stations on the JR Chūō-Sōbu Line that connects the western Tokyo municipalities of Mitaka and Musashino (as well as Chiba Prefecture in the east) with central Tokyo. To name but a few, Ibuse Masuji (1898–1993), Yosano Akiko (1878–1942), and Dazai Osamu (1909–1948) all lived in the area, which from the 1980s onwards also became closely connected to the literature of Murakami Haruki (b. 1949). Dotted with countless cafés and small boutiques, Kichijōji's former reputation as an artist colony still resonates today. Needless to say, Fumiya's miserable life in Kichijōji does not fit in with the area's fancy image.

Starting out in the western suburbs, Fumiya and Fukuhara head for central Tokyo, the symbolic center of Japan. In a sense, theirs is also a journey to the past. However, the past they revisit is not a collective, public one tied to the numerous historical sites they stop at while en route. Rather, their walk serves to connect the emptiness of their present—both men lost the woman they love (in the film, Fumiya never even had a lover)—to memories, and, consequently, all destinations are related to unresolved issues in their personal histories.

WALKING AS RITE OF PASSAGE

Fukuhara is the one who initiates the walk and, despite its seeming randomness, stays in control of the route throughout the book. (In the film the characters are simply shown walking without ever deliberating about the route.) For this reason, I will begin by mapping out the meaning this stroll across the city has for Fukuhara, addressing some of the questions that Fumiya does not get a satisfying verbal answer to in either work: Why is Fukuhara determined to turn himself in at Japan's highest police authority when he could do so at the local police box? Why does he insist on walking, and why does he not take the direct route but zigzag across town? Why is he ready to pay Fumiya, a total stranger, a million yen for accompanying him? As mentioned above, the walking route itself does not play a prominent role in the film. However, while many of the specific locations discussed below can only be clearly identified in the novel, the symbolic meaning of the walk is very similar in and central to both texts.

Given that Fukuhara will most likely be incarcerated for the rest of his life, the walk may be read as a rite of passage to a new existence as prisoner. Ethnographer Arnold van Gennep observes that, throughout the world, significant changes in social status (such as the one that lies ahead of Fukuhara) are commonly accompanied by rites of passage (1999, 21, 184). These rites frequently involve broad spatial movements and typically consist of three phases to which the narrative structure of *Tenten* and *Adrift in Tokyo* can be linked. Fukuhara's discontinuation of his business following the homicide (as well as Fumiya's termination of his rental contract, for that matter) can be seen as representing the first phase of *separation* from a previous world. The two men's zigzag walk across Tokyo corresponds to van Gennep's phase of *liminality* during which the transition from a former status to the next has not yet been completed. The final phase of *incorporation* begins as Fukuhara enters the Metropolitan Police Department in the end.

In *Tenten* and *Adrift in Tokyo*, the narrative focus lies on the second phase. If understood as representing the liminal phase in the transition to a minutely regulated, unfree life, both the extended duration of the walk—in the film and the novel, they spend several days on the road—as well as the spontaneity with which Fukuhara and Fumiya determine their next destination attain a deeper meaning. Fukuhara is savoring and at the same time celebrating the civil liberty to go where and whenever he likes for a final time, and his somewhat pretentious choice of the country's highest police authority as the location for his self-determined surrender is part of this mise-en-scène. The walk allows Fukuhara to keep his dignity, and to get ready for his new life. Although not always eloquently verbalized, it represents a phase of self-reflection, remorse, and mourning both in the novel and the film. In the novel, Fukuhara's tireless efforts to solve whatever unresolved issues there may be—not just in his own or Fumiya's life, but also in the lives of people they meet on the way—also signal a desire for closure.

Fukuhara is prepared to follow the rules of ritual. He appears in front of Fumiya dressed in a formal suit and leather shoes (sneakers in the film)—"it wasn't an attire suited for walking all the way to Kasumigaseki" (Fujita 1999, 46–47)—and does not seem to care about the amount of money he spends along the way. For instance, he tosses a 10,000-yen note in the collection box at Igusa Hachiman Shrine, one of their first stops just northwest of Kichijōji Station, and does not bat an eyelid as Fumiya deliberately orders the most expensive kinds of sushi—a food often associated with funerals—as they have dinner on the first evening in the novel. Perhaps money has simply lost its mundane meaning for the prisoner-to-be. But, considering that rituals (and, in particular, religious rites) are closely connected with money in Japan, the generosity of the payment Fumiya is to receive in the end takes on a somewhat spiritual nuance.

Fukuhara's choice of travel companion may be related to the loan shark's own family history. Towards the end of their walk, he takes Fumiya to Yanaka Cemetery, which spreads out behind Nippori Station on the northwestern corner of the Japan Railways Yamanote circle line. Yanaka is one of the few areas of central Tokyo left largely untouched by both the 1923 earthquake and the 1945 air raids. Sprinkled with numerous small temples and home to one of the city's largest cemeteries, with over 7,000 graves—among them many belonging to important political and cultural figures—this picturesque area is overwhelmingly quiet despite its central location. It turns out that their visit falls on the anniversary of the death of Fukuhara's son, who died soon after he was born and whose grave is there. Had he lived, he would probably have been around Fumiya's age; the reader is thus led to speculate that Fukuhara is projecting a part of himself on his orphaned counterpart.[3]

The ceremonial character of Fukuhara and Fumiya's walk is further underscored by a musical metaphor early on in the story. When the two stroll by Musashino Art University (apparently Nihon University in the film) on their way to their first destination, Zenpukuji Park (just north of Kichijōji), Fukuhara catches the sound of someone playing the piano. Fukuhara instantly stops to immerse himself in the music, which he identifies as Maurice Ravel's *Pavane pour une infante défunte* ("Pavane for a Dead Princess," written in 1900). In the novel the music will only be "audible" to those who are familiar with Ravel, but in the film the audience can actually hear it—and possibly recognize the melody when it is played again later in the film's climatic scene. In this first instance, Fukuhara loses himself in the music to such a degree that he does not even notice a woman trying to pass by him on a bicycle. In the film, she even gets into a car accident without Fukuhara noticing it. Fumiya is taken by surprise by this unexpected love for classical music on the part of Fukuhara, but the piece is clearly symbolic of their walk.

A pavane is a solemn kind of dance that enjoyed great popularity at the courts of sixteenth-century Europe, and that survived well into the twentieth century as a musical form. The dance was typically used at the commencement of grand royal ceremonies. Danced in pairs, a pavane proceeds slowly and contains no running passages; in rather simple steps the two partners make circling movements across the room. Although at this point neither the reader nor Fumiya know of Fukuhara's accidental homicide, and of the existence of his own "dead princess," this scene still links the seemingly random zigzag course the two men take across Tokyo to an old, venerable ceremonial. The walk becomes readable as homage to Fukuhara's beloved wife. In point of fact, the only two destinations that Fukuhara insists on including in their route to Kasumigaseki—the Igusa Hachiman Shrine, the place where he and his wife became a couple, and Yanaka Cemetery, where their son's grave is—are related to her and their common family history.

Just as a pavane consists of advances as well as retreating steps, Fukuhara is not in a hurry to reach his final destination. After offering an unusually long prayer at the shrine, in the novel he begins asking Fumiya questions about Misuzu, the sex worker with whom he is still in love, and decides they should stop by at the sleazy Ikebukuro striptease bar where she performs. Again, they do not go there right away. They first head for nearby Nishi Ogikubo, a neighborhood near Kichijōji where Fumiya lived with his biological father from age three until second grade. Fukuhara is curious to find out whether the girl Fumiya first kissed as an elementary-school student still lives in the area, and what has become of her. Thus, while the bouncing alternation between Fukuhara's and Fumiya's memories is reminiscent of the back-and-forth of a pavane, the resulting zigzag route is at the same time reflective of the fragmented, associative character of memory itself.

CLOSING THE DOUBLE CIRCLE:
FUMIYA'S RETURN TO IKEBUKURO

Fumiya is motivated by entirely different reasons when he shows up in Inokashira Park to accompany Fukuhara on his strange journey. Fumiya simply does not have much of a choice. While he does not have much to lose either, chances are that he will be a debt-free man at the end of the walk—if Fukuhara keeps his word. In this sense, Fumiya, too, is going through a transitional phase, but he is too anxious and suspicious of Fukuhara to notice right away. However, over time Fumiya's initial wariness gives way to trust and he gradually opens up. This becomes particularly obvious in the film in non-verbal ways, as seen, for example, in Fumiya's facial expressions and increasingly relaxed body posture. In the film's climatic scene—a rollercoaster ride discussed in detail below—the growing emotional closeness is translated into physical contact as the two men squeeze themselves into the tiny car. The first-person narration in the novel conveys to the reader that Fumiya does enjoy the walk even if he answers otherwise when asked. After a few days he even begins to dread the end: "I wondered how many kilometers were left to the Metropolitan Police Department. Seriously, I wished for Kasumigaseki and Sakuradamon to disappear to the other side of the world" (Fujita 1999, 368).

Thanks to Fukuhara's inquisitiveness, the reader soon gets to know the details of Fumiya's unhappy upbringing (the film's audience learns only that he is an unloved, abandoned child with apparently no social life to speak of). Although Fumiya shows no particular interest in digging up old childhood memories, he lets Fukuhara drag him to Nishi Ogikubo (represented by nearby Asagaya in the film) on the first day to look for his former home. It turns out that it was demolished and replaced by a coin parking lot. The house of his former classmate Naomi is unchanged, however, and her father—a tatami maker who is still furious at Fumiya's father for scamming him (in the novel) and for seducing his wife (in the film)—directs the two visitors to a nearby cosplay bar when they inquire about his daughter's whereabouts. In the novel, it turns out that Naomi, once the brightest girl in class, is what a couple of years later would be termed a NEET ("Not in Education, Employment, or Training"[4]). Cosplay (dressing up as a manga or anime character) is her greatest and, apparently, only passion, allowing her to escape the monotony of everyday life. On this evening, however, a case of theft brings back reality. In the novel, similar disappointments follow as Fukuhara's former lover, whom they accidentally run into later on this first evening, is arrested for prostitution when they visit her small bar close to Nakano Station, another important, more central stop on the Chūō-Sōbu train line and terminus of the Tōzai subway line.

In the novel, they spend the night at a cheap hotel near Nakano Broadway, a massive, four-story shopping complex built in 1966. By the mid-nineties, Nakano Broadway had transformed into a mecca for fans of popular culture, dedicated almost entirely to anime, manga, and collectibles. Although Fumiya and Fukuhara do not enter the complex, their flying visit at the cosplay party a few hours earlier still resonates. The crowd of adults dressed up as manga and anime characters makes a lasting impression on Fukuhara, causing him to realize that his wife, too, must have felt an urge to slip into a different personality. Apparently, she had wanted to escape the constrictions of her marriage and used every opportunity to date younger men. Fukuhara gave her what proved to be a fatal blow when he learned that among the many men with whom she spent time, there was one she could not forget even though he had been the only one she did not sleep with.

As this example shows, love relationships—which are almost absent from *Adrift in Tokyo*—are generally portrayed in a rather clichéd and latently sexist way in *Tenten*. Yet, the text is interspersed with self-irony. Fumiya, for example, starts feeling uncomfortable because he himself recently had a corresponding experience, and therefore starts wondering whether Takako, the married woman with whom he spent a curious night, could have been Fukuhara's wife. Fumiya is soon relieved to learn this is not the case. In the context of this chapter, the episode is important not for its apparent comical qualities but because it represents a piece in the puzzle of Fumiya's relationship with women, which in *Tenten* is closely related to place—and, with the exception of the encounter with Takako, is non-existent in the film adaptation.

Tenten's Fumiya was born in Ikebukuro, where he lived with his biological parents until his mother left the family when he was three. He then moved to Nishi Ogikubo, was adopted by the Takemura family in second grade and spent his teenage years in Nagano Prefecture before coming back to Tokyo to study. His early childhood memories of Ikebukuro are, thus, as faint and vague as that of his birth mother. His father burned the family's photo album, so all he remembers about her is the red miniskirt she often wore. This piece of clothing acquires pivotal importance in Fumiya's subconscious; all women he feels attracted to throughout the story wear red miniskirts. Moreover, whether directly or indirectly, all of these women are connected to the place where Fumiya was born and abandoned by his mother.

Located in Toshima Ward in northwest-central Tokyo, Ikebukuro is a major transportation hub. Shared by Japan Railways, the Tokyo Metro, and the Seibu and Tōbu railway lines, Ikebukuro Station is Japan's second busiest if measured by the number of passengers (JR Higashi Nihon). In terms of retail space, the adjacent Seibu and Tōbu department stores are among the largest in the world. While west of the station, Rikkyō University, an elite private school, and the Tokyo Metropolitan Theatre can be found, until around the early 1990s, the area's image was dominated by the red-light district that stretches from North Ikebukuro, where Fumiya was born, to the east side of the station. To this day, Ikebukuro is known as the headquarters of Kyokutōkai, a yakuza organization. There are a number of literary works set in Ikebukuro, most of which—like *Tenten*—play on the area's somewhat sleazy reputation (e.g., Ishida Ira's [b. 1960] *Ikebukuro West Gate Park* series, published from 1998 to 2014). In *Tenten*, the bar girls' striptease performances are described in minute detail. The manager's association with organized crime, too, fits well with the image of Ikebukuro that was still alive when *Tenten* was published.

The significance of the red miniskirt becomes obvious in several instances. It is Takako's bright red skirt that catches Fumiya's attention in the classy Shinjuku hotel bar where he had taken Misuzu on their first date.

Takako's connection to Ikebukuro is an indirect one, but the association with a mother figure is very strong in this scene. However, the quasi-Oedipal desire is transformed into a non-sexual one as Fumiya and Takako—who is old enough to be his mother—go up to her hotel room. They cuddle up under the sheets, enjoying each other's warmth, just like a mother and her baby would.[5] In contrast, Misuzu, who also wears a red miniskirt and high heels of the same color when Fumiya first sees her, is much closer to him in age. Their predominantly physical relationship also bears undertones of incest, though, because it is mainly Fumiya's striking resemblance to Misuzu's younger brother that attracts her to him. Given that Fukuhara's mission is to leave no unfinished business on his walk—this includes plotting to liberate Misuzu from the clutches of both her violent bar manager as well as her repressive family—Misuzu's resolution to enter a convent at the end of the novel implies some sort of atonement. However, with the stereotypical triad of mother, whore, and saint now completed, the former whore's renunciation of physical pleasure must also be read as reifying the latently negative attitude towards female sexuality that runs through the novel.

Fumiya loses Misuzu for a second time at the end of the novel, but he gains much more than the promised one million yen from the walk. Ikebukuro looms large in his consciousness. While Fukuhara and Fumiya make many detours before going to Ikebukuro, the story already delves into its maze of streets much earlier. After Fukuhara's former lover is arrested in her Nakano striptease bar during the two men's visit, Fumiya finally gives in to Fukuhara who has been asking about his relationship to Misuzu from the start. Although they are walking from Nakano to nearby Tetsugakudō Park, and continue on to bustling Takadanobaba and through the quiet residential area of Shimo-Ochiai—both located just south of Ikebukuro—the Ikebukuro of Fumiya's memory supersedes the present. Fumiya's flashback is interrupted several times, but it takes up more space in the novel than the description of the encounters they have along the way.

Fumiya's account arrives in the narrative present shortly before they reach Ikebukuro, the place where he was born and abandoned by his birth mother, and later fell for and eventually lost Misuzu. As the past and present merge, Fumiya completes a circle, both in the geographical as well in the biographical sense. Fumiya's transition is as profound as Fukuhara's. Although Misuzu is forever lost to him, her decision to enter a convent also relieves him of his obsession. Moreover, it turns out in the end that Makiko, the manager of a bar who greatly helped out the two men en route, really is Fumiya's birth mother—an unexpected and unwanted revelation that adds to the feelings of loneliness that overwhelm Fumiya after Fukuhara and Misuzu are gone.

What will I be doing from now on? All of a sudden I feel awful as if I had been thrown into a pitch-black hole. If possible, I want to continue walking forever, for I am afraid to lose my way if I stop. [...] I fear that even the road I am walking on might disappear. Although I have no idea where I am headed, I make determined strides forward, stomping my feet on the street until they hurt. (Fujita 1999, 418–19)

Fumiya needs to restart his life with no clear route ahead of him. As readers, we realize how much he has changed and grown as a person in the course of the walk. More than that of Fukuhara, Fumiya's journey may be read as metaphor of the search for identity, and for a place in this world.

ENCOUNTERS WITH THE UNEXPECTED AND THE UNRELIABILITY OF MEMORY

Similar to *Tenten*, recollections of the past play an important role in *Adrift in Tokyo*. However, while memories are closely linked to specific locations in the novel, the spatio-temporal connection is far weaker in the film. The Tokyo cityscape and the two men's individual memoryscapes are instead interconnected by encounters with the unexpected. Unforeseen turns and betrayed expectations are a frequently employed stylistic device in the film. Naomi, the girl that Fumiya remembers as having fallen in love with him in elementary school, is a good example. When they meet her at the cosplay event, she remembers Fumiya, but for a different, highly embarrassing episode not included in the novel. Determined to give her one of those fashionable, but way too expensive, Lacoste T-shirts for her eighth birthday, Fumiya had glued a crocodile he cut out of one of his socks onto a cheap polo shirt. When Naomi opened the present, the crocodile fell off, and Fumiya became the party's laughing stock. Reminded by Naomi of this humiliating moment, Fumiya feels vindicated in his general dislike of memories—he explicitly states that he burnt all of his childhood photos upon entering university.

Fukuhara, too, must learn that indulging in reminiscences cannot bring back the past. After he offers his long prayer at an unidentified Hachiman Shrine (which is much smaller than the impressive Igusa Hachiman Shrine appearing in the novel), the two men stop at a nearby restaurant specializing in *ōgyōchī*, a Taiwanese desert made of a tropical variety of fig and eaten with lemon syrup. While this bright yellow jelly is hugely popular in Taiwan and Singapore, it is not commonly found in Japan. The dessert's significance for the film lies in the way it is written in *kanji*, which mean "eggs of love." Fukuhara recounts that he and his wife always came to eat *ōgyōchī* to reconcile after a marital dispute. This time, however, there is a serious marital conflict going on in the back room of the small dining area, where the shop owner appears to be beating up his wife despite the presence of customers.

Miki Satoshi's film expands on the comical aspects of Fujita's novel. Outcomes that run counter to expectations are a key element of any comedy. However, on a deeper level, the comical here also serves to expose memories as untrustworthy, if not treacherous. Even more importantly, the film's climatic scene (which is not included in the novel) illustrates how memories are malleable, and can be completely made up. The scene in question takes place at Kōrakuen, a central-Tokyo amusement park located near Suidōbashi Station on the Chūō-Sōbu line. The area was developed to accommodate sports and amusement facilities in the late 1930s, when a baseball stadium, a velodrome, a roller-skating rink, and an ice-skating rink were built there. The amusement park featured in *Adrift in Tokyo* opened its doors in 1955, and was renamed Tokyo Dome City Attractions after being renovated in 2003.

Fumiya visits the park with his surrogate family. As in *Tenten*, a strange sort of bond has developed between him and Fukuhara in the course of the walk, and their relationship grows even closer when they visit Makiko (who, in contrast to the novel, is not related to Fumiya in the film). Makiko had previously acted as Fukuhara's wife at someone else's wedding, and displays a photo taken on that day in her living room. From the way Makiko's live-in niece Fufumi reacts to Fukuhara's sudden appearance, the viewer is led to speculate that Makiko had told her Fukuhara was her husband. Instead of admitting to the lie when he suddenly shows up, Makiko claims that he just came back from years of working overseas, and spontaneously introduces Fumiya as their son. Although it remains unclear whether Fufumi believes her, she cheerfully accepts the ad hoc explanation. Makiko and Fukuhara have no difficulty acting like an old married couple, but Fumiya, who never experienced ordinary family life, is an awkward actor at first, not least because of the somehow too formal, polite way he addresses his "father" as *otōsan*. When he finally settles for the somewhat rough but, at the same time, intimate *oyaji* instead, both Fumiya and Fukuhara instantly identify with their roles.

The night before they visit Makiko, Fukuhara learned that Fumiya has never even once in his life been on a rollercoaster. Thus, the "family" decides to visit Kōrakuen (as well as Ueno Zoo, to which he has never been, either). When Fumiya and Fukuhara scream for their lives as the rollercoaster picks up speed, something strange happens. The film becomes grainy, colors fade, and the camera shakes as if handheld. All of a sudden Fumiya is a child again, with his father sitting next to him in the rollercoaster, laughing, and putting an arm around his son. Down on the ground, his mother and sister are waiting, cheerfully waving their hands. However, it is important to note that, while the scene closely resembles an old family video, what we see is *not* a flashback, but a fake memory. Fumiya's father is most obviously a younger version of Fukuhara, and, judging from the clothes they wear, his young mother and little sister are none other than Makiko and Fufumi.

The importance of this scene is underscored by the melody played by a carousel organ, which is a merry version of Ravel's *Pavane for a Dead Princess*. The diegetic tune slowly transforms into an extra-diegetic piano version shortly after Fumiya and Fukuhara wedge themselves into the tiny seats of the rollercoaster's front car. The "family video" itself is silent, all we hear is the *Pavane*. The music is unlinked from Fukuhara's dead wife in this scene, but it is still related to both nostalgia and grief. There is nostalgia for the happy childhood Fumiya never experienced, and grief for the imminent loss of the blissful "family life" Fumiya is now experiencing for the first time. In terms of memory, the scene is also key. As mentioned, as if to free himself of sad memories, Fumiya has previously burnt all objects reminding him of his childhood. The fake memory of a happy family outing that the rollercoaster ride evokes may thus be read as expressing both Fumiya's loneliness and his desire for ordinariness. Although a fake, the flashback at least temporarily fills in a gap that has been nagging Fumiya for more than twenty years. In its climatic scene, the film suggests that memories are subjective and possibly incompatible with those of others. *Adrift in Tokyo* also implies that the archive of our memory is retrospectively changeable and ultimately as fluid as the identity it helps to construct.

FOOD, FAMILY MEALS, AND AN ATMOSPHERE OF NOSTALGIA

In *Adrift in Tokyo*, Miki Satoshi makes frequent use of a plot device that is commonly employed in Japanese film and television drama to indicate the state of relationships among characters, namely food and shared meals (Freedman and Iwata-Weickgenannt 2011).[6] Mrs. Fukuhara's co-workers, for example, talk at length about food and even go out for lunch together (although, significantly, they are not shown eating). They seemingly vie for the best story about tasteless, disappointing dishes, which gives these scenes a comical touch. As if reflecting their precarious working conditions, they never share a satisfying meal.

Fukuhara and Fumiya's food relationship also starts out inharmoniously. Fukuhara accidentally leaves a stain on Fumiya's suede leather jacket when he offers him a skewer with grilled rice balls in Inokashira Park. Their next meal is in the *ōgyōchī* shop, and, although the owners get into a violent fight during their visit, Fukuhara and Fumiya share private details over the sweet-and-sour dessert. Their third meal—*tonkatsu chazuke*, cutlets over rice soaked in green tea—marks a change as it clearly resembles the strange and uncommon dishes that they later share with their "family members," Fufumi and Makiko. As they are enjoying this curious dish, Fukuhara has Fumiya guess what his last supper as a free man will be. It turns out that it is neither sushi (which Fukuhara will save for the day he is released) nor ramen noodles (which leave a strong aftertaste), but Japanese curry and rice, a choice that Fumiya gives a nod to.

When they stay at Makiko's, the number of meals shown in the film increases, and they also become more elaborate. On the first morning, Makiko cooks them a full Japanese breakfast, including steamed rice, miso soup, grilled fish, and an assortment of pickles which Fukuhara enjoys while reading the newspaper. With reading glasses on the tip of his nose and wearing a *hanten*, a padded jacket traditionally worn over a kimono, he looks (and behaves) like the stereotypical man of the house. Mainly thanks to Fufumi, the food they share at Makiko's house also becomes stranger. For instance, Fufumi insists that mayonnaise makes sukiyaki tastier. Even though Fumiya pretends to gag when he tries the combination, his extra-diegetic narration admits that it actually did not taste that bad, and that he simply felt like exaggerating to add to the fun. The next morning, Fufumi offers her "brother" a glass of milk with just a little bit of salt, claiming that the addition made it taste sweeter. Her suggestion to put leftover curry over spaghetti falls into the same league. Fufumi's rather unsophisticated variations will never make it into any standard cookbook, but are more likely to become a unique family tradition. Her playful attitude towards food is very much in tune with her position as the youngest member of the "family." By taking delight in food experiments—by playing the child—Fufumi allows the "family members" to share a unique culinary experience. At the same time, she creates an atmosphere of nostalgia that, despite its inauthenticity, brings closer together people who were, until very recently, essentially strangers.

The importance of meals as barometers indicating the state of emotional ties between the characters becomes especially obvious towards the end of the film. When Fumiya gets up one morning, he finds the women in the kitchen, already preparing for dinner. He pales as he hears Makiko say that *curry* needs to be cooked for several hours in order to bring out the flavor of the spices. She keeps on chattering that curry is best cooked the day before, and that Fukuhara really should have told her earlier, but Fumiya is not listening. It is through his choice of evening meal that Fukuhara signals to Fumiya that their journey has come to an end. When they eat what appears to be a delicious dish, Fumiya's eyes well up with tears. The next morning, he walks with Fukuhara to Sakuradamon. When they reach the moat around the Imperial Palace, Fumiya starts walking backwards "to rewind the time." In the final scene, Fukuhara hands Fumiya a thick bundle of 10,000-yen bills. As Fumiya starts to count the money, the bill on top is blown away by the wind. While he hastily collects it, Fukuhara quickly crosses the street and disappears.

In her analysis of Tokyo in twentieth-century cinema, Catherine Russell points to the long history of using traditional Shitamachi settings—intimate, small-scale neighborhoods—as a trope. She argues that Shitamachi's "narrow streets, small shops, inns and bars, and the street lighting render the city as a kind of interior space," adding that, when these traditional neighborhoods disappeared in the postwar period, "other small neighborhoods were explicitly depicted as nostalgic places, where a sense of community persists within an otherwise oppressive urban environment" (2002, 216–17). *Adrift in Tokyo* fits this pattern. The film shows Tokyo to be enormously large, a place where it is easy to get lost among the crowd. Especially when Fukuhara and Fumiya separate for a few hours and miss each other at the agreed-on meeting point, the anonymity of the city—in this scene represented by the glittering neon lights of East Shinjuku, one of the largest commercial districts—appears overwhelming. The camera draws back, and Fumiya looks (and feels) small and insignificant. Yet, Fukuhara manages to find him without difficulty, and they retreat into Shinjuku's so-called Golden City (Gōruden Gai), a small corner of Tokyo with a strong retro atmosphere, characterized by the kind of narrow streets, small shops, inns and bars to which Russell referred. From there, Fukuhara and Fumiya continue their peculiar journey through the back alleys of one of the world's largest cities, and the level of nostalgia further rises as they reach Makiko's house soon thereafter. Like the novel, the film adaptation shows how a big place can have a human scale, and zooms in on intimate, personal experiences. The Tokyo described in *Tenten* and *Adrift in Tokyo* is full of loneliness and alienation, eccentricity and weirdness, warmth, friendship, and emotions, coincidental encounters and goodbyes.

NOTES

1. To distinguish between the two texts, I will in the following refer to the novel as *Tenten* and use the English title when referring to the film.
2. For a compelling analysis of the social criticism in *OUT*, see Seaman 2006.
3. While the excursion to Yanaka does not take place in the film, Fumiya learns from another character that Fukuhara once had a son. From early on, their relationship resembles that of an estranged father and son. When they are put in a situation where they must pretend to be related, they are surprised by how natural it comes to them.
4. Introduced in 2004 by Genda Yūji and Maganuma Mie, the term quickly gained currency in Japan. Although meant critically, it was embraced by those it designates as well.
5. The encounter between Fumiya and Takako is also included in the film but shorn of the comforting nuance it has in the novel; instead, it is designed to provoke laughter.
6. In the novel, too, meals serve a similar if less prominent function. For more on food, gender, and sexuality in Japanese literature, see Aoyama 2008.

WORKS CITED

Aoyama, Tomoko. 2008. *Reading Food in Modern Japanese Literature*. Hononlulu: University of Hawai'i Press.
Benjamin, Walter. 1991 [1929]. "Die Wiederkehr des Flaneurs." In *Gesammelte Schriften III: Kritiken und Rezensionen 1912–31*, 194–99. Berlin: Suhrkamp Taschenbuch Verlag.

Fujita Yoshinaga. 1999. *Tenten* ("From Here to There"). Tokyo: Shinchō Bunko.
Freedman, Alisa and Iwata-Weickgenannt, Kristina. 2011. "'Count What You Have Now. Don't Count What You Don't Have:' The Japanese Television Drama *Around 40* and the Politics of Women's Happiness." *Asian Studies Review* 35 (3): 295–313.
Genda Yūji and Maganuma Mie. 2004. *Nīto, Furītā demo naku shitsugyōsha demo naku* ("NEET—Neither Freeter Nor Unemployed"). Tokyo: Gentōsha.
Gennep, Arnold van. 1999 [1909]. *Übergangsriten* ("Les rites de passage"). Frankfurt: Campus Verlag GmbH.
Hutcheon, Linda. 2006. *A Theory of Adaptation*. New York: Routledge.
Jinnai, Hidenobu. 1995 [1985]. *Tokyo: A Spatial Anthropology* (*Tōkyō no kūkan jinruigaku*). Translated by Kimiko Nishimura. Berkeley: University of California Press.
Kirino Natsuo. 1998. *OUT*. Tokyo: Kodansha.
JR Higashi Nihon. 2016. *Kakueki no jōsha ninin* ("Passenger statistics per station"). Accessed 4 December 2016. http://www.jreast.co.jp/passenger/index.html
Russell, Catherine. 2002. "Tokyo, the Movie." *Japan Forum* 14 (2): 211–24.
Satoshi Miki. 2007. *Tenten* (trans. *Adrift in Tokyo*). Style Jam, Geneon Entertainment, Zack Corporation, and Aoi Promotion.
Seaman, Amanda. 2006. "Space, Gender, and Power in Kirino Natsuo." *Japanese Language and Literature* 40 (2): 197–217.
Yiu, Angela. 2006. "'Beautiful Town', the Discovery of the Suburbs and the Vision of the Garden City in late Meiji and Taishō." *Japan Forum* 18 (3): 315–38.

Chapter Three

On Möbius Strips, Ruins, and Memory

The Intertwining of Places and Times in Hino Keizō's Tokyo

Mark Pendleton

"I have built Tokyo from burned-out ruins to a great city," writes Hino Keizō (1929–2002) in his 1985 novel *Yume no shima* (1985, trans. *Isle of Dreams* , 2010). "But I have therefore destroyed something invisible, including . . . myself" (Hino 2010, 79). Hino's novel explores the relationship between individual subjectivity and cycles of destruction and renewal in the postwar Japanese city through the story of a widower's encounters with a strange humanoid figure in a dystopian landscape inspired by a reclaimed island in Tokyo Bay constructed partly out of trash.[1] The real-life Yumenoshima is one of several such material reminders of Tokyo's proliferating postwar problem with consumer waste (Kuehr 1996).[2] Despite winning the thirty-sixth annual Geijutsu Senshō ("Arts Award"), a prestigious annual prize awarded by the Japanese government,[3] the novel has received little critical attention in Anglophone scholarship beyond somewhat oblique references to Hino's concern with questions of production and (over)consumption in the Japanese city, which lead to descriptions of him as an "environmental" writer (Thornber 2012, 485). Scholars writing in Japanese, however, have analyzed Hino's novel through its focus on the materiality of the city of Tokyo, how it represents the city's past, and how people in Hino's time related to those histories—what we might call memory (e.g., Satō 2011; Satō 2004; Matsushita 1997; Andō 2012).

In this chapter, I build on this existing Japanese scholarship and the availability of *Isle of Dreams* in an English translation (Hino 2010) to argue that the novel should be read not solely as an environmental text but also as a "memory text"—one that intervenes in a postwar memory politics manifested in various specific sites across Japan, most notably Tokyo. Annette Kuhn has characterized memory texts as montages "of vignettes, anecdotes, fragments, 'snapshots' and flashes that can generate a feeling of synchrony: remembered events seem to be outside any linear time frame or may refuse to be easily anchored to 'historical' time" (2010, 299). *Isle of Dreams* embraces a similar concern with how contemporary experience is connected to historical time. Hino frequently employs images relating to past events, but the nature of their connection to history is more reflective of a loose intertwining than one of linear causality.

Intertwining can also be seen geographically in the novel, with the plot constantly moving between Tokyo's center and its peripheries. Tokyo's center has moved over time, from the old downtown Edo heart around Nihonbashi and Kyōbashi in what Seidensticker (1983) famously described as the "low city" (Shitamachi) to the east, and then in an ever westward pull from the late Meiji period onwards—into the "high city" (Yamanote) of Marunouchi and, ultimately, beyond to the new developments of Shinjuku and Shibuya. In contemporary times, we might think of a center bounded by the Yamanote loop line (see Pendleton and Coates 2018) or, to borrow from Roland Barthes' (1982 [1970]) famous description, the area surrounding the "void" of the Imperial Palace at the heart of Tokyo and the nation itself. If the exact location of the center is contingent on time and perspective, however, its peripheries are perhaps easier to identify. Suburban sprawl moves in all directions from the central city, to Tama and Hachiōji in Tokyo's west, Kanagawa Prefecture to the southwest, and into Saitama and Chiba Prefectures to the north and east respectively. These remain connected to the center through a radial network of transportation systems. To the southeast is the peripheral space of Tokyo Bay, a space that, as we will see below, has increasingly been filled in through land reclamation projects over the course of the twentieth century, and which is the primary peripheral zone explored in Hino's novel.

Intertwining also features in Hino's own descriptions of his approach to writing; he sees this as akin to constructing Möbius strips—formed from the city and its periphery and from Japan's pasts and presents (Sano 1985, 138). While this Möbius-strip metaphor is useful, I suggest in this chapter that it is not fully adequate to describe the complex intertwinings at play. Japan's postwar memory politics—a politics of defeat, loss of empire, and crumbling postwar visions of progress and peace—are made visible in Hino's novel through specific, dystopian and peripheral terrains in 1980s Tokyo. The city functions as a central actor in the novel, filled as it is in Hino's vision with, on the one hand, gleaming new structures reflecting capitalist progress and, on the other, forgotten imaginations of alternative postwar futures, rotting corpses, and decaying buildings.

Appearing at the peak of the 1980s "bubble" period and utilizing the geographical peculiarity of the reclaimed islands in Tokyo Bay, *Isle of Dreams* speaks to a sense of cultural decay and memory loss associated with the apex of the postwar vision of economic growth and prosperity. The novel also presages the material manifestation of ruination in the economic and social collapses of post-bubble Japan, and the prospect of renewal from the ashes of these various perceived national defeats. However, this process is less than perfect and highly uneven. Hino's Möbius-strip metaphor—a metaphor that combines contiguity, linearity, and circularity—takes us some way towards an embrace of the messiness of the relationship between place and time. It is best understood, however, when read alongside another key motif of Hino's writing—ruination. To talk about memory, imagination, and the city in Hino's Tokyo, is to talk about a decaying Möbius strip—continuous and cyclical, yes, but also uneven and slowly disintegrating.

HINO KEIZŌ AND THE RUINS OF TOKYO

In a discussion of the work of the much more internationally famous Japanese novelist Murakami Haruki (b. 1949), Matthew Strecher notes that *Isle of Dreams* vied unsuccessfully with Murakami's *Sekai no owari to hādo-boirudo wandārando* (1985, trans. *Hard-boiled Wonderland and the End of the World*, 1991) for the 1985 Tanizaki Jun'ichirō Prize. As it turns out, Hino went on to win that prominent award for contemporary literature the following year for another novel, *Sakyū ga ugoku yō ni* ("As the Sand Dunes Move," 1986). Both Murakami's *Hard-boiled Wonderland* and Hino's *Isle of Dreams* are set in Tokyo, and Strecher argues that at the peak of Japan's bubble economy writers were increasingly turning to the city as a setting through which contemporary concerns could be explored. Tokyo, in Hino and Murakami's works, is "presented as a façade of sanity, masking the turmoil and despair of the postmodern age that lurk[s] beneath the surface" (1998, 369). This move towards the city marked a partial turn away from an emphasis in earlier literature, particularly of the Meiji and Taishō periods, on the imagined spaces of the countryside. This was particularly evoked through the nostalgic *furusato* of the ancestral hometown which, in translating as "native place," Stephen Dodd has suggested was connected to a "sense of uprootedness and loss experienced by many writers during Japan's period of modernity" (2004, 1).

For many writers active in the 1980s, such as Murakami and Hino, it was not the idealized landscapes of rural and regional Japan that provided the metaphors of "what it meant to be Japanese" (Dodd 2004, 3). Instead, it was the city itself. *Isle of Dreams* is particularly representative of this period, Strecher suggests, as it "deals almost exclusively with the theme of the beautiful, empty shell of Tokyo in the 1980s" (1998, 369). Authors like Hino deployed the city as a canvas on which to project larger issues of capitalist excess, national belonging, and personal identity. For Hino, the reclaimed lands in Tokyo Bay were particularly evocative settings, representative as they were of both the potential and the destructive reality of postwar economic growth. This relationship among beauty, emptiness, and the city can be seen in the ways in which the protagonist of *Isle of Dreams* regularly describes in loving terms the locations in which he moves.

> This evening, too, the sunset on the reclaimed land was beautiful, particularly here on Site #13, devoid of buildings other than a row of level warehouses along the eastern bank. On the southern edge where he had recently been, the lone ventilation tower of the seabed tunnel soared into the sky, but this was the most extensive and the emptiest area and would remain so until the inner and outer sections of the Central Breakwater Reclaimed Land Site were filled in. (2010, 52)

While Tokyo was an essential setting for many writers writing in the 1980s, in interviews Hino rejected common critical descriptions of *Isle of Dreams* as exclusively focused on the *contemporary* city (e.g., Kanno 1987; Kojima, Akiyama and Katō 1985). These Japanese-language reviews tended to eschew questions relating to Tokyo's pasts in favor of a focus on contemporary social issues. For Hino, however, it was important to read the social isolation and emptiness of the contemporary urban landscape of Tokyo as also reflective of a historic landscape of ruination and the simultaneous burying of this landscape in memory. One such comment can be found in an interview with Hino published in the *Suntory Quarterly* magazine: "From soon after *Yume no shima* came out, whenever you opened any magazine [to read about the book], you would just see the words city, city city.... But for me, one more thing is more clearly apparent—the ruins in the background" ("Yume no shima" 1987, 27).

These "ruins in the background" had their origins in the firebombed landscapes of 1945 Tokyo, a city that Hino returned to as a teenager after several years abroad in Japanese-occupied Korea. In their discussion of the work of Tokyo war photographer Ishikawa Kōyō (1904–1989), David Fedman and Cary Karacas point out that "despite America's rhetorical commitment to precision bombings, these attacks on strategic sites often took housing and civilians with them" (2014, 967–70). On the night of March 9, 1945, in particular, Ishikawa was confronted with "scenes from hell," in which tons of incendiaries were dropped on the city, before flames enveloped the landscape. While aerial authorities' photographs may have suggested that "nothing remained after the conflagration," Ishikawa's focus on the social reality of the bombings on the ground revealed "the civilian suffering that occurred at the scale of the lived urban spaces and, most principally, the body" (2014,

970). This dual landscape of destruction—of both the city and its residents—is what Hino was to return to some months later. It is therefore not surprising that the destroyed city functions as a formative memory trope in his descriptions of his writing and in the works themselves.

> I lived in Tokyo until I was five, and then moved to Korea. . . . I knew prewar Tokyo. After that time, I lived in Korea for ten years and then graduated high school the year after the war. While I was in Korea, I was nostalgic for that Tokyo. I just thought, "I want to go home to Tokyo, I want to go back." But when I finally returned, Tokyo just wasn't there. It was simply a ruin. Tokyo had completely disappeared. ("Yume no shima" 1987, 27)

Hino was part of a generation of Japanese people who grew up with this experience of loss, their youthful memories shaped by the destruction of much of the urban landscape of Japan and the deaths of so many. These memories were again reshaped by postwar processes of destruction and reconstruction in the service of progress. Scholars have referred to this generation who experienced the war defeat firsthand as the *yakeato sedai* (or "burnt-out ruins" generation) (e.g., Rosenbaum and Claremont 2011). Roman Rosenbaum argues that this generation cannot be held directly responsible for Japan's imperial and wartime aggression, due to its members' relative young age during the war years (2011, 5). Despite this lack of direct war responsibility, however, it is a generation also characterized, according to Rosenbaum, by a sense of responsibility for the construction and maintenance of a peaceful postwar Japan that arose from a recognition of the wartime activities of their parents and their experiences as victims of war. Rosenbaum explains this by arguing that "Victor's justice . . . erases memory but victim's justice leads to a much deeper, often artistic expression of self-interrogation" (Ibid., 5). *Isle of Dreams* and Hino's oeuvre more generally represent an example of this generational self-interrogation of the past through fiction, a process that requires a consideration of the legacies of war and empire, but also of what had happened in the postwar. For writers like Hino, ongoing processes of social ruination over the decades after the end of the war became as important a theme to explore as the war-ravaged landscapes of the *yakeato* themselves.

The radical transformation of Tokyo did not end with the ruinous events of 1945 but continued in the decades after, as economic prosperity fueled a seemingly never-ending process of economic and geographical expansion. Hino's life course also followed that of a re-emergent postwar Japan. As a student at the University of Tokyo after the war, he became involved in literary circles. He put out a *dōjinshi* (self-published magazine) called *Nijūdai* ("Twenties"), along with poet and literary critic Ōoka Makoto (b. 1931) and writer and critic Sano Yō (1928–2013), and the same group later created the literary journal *Gendai bungaku* ("Contemporary Literature")

(Yamanouchi 2009). After graduation, Hino joined the staff of the *Yomiuri shinbun* newspaper, and was assigned to the foreign desk—all the while maintaining his connection to the literary world, primarily through the writing of works of literary criticism. He was a prominent figure in Tokyo's postwar literary scene. He associated with editors and writers for the magazines *Gendai hyōron* ("Contemporary Criticism") and *Gendai hihyō* ("Contemporary Critique"), such as Okuno Takeo (1926–1997), Yoshimoto Takaaki (1926–2012), and Yamaguchi Hitomi (1926–1995). Hino subsequently served periods overseas as a foreign correspondent in South Korea and Vietnam in the 1960s, before turning his attention to writing fiction, along with reportage and criticism, in his late thirties. In 1974 one of his novels was awarded the Hirabayashi Taiko Literature Prize, a prize awarded between 1973 and 1997 to novels and works of criticism written by authors who had devoted their careers to literature without significant recognition. That same year, he received Japan's leading literary award, the Akutagawa, for another of his novels.

By the mid-1980s, when Hino was writing *Isle of Dreams*, he had witnessed over forty years of change in Tokyo—cycles of destruction and renewal—occurring alongside, and often in contrast to, a postwar teleological narrative of progress centered on a myth of permanent growth. Speculative, debt-fueled expansion precipitated the post-1989 collapse of the economy into the seemingly interminable Lost Decades, characterized by stagnation and decline, albeit a decline that is unevenly felt and the meaning of which remains heavily contested (Gordon 2015). In 1985, however, much of this was yet to come. The bubble economy continued to be propelled forward—or, in the case of construction, upwards into ever higher skyscrapers. Perhaps not surprisingly, then, Hino's protagonist in *Isle of Dreams*, Sakai Shōzō, works for a construction company. Sakai sees in Tokyo "the beauty of contemporary buildings, sharply geometrical in form, devoid of superfluous décor, adroitly bringing to the fore a texture that was both mineral and metallic" (2010, 2). In contrast to the beauty Sakai found in the vertical materiality of the city, however, the primary action of the novel, and its turn towards darker themes, is located in settings with roots in much earlier expansionary desires, namely, the reclaimed islands of Tokyo Bay.

Tokyo is built around a large bay with an area of some 1500 square kilometers. Despite its scale, Tokyo Bay is largely devoid of natural islands, a relatively unremarkable feature that only became a source of some concern in the mid-nineteenth century. The unannounced arrival in 1837 of U.S. merchant Charles W. King at the entrance to what was then called Edo Bay led to a realization of the danger this exposure created for the seat of Tokugawa political power. Under the direction of Egawa Hidetatsu Tarōzaemon (1801–1855), work began on bolstering defenses in 1839. The subsequent arrival of U.S. Commodore Matthew Perry (1794–1858) in Edo Bay in 1853, with the demand that Japan open up to foreign trade, led to a rapid expansion of these plans, including the construction of six new artificial battery emplacements in the bay. Only two of the six remain, with #6 designated as a place of great scientific value due to its plant- and birdlife—and, thus, off-limits to human visitors. By contrast, #3 was opened as a free-standing island park in 1928. Through land reclamation it can now be accessed on foot from the northern end of the larger artificial island of Odaiba. The park contains remnants of its military past in the form of the ruins of barracks, an explosives warehouse, and an ammunition storehouse. Odaiba itself more commonly attracts visitors as a leisure and entertainment destination, featuring a convention center, shopping malls, sporting facilities, and a large *onsen* facility, alongside various corporate buildings constructed in futuristic styles at the tail end of the bubble period.

The land reclamation that created Odaiba is representative of the larger encroachment of Tokyo onto its oceanic surrounds, a process that accelerated through the twentieth century. Prewar plans for floating airports as temples to a particularly imperial modernism gave way in the postwar to expansionist ambitions to accommodate the growing concentration of population and capital in Tokyo. For scholars like Jinnai Hidenobu, the gradual takeover of the bay was one of the key elements in the historical evolution of Tokyo residents' relationships to the city (1988). This evolution also involved the dramatic reduction in the number of waterways that were part of Tokyo's urban landscape, through burial, diversion, and other means of control. Tokyo moved away from its nineteenth-century position as a "Water Capital" rivaling European cities like Venice, becoming a city where the waterways were distinctly marginal (Ibid., 177–81).

INTERTWINED LANDSCAPES:
THE CENTER AND THE PERIPHERY

Waterways are a key feature of the evolving historical relationship Tokyo residents have with their city. However, the core setting for Hino's novel can be found in a specific waterfront location, the island of Yumenoshima, one of several artificial islands constructed from waste materials at the northern end of Tokyo Bay. As with Odaiba, continuing processes of land reclamation have resulted in Yumenoshima becoming contiguous with the rest of the metropolis; a series of bridges and train lines connects Yumenoshima to various other artificial islands and areas of reclaimed land, including nearby Tatsumi, Shiomi, and Kasai—and through these to central Tokyo. Yumenoshima is also primarily a recreation destination, with a park occupying the bulk of the island's landmass. Yumenoshima Park houses a large enclosed tropical botanical garden, indoor and outdoor sports facilities, a marina and barbeque areas as well as waste processing facilities. It is also home to the memorial to the victims of the 1954 Lucky Dragon incident, in which a boat—the Daigo Fukuryū Maru (Lucky Dragon #5)—carrying twenty-three Japanese tuna fishermen encountered fallout from a U.S. nuclear test on Bikini Atoll, with one crew member dying as a result of nuclear radiation, and others suffering from radiation sickness. This incident has been cited by some historians as a catalyst for the emergence of Japan's postwar anti-nuclear movements (e.g., Orr 2001, 47–48; Dusinberre and Aldrich 2011). The boat was renamed the Hayabusa Maru (Falcon) and continued to be used as a training vessel by Tokyo University of Fisheries before being discarded in 1967 at the Tokyo Municipal Waste Facility #15, adjacent to Yumenoshima. It was subsequently salvaged and restored as the centerpiece of the memorial.

The Lucky Dragon's story of abandonment and reuse is just one outcome of various attempts to address the massive increase in waste production in the city over the decades after the end of the war. The Tokyo Metropolitan Government revived prewar plans and began using landfill to create or expand artificial islands. Yumenoshima was the key location for urban landfill between 1957 and 1966, accumulating over ten million tonnes of refuse (*Tokyo Metropolitan Government* 2016). Minobe Ryōkichi (1904–1984), who served as the Communist and Socialist Party-backed governor of Tokyo between 1967 and 1979, ultimately declared a "war on garbage" in 1971, aimed at reducing the reliance on landfill sites through the creation of incinerators, and implemented various education campaigns around garbage production and management (Hein 2004, 205–7). Despite significant progress in these areas, waste disposal facilities in the bay continued to proliferate, so that by the end of the 2014 fiscal year some 106.52 million tonnes of waste were located in Tokyo Bay across a cumulative area of 7.61 square kilometers (*Tokyo Metropolitan Government* 2016).

The siting of these postwar wastelands on the periphery of the metropolis is not arbitrary. For art historian Ignacio Adriasola, the "haunted landscape where Tokyo meets the bay . . . [indicates] the paradoxical centrality of the periphery to modernity" (2015, 201). Adriasola traces the creation of this central position of the periphery to the emergence of architect Tange Kenzō's (1913–2005) never-quite-realized 1960 masterplan "Tokyo Megalopolis," which sought to "circumvent the disorder of the city by colonizing the wasteland into an officially sanctioned 'order in liberty' that rearticulated the center into an axial node" (Ibid., 202), an outcome of the particular historical reconstruction of the city as a capitalist utopia of urban hyperdensification (Ibid., 208). While processes of reconstruction and hyperdensification emerged most notably in the 1960s, like the story of Yumenoshima, they are themselves linked to earlier imperial histories.

> While in the plan Tange aspired to create in the bay a blank slate for Tokyo as megalopolis—the capitalist utopia of the future—its mysterious links to the preexisting built environment speak of an unresolved relationship to the city and the nation's past and memory. . . . This monumental gesture was the expression of the dream of growth, a dream that was the fruit not only of utopian capitalism but also of the repressed memory of empire: for Japan's ascendancy inevitably relied on a new form of colonial exploitation of the continent. Notably, such anxieties materialize in the periphery. The urban periphery's elision in the plan—its presence as an absence—reveals it as the ghost that returns to haunt Tange's blueprints of the future. (Ibid., 213–14)

Hino's vision of the peripheral landscape of Yumenoshima also contains a similar sense of a haunting ghostliness, a creeping crisis of both environment and mnemonics. Hino describes the relationship these liminal geographical sites have with the city itself through the metaphor of a Möbius strip—intertwined and simultaneously linear and circular, this metaphor also connects his fictional narratives to social processes of memory-making and imaginings of the future.

> [T]he front all of a sudden becomes the back and the back the front. Rubbish is a destroyed thing with negative value while cities are seen as positive. However, my Tokyo is the Tokyo of the *yakeato* (burnt-out ruins) of the postwar. Cities are eminently destructible things. That everything in the universe is breakable or in a state of ruination suggests that life itself is transient. In contemporary terms, this is often called the law of entropy. But on the other hand, grass soon grows on earth made from garbage, manmade things revert to nature, and a new Tokyo is born. This kind of large-scale circulating energy flows throughout the universe. (Sano 1985, 138)

While ruination is central to *Isle of Dreams,* as we will see below, Hino's interest in thinking through the meaning of the ruined city for postwar Tokyo began well before the publication of *Isle of Dreams* with two *yakeato*-themed essays, *Yakeato ni tsuite* ("On the Burned-out Ruins [of the Postwar]," 1955) and *Haikyoron* ("Ruin Theory," 1959). These essays were originally published in literary journals before being gathered together with other critical writings by Hino in a 1967 volume titled *Sonzai no geijutsu: haikyo o koeru mono* ("The Art of Existence: Beyond the Ruins," 1967). In "On the Burned-out Ruins," Hino considered what impact the city's state of destruction in the immediate postwar period had on people's relationship to what came afterwards, with the decade-long U.S.-led Occupation of Japan's main islands and ongoing attempts to address responsibility for the war. He does this through a discussion of Erich Maria Remarque's (1898–1970) 1929 novel *Im Westen nichts Neues* (*All Quiet on the Western Front*), a landmark exploration of the banality of war. Hino selectively quotes from a segment that appears early in Remarque's novel: "This book is to be neither an accusation nor a confession.... It will try simply to tell of a generation of men who, even though they may have escaped (its) shells, were destroyed by the war" (Hino 1967, 7). For Hino who, like Remarque, was writing as part of a war-scarred generation, war leaves behind ruins—material and psychological.

Tokyo's ruinous past has a dual function in postwar history that is made visible, Hino argues, through people's relationship with that past and to the materiality of the landscape itself. He writes:

> It is a curious way to put it, but the *yakeato* for us does not only have a negative sense of something no longer being the thing it once was, but also has a positive sense of the true essence of that thing being revealed. Streets and houses and tree-lined avenues did not meaninglessly disappear. Steel and stone and cement and earth were actually made visible. Meaningful things that people found familiar, whether beautiful or not, disappeared... and were revealed in all their nakedness. (Ibid., 8–9)

He continues:

> The stone and iron and cement lying around in the *yakeato* were to us both a symbol of our meaningless existence and an ideal form. On that unlucky site existed purely exposed materials. Those materials simply exist, shorn of all human meaning, yet I also sensed in that meaninglessness a fixed and absolute certainty. (Ibid., 10)

For literary critic Satō Izumi, Hino's personal memories and the various political events they reference have, like the Möbius strip of the city and its periphery, become "intertwined" (2004, 140). The same is true of history and the text. Hino's protagonist, the salaryman Sakai, is "not a go-getter but... is nonetheless conscientious and earnest" (2010, 34). In many ways, he is typical of what Vera Mackie calls the "archetypal citizen" of postwar Japan (2002, 203), a salaryman not unlike Hino himself, with his own history of working in Japanese corporate media. Sakai and the author share other biographical similarities. The Chinese characters for Shōzō are made up of the Shō from the *nengō* (era name) of the wartime emperor Shōwa and the number three, representing the year of Sakai's birth (Shōwa 3 = 1928). Hino himself was born in 1929, the fourth year of the Shōwa era.

Despite this "intertwining" of the personal and the fictional, however, Satō argues that we should not read Hino, as some have, as writing in the style of the *shishōsetsu* (confessional "I-novel") popularized in the early twentieth century. This is a style which, in Irmela Hijiya-Kirschnereit's classic formulation, is marked by a bringing together of factuality—that the work reproduces "the reality experienced by the author" (1996, 174)—with a *focus figure,* who is more than a simple "combination of the characters of first-person narrator, hero, and author" but "is in evidence in all the relevant levels and aspects of the work," from the narrative to the temporal structure, plot, and philosophy (Ibid., 179–94). Rather than a primary orientation to the focus figure of the "self," however, Satō argues that Hino's works orient from place (*basho*), with his key interest lying in how to work "from a specific site to a place beyond" (2004, 140). Place in Hino's work, like the focus figure in a *shishōsetsu*, shapes "all the relevant levels and aspects of the work." In *Isle of Dreams*, the intertwining of history and memory emerges from the intertwining of place and text through the figure of the city.

The city functions as a protagonist in the novel, as Hino allows his human protagonist to explain. Despite Sakai's work in construction and his regular excursions around the city, "the bay was for him a complete blind spot" (2010, 24).

> Allowing his eye to wander the entire map of the city, including the bay, he was surprised to see how deeply into the heart of the metropolis the water penetrated. The focal point, if judged from population distribution, would lie in the western region, beginning in Shinjuku, but when one looked solely at the old city, radiating out from the Imperial Palace and wedged between the two rivers—the Tamagawa in the west and the Arakawa in the east—nearly a quarter of the area was submerged. It seemed to Shōzō as though land reclamation had advanced, quite beyond the reality of the capital's increasing refuse outflow, as though some immense and invisible force had suddenly begun filling in what the water had gouged away. . . . When in his mind's eye he saw Tokyo's last forty years compressed into the space of mere minutes, as he looked out on the rows of barracks that had risen from the brown-red ashes assuming the outward form of domestic dwellings, filling the old city in the twinkling of an eye, and now moving slowly but inexorably into the suburbs, even as in the urban center high-rises were sprouting up with expressways and subways ringing the city, it was as though a single, seething, subterranean mass of slime mold had been formed from an infinite number of microorganisms and was now projecting its crowned stalks skyward. (Ibid., 24–25)

The geographical particularities of Yumenoshima—its creation from waste, its historical antecedents, its simultaneous position as peripheral and central to the city—combine to provide Hino with the means to move readers beyond the specifics of the site, to a place where we are challenged to think about how memory, history, and the contemporary city interrelate.

INTERTWINED MEMORIES: TEXT AND TIME

Hino's *Isle of Dreams* opens with a statement of intent that indicates its function as an intertwined and synchronous memory text: "When our consciousness begins to change, for better or for worse, events around us seem to fall into line, starting with mere coincidences, hardly worth noting. Of course, how could it be otherwise?" (2010, 1). For protagonist Sakai Shōzō, internal processes of imagination and memory relate directly to the external environment and the broader social context.

Sakai's story begins at a time and in a place that could not be any more commonplace: a lunch break from his job at the firm where he works, followed by a regular, post-lunch walk. The pattern is one that could have been replicated on any day, as Sakai wandered around the unspecified "central" location of his office complex, not far from the bay. Sakai notices the shifting seasonal landscape before turning his attention to his fellow corporate workers and then ultimately to the urban landscape of the bayside district full of "the beauty of contemporary buildings" (Ibid., 2). On this day, as he ingests this quotidian scene, Sakai wanders further down the street than he typically does, thinking "of nothing in particular, nor did he reminisce" (Ibid., 3). He continues until he stumbles across a nondescript building with a copper plate reading "Mitsubishi House #21." He recalls that the building once housed the Soviet Cultural Center, which, "as a student just after the war, he had indeed sought out . . . to read literary magazines" (Ibid., 4).

Sakai is not particularly concerned with actively reliving the past. Hino describes him as "by nature, not strongly inclined to indulge in nostalgia, and since his wife's death from a sudden illness three years before, he had come all the more to regard the past as forbidden territory" (Ibid., 4). Yet the past is not dead, to borrow the William Faulkner (1951) aphorism, as Sakai very quickly comes to understand in a passage that illustrates the intertwining of memory and place that is central to Hino's novel.

> He attempted to think calmly, but he sensed his exuberance of a moment before fading, though this had neither to do with the Soviet Union nor with his years as a student. He was rather haunted by the eerie intuition that something unexpected had broken into this new urban neighborhood that he had come to see as his own exclusive world.
>
> It was ridiculous for a grown man to allow himself to be perturbed by such trivialities. Nothing had, in fact, happened. Yet even as he told himself this, the feeling grew within him on his way back to the office that, little by little, fissures had sprung up in his perception of reality, a perception that hitherto had quite naturally led him to assume a tacit understanding between the district and himself. (Ibid., 5)

Tokyo in *Isle of Dreams*, then, functions not simply as a passive prompt to individual memory, but as a central actor in the construction and deployment of memory writ large. The city is an historical phenomenon both shaped by and continuing to shape the geographical and social landscape.

Sakai spends his spare time exploring the city. He often rides a bus, a form of transport that allows him to look out at the passing landscape and, when confronted by a new piece of construction or an interesting piece of architecture, disembark and explore. One Sunday afternoon, he sets off for

Ginza, a popular and largely high-end shopping district. As he travels through Sukiyabashi (near Yūrakuchō Station), he decides instead to travel on to Harumi Wharf at the end of the route, which takes him across areas of reclaimed land on the edges of Tokyo Bay. Harumi was originally the planned location for the proposed, but never realized, 1940 World Expo marking the mythological 2600th anniversary of the establishment of the Japanese Imperial Family (Collins 2007)—another example of the paradoxical centrality of these peripheral bayside locations to the story of the Japanese nation. Like the proposed 1940 Tokyo Olympics, the exhibition was cancelled because of the onset of the second Sino-Japanese War in 1937. Harumi is for Sakai a place from which he thinks that the city "was at its most beautiful . . . [like] Manhattan, as viewed from the harbor" (2010, 11). As he passes Tsukiji—home of Tokyo's major fish market—and crosses Kachidoki Bridge onto the reclaimed land of Tsukishima, the bus fills with youths, who then disembark *en masse* and head into a large, oddly shaped building. Intrigued, Sakai follows them inside, where he encounters a large space filled with cosplayers and tables laden with zines, self-published collections of writing and art photocopied and distributed through fan communities—not dissimilar to the *dōjinshi* that Hino himself self-published in his university days. For Sakai, this space and its teenage inhabitants suggest to him something about the alienation of the transformed capitalist city and the relationship between the center and the periphery: "[T]here was something about these costumed boys and girls, roaming aimlessly, that clung to them like a dismal shadow. Had Tokyo's neighborhoods become such dreadful places that it was only here, on this artificial island, that these children could act out their fantasies?" (Ibid., 13).

Wandering away from the "zine" fair, Sakai ends up at a fence overlooking the Tokyo skyline and its proliferating mass of skyscrapers. As he stands and watches, the landscape begins to change, with the sky shifting from yellow to red and then to a dark purple.

> The shadows of the crowded clutter of the buildings grew still darker, and a desolate, ominous aura crept over all that Shōzō could see before him. The ragged, blood-red clouds, driven by an untold wind, were scattering in sundry directions and with ever-changing shapes across the sky. It was as if across the entire western horizon, tongues of fire, fanned by that wind, were flickering behind the vast array of buildings. (Ibid., 15–16)

This scene immediately evokes Tokyo at the end of the war, a picture seared in Shōzō's imagination and framed by the collective memory of the *yakeato*.

> *So it had really burned!* thought Shōzō. It had been in the spring, about now, just before the end of the war. There had been massive air raids, night after night, from the area around the mouth of the Sumida River to Shinagawa and

Ōmori. Had he been standing here then, he would have been engulfed in an inferno, emanating not only from the west but also from the north and south. Every night it had been a virtual circle of fire, a fire that surely must have reached as far as the water's edge, set the sky ablaze, and illuminated the sea. Yet of that Shōzō had no personal memory of his own, and so in his imagination he instead saw flames pouring out of every window of the Tokyo World Trade Center Building, Tokyo Tower collapsing in burning rubble, and, in the ferocious heat, all the countless new high-rises glowing and twisting. The fire was raging all around him. Even the rows of gas tanks behind Toyosu Wharf were bright red, sending up wave upon fiery wave. . . . [I]t was for Shōzō as though he had indeed had a vision of portentous turbulence, descending on Tokyo and whirling through the streets like roaring flames. (Ibid., 16)

In this scene, Sakai scans the waterfront horizon, from the mouth of the Sumida River on Tokyo's east side around to Shinagawa and Ōmori in the southwest. In doing so, his eye passes over the Tokyo World Trade Center Building, Japan's tallest skyscraper when it was constructed in 1970 in the waterfront area of Hamamatsuchō, and home to various corporate offices; Tokyo Tower, a communications tower which at 333 meters was Japan's tallest structure from its construction in 1958 until it was surpassed by Tokyo Sky Tree in 2012; and the artificial island of Toyosu, home from 1954 to 1994 to a massive oil and gas production facility which helped to provide energy to city residents. Scanning across the architectural and industrial outputs of the postwar economic boom, Hino (through Sakai) reorients the waterfront periphery as a site from which to view the postwar processes that rebuilt Tokyo. These waterfront zones provide a means through which the reader views the city anew, both as a site of constant growth and construction—the capitalist utopia that Adriasola discusses—and as a location from which Hino's concerns around unresolved historical memory and contemporary alienation can be realized. For Hino, these explorations into the nature of historical memory and social alienation begin with an encounter between Sakai and a strange person.

As Sakai departs the waterfront, he is borne down upon by a speeding motorcyclist who nearly collides with him before coming to a halt nearby. The rider, a "strange girl," has a brief and stilted conversation with Sakai before departing, leaving Sakai to note that the encounter had been neither "a dream nor an illusion." As Sakai inhales the lingering smell of the motorcycle's gasoline, he senses however that the encounter had been something "quite alien to the world he had previously known and experienced," as though "a black wind, full of an eerie life force, had suddenly passed through his body" (Ibid., 21).

This peculiarly transformative encounter with the woman leads Sakai repeatedly back to the reclaimed lands. While he does not actively seek out the motorcyclist, he has a "half-expectation" that she may reemerge, not from the city, but "from behind the gray, domed building through which the crowd of children had recently drifted" (Ibid., 23). On one trip, Sakai takes a different route, catching a taxi to Shinagawa before boarding a bus heading east and "traversing the area of reclaimed land" (Ibid., 25). He alights on Odaiba, near the Museum of Maritime Science, and heads towards a patch of undeveloped land from which he can see across the water to Ōi Pier, where container vessels dock to load and unload the vast quantities of goods through which Tokyo's postwar economic boom materialized. His previous stops had been on the reclaimed lands of Tsukishima and Harumi; by this point these reclaimed lands had been so developed that they no longer appeared obviously artificial. As he traveled further that day, he saw wide-open spaces, filled with weeds, a sight largely alien to bubble-era Tokyoites, more accustomed to the "beauty" of concrete and newly constructed buildings.

> Only recently had he experienced how the broad, deserted stretch of asphalt along the Harumi Wharf could chafe at the skin of the soul, but there the scent of the city had wafted in across the surface of the narrow stretch of water. It had been as though, depending on the wind, one might hear the hubbub of the city.
> Where he now stood was a true wilderness, but one with neither the smell of millennia nor the gravity of earth. Had it been ten years since the construction of this artificial land? Twenty? (Ibid., 28)

His explorations through Tokyo's peripheral spaces and his reflections about origins and history begin to penetrate his subconscious, as his dreams also become more frequent, vivid, and filled with historical motifs of ruination and war.

> He finds himself, for example, in an old, dilapidated wooden house. A small, plastic model airplane, a fighter from a World War II American warship, comes careening in and crashes into the rotting wall planks, lodging itself there before bursting into reddish yellow flames that slowly spread from the planks to the ceiling. (Ibid., 41–42)

His daily life is also gradually taken over by thinking about the sites where he spends his weekends. In one phone conversation with a school friend who works for the Tokyo Metropolitan Government, he discusses some of the reasons why these explorations are becoming so important, again connecting his contemporary explorations with themes of war defeat, postwar reconstruction, and urban alienation.

> It's something quite new. I feel drawn to it, though I myself don't know why. Perhaps one reason is that it reminds me of the burned-out ruins of our childhood. It's just that it's wistfully familiar, as though I were taking a journey home.... [R]ecently I've had the strange feeling that I need to verify some

sort of starting point. We've been working like madmen for thirty years. Who *are* we, and what have we been doing? . . . I don't think I'm merely reminiscing. We've been cramming buildings onto narrow strips where every cubic foot is worth its weight in gold. So the sight of such vast, empty space is quite moving. The very idea of man-made land makes one imagine what sort of habitations might be built there. There's something hallucinatory about it, quite contrary to my nature. . . . I feel that I become a different person there. (Ibid., 43–44)

The friend arranges for Sakai to access part of the site where waste disposal is ongoing. It is there that waste becomes central to his understanding of the relationship between past, present, and future, "as a circular flow, an immense yet invisible cycle—devised, planned, and carried out by humans, to be sure, but nonetheless driven by a mightier power behind it all" (Ibid., 45–46). Later, he encounters a group of motorcyclists racing around the reclaimed island. An accident occurs and the riders take off, leaving an unconscious rider behind—the mysterious woman from Sakai's earlier encounter. Sakai bundles her into a taxi and takes her to a hospital, where she is held overnight. When he returns the following day, she has disappeared, leaving only a name—Hayashi Yōko—and an address, another bayside location, this time in Minato Ward's Shibaura district, a light industrial area (just outside of the central Yamanote loop line) that, by the time Hino wrote the novel, had begun its transformation into a nighttime entertainment district serving nearby corporate workers. Shibaura is also built on reclaimed land, constructed over former canals. Sakai pays Hayashi's medical bill and sets out to find her.

Arriving at the address in Shibaura, he knocks on the door. It is opened by a woman he had encountered previously dressing mannequins in a store window. This woman warns Sakai about meeting Hayashi again, a woman she describes as "in a way my sister" but at the same time "bad" (Ibid., 71), a threat evocative of Sakai's own sense of a changing self. This warning is accompanied by a vague threat of "ruin" (*hametsu*)—not in a physical or material sense (a widower, Sakai has no family and little in the way of fortune), but "quite literally, what you *are*" (Ibid., 72). As Sakai leaves the Shibaura warehouse, his mind turns back to the mannequin display made "with figures that inspired a sense of melancholy that was close to sorrow" (Ibid., 74). The following week, he walks past another display in a travel bureau, clearly designed by the same woman. It features mannequins of a man and woman lying on a tropical island with the tagline, "For all of you now wasting away in Concreteland, the Isle of Dreams is here!" (Ibid., 77). Later he heads towards the real Yumenoshima, thinking, "Whoever had come up with the name must have been wonderfully imaginative. Or perhaps bitingly cynical" (Ibid., 82).

On Yumenoshima he fully expects a third encounter with the motorcyclist and, sure enough, this occurs—although this time, she is accompanied by a young boy and has several bags balanced on the back of her motorcycle. After taking the boy to the edge of the reclaimed land, she returns for Sakai and they rendezvous with the boy. They then hike to a small wharf where the woman and the boy inflate a rubber dinghy to continue on to an "off-limits" island offshore. The island is dark, with detritus of century-old human habitation—the boy says the island was a Meiji-era battery (suggestive of Battery #6)—and a wild, writhing mass of lifeforms, such as moths, bats, snakes, vines, and "primeval forests." Beyond the forest lies a stone chamber, where Sakai and the boy strike up a conversation.

> "By and by, Tokyo will become unlivable." The boy spoke as if he were talking about the weather.
> "Why?"
> "Don't know. It'll hollow out."
> "Do you think it will be destroyed? Through war or earthquakes?"
> "By something else, I think. There'll be a lot more high-rises, grand and beautiful, sparkling bright. But, mind you, there'll be no one there. There'll be nothing moving. It'll be, you know, like those souvenirs they sell, with sea bottoms or miniature landscapes, all enclosed in glass. Something like that."
> "And when will this happen?"
> "Don't know. It just appears to me in that way." (Ibid., 106)

Later, Sakai has sex with the woman and is awoken the following morning by a raucous sound of squawking birds. The trio then explores the island, stumbling first across the ruins of a house.

> This house must have been inhabited by samurai assigned to manning and maintaining the battery. Though Shōzō had never been the least interested in such things, he thought he saw rising from the piles of scrap lumber the fears and anxieties of those men, haunted as they were by the sight of [U.S. Commodore Matthew Perry's] black ships. Impossible as it was to imagine their nature and character, the story now oozing forth—of material crumbling to wood dust and becoming the food of mushrooms and insects—would itself die in a decade's time, when all had rotted away. (Ibid., 117)

They then come across a horrific scene of dozens of dead and dying herons and seagulls hanging upside down, having been trapped by strong nylon fishing line wrapped around the trees. The sight prompts Sakai to reflect, "The place to which . . . the woman had lured him was no teeming, wriggling, entangling, breathing isle of dreams, of birds and beasts, fish and insects. It was a new form of Nature, into whose depths oil, iron, concrete, styrene and vinyl had already been absorbed" (Ibid., 121).

The woman is overcome and collapses, with Sakai and the boy forced to transport her to safety. As she rests, she moves through a series of emotional states, speaking in different voices—at one point the hoarse, somber voice of an old woman; at another, her own higher-pitched voice (Ibid., 126). She cries out various statements of semi-lucidity, before her face freezes, "entirely expressionless, like a mask, a mask without eyeballs—no, like the face of a mannequin" (Ibid., 126). Sakai feels that the forest is collapsing around him, a sensation that is broken by the woman awakening. He is left, however, with "a sense of having envisioned something, of having grasped that even this primeval forest would someday go to ruin—and that this might not be cause for sorrow" (Ibid., 131).

Back home, Sakai takes a week off from work feigning illness, but returns every evening to the artificial bay by the battery to wait for the woman and the boy to return (Ibid., 139). Eventually they reappear and Sakai returns with them to the island. He suggests burying the birds and, while doing so, he stops to look out at the skyscrapers across the water.

> *We built them in the midst of burned-out ruins*, he thought.
> The memory of the refuse he had seen on the outer portion of the Central Breakwater flashed across his mind. *The rows of office buildings that have arisen by sucking and swallowing energy from the surrounding earth are becoming an immense cycling system, ceaselessly devouring dreams, disgorging waste, and bringing forth new land. If the forgotten fortress in the forest is a ghostly specter that at any moment may vanish, the white high-rises are rows of luminous shadows. When one day the vital energy of both ancient nature and today's city ebbs, there will be born on this artificial land, still desolate and half-formed, a new, sylvan city, a buoyantly breathing, inorganic forest, inhabited by mannequins brought back to life.* (Ibid., 145–46)

CONCLUSION: ON MÖBIUS STRIPS, RUINS, AND MEMORY

Much can be noted about *Isle of Dreams*, including its questionable gender politics (the figure of Hayashi Yōko is a curiously dehumanized foil for Sakai's explorations of national history and personal identity), its examination of grief and mental illness at the peak of postwar capitalist alienation, and of course its commentary on Japanese consumption at the height of the bubble era. For the purposes of this chapter, however, the elements of intertwined place and memory are key. Memories of war and its aftermath uneasily intertwine with social histories. Peripheral landscapes indirectly reflect and yet speak to the concerns of the center. Together, this intertwining of places and pasts offers a commentary on the contemporary city, which is captured most clearly in Sakai's final internal monologue.

> The light is quickly fading. It is growing dark. The sky is an undulating black, the earth a transparent black. Only the topsy-turvy streets of Tokyo still shine—and ever brighter, in phosphorescent bright gray.
> Floating faintly beyond them is the landscape of the burned-out ruins. Amid the pale brown expanse are collapsed walls, bare tree trunks, burning streetcars, a violently swirling sky, the sound of wailing voices....
> It is no superimposed image. The ruins themselves have twisted, moved, and bulged, the silhouettes illuminated in the phosphorescent light, swelling and spreading of their own accord between the black sky and the empty earth. (Ibid., 149)

A Möbius strip is a curious object. Draw a straight line from a single starting point on one side of the strip, and, by the time you complete a loop, your line is on the reverse side of the object. Continue in the same direction and you are back at your point of origin. Front becomes back and then front again. In the intertwining of place and person, and past and present, Hino's deployment of the Möbius-strip metaphor is useful. However, it is perhaps inadequate to give a complete picture of Hino's understanding of the relationship among past, present, and future.

An afterword to the Japanese version of *Isle of Dreams* dated September 1985 does not appear in the English translation. In it, Hino writes about his memories of exploring the artificial islands twenty years earlier. After the evening deadlines, he would often wander down from the *Yomiuri* newspaper offices in Nishi Ginza towards where the Sumida River opens into Tokyo Bay (1985, 196). He writes, "Just fifteen or so minutes from the center of Tokyo by foot, bus or subway, there's a bleak and desolate world. It's like they were creating another world entirely." For Hino, the mnemonic-historical element of his work is central to understanding how the city of Tokyo is constructed as a place that emerges in cycles of creation and destruction, and in how people perceive themselves within historical time.

> So I watched this process of prewar Tokyo disappearing and a new Tokyo appearing in its place. This was not a building up of an existing city, but instead happened on the terrain of the burned out ruins [of war]. That had happened before in the same way, so we have to accept that one day it will happen again. I began to think of a city as something that is created and propagated, and then, like a living organism, spreads wider, more complex, more beautiful. Like an organism, however, it will one day die, and then, perhaps, be reborn. ("Yume no shima" 1987, 27–28)

It might be tempting to read Hino's text as a simple critique of linear postwar narratives of progress through an embrace of a more spiritualistic notion of cyclical time and reincarnation. However, when we look at Hino's text alongside his other writings, the picture becomes more complicated. Hino does not suggest that history moves ever-forward. Nor, however, is historical time in Hino's worldview perfectly cyclical. The past is never perfectly reproduced in the present. This speaks to much scholarship in memory studies over the past several decades, which has shown us that the past is constantly in a process of creation, reinvention, and redeployment; memory tells us much more about our contemporary moment than the historical event it purports to speak of. Memory reflects a specific orientation towards time, which, as Susannah Radstone has written, is characterized by "non-linearity, circularity or timeliness" (2005, 138). As such, it poses a specific challenge to history and its writing, especially given that history has often been understood to be concerned with linear causality. Annette Kuhn uses similar language in arguing that in memory texts time rarely "comes across as continuous or sequential" (2010, 299).

Hino is not the only person to draw on the image of the Möbius strip to describe the relationship among memory, history, and place. French theorist Pierre Nora coined the phrase *lieux de mémoire* in his classic text "Between Memory and History" to describe those places and objects in which "memory crystallizes and secretes itself" precisely because of its separation from a continuity of lived experience (Nora 1989, 7). Nora argues that these *lieux* (or places) of memory are:

> created by a play of memory and history, an interaction of two factors that results in their reciprocal overdetermination. To begin with, there must be a will to remember. . . . One is reminded of the prudent rules of old-fashioned historical criticism, which distinguished between "direct sources," intentionally produced by society with a view to their future reproduction—a law or a work of art, for example—and the indiscriminate mass of "indirect sources," comprising all the testimony an epoch inadvertently leaves to historians. (Ibid., 19)

Nora reminds us that *lieux de mémoire* are "mixed, hybrid, mutant, bound intimately with life and death, with time and eternity; enveloped in a Möbius strip of the collective and the individual, the sacred and the profane, the immutable and the mobile" (Ibid., 19). For Nora, however, while the purpose of *lieux de mémoire* is precisely "to stop time . . . it is also clear that *lieux de mémoire* only exist because of their capacity for metamorphosis, an endless recycling of their meaning and an unpredictable proliferation of their ramifications" (Ibid.). Sites of memory, then, are fundamentally about processes of intertwining, while also not remaining static.

Such *lieux* are perhaps most vividly encountered in Japan in the memorial sites of Hiroshima and Nagasaki which evoke a permanent and falsely unique national atomic victimhood (Orr, 2001). They also run the risk of solidifying memory in certain ways. There is a need to ask, as Lisa Yoneyama has done in the context of Hiroshima, "How acts of remembering can fill the void of knowledge without re-establishing yet another regime of totality, stability, confidence, and universal truthfulness?" (1999, 5). Yoneyama is concerned here with the metamorphological capacity of memory, a concern that Hino also latches onto with his choice of the liminal waste-filled islands of Tokyo Bay as setting for his "direct source" of a novel. Hino's novel is not an indirect artifact left for future historians to inadvertently discover but is instead an outcome of what Nora suggests is the "will to remember." In *Isle of Dreams*, we have an example of a specific attempt by Hino to spatially reorient memories of war in Japan and, in so doing, contribute to the continued metamorphosis of how people in Tokyo understand their connections to the collective memory of the city's pasts. Similar intentions can be found in more contemporary Japanese scholarship, such as in the East Asian *lieux de mémoire* project (Itagaki, Chon, and Iwasaki 2011).

What Hino presents in *Isle of Dreams*, then, is a complex understanding of how people relate to the Möbius strip of the evolving historical landscape of Tokyo. This represents contiguity between center and periphery; the landscape and our relationship to it; and an unsettling co-existence of linear and non-linear narratives of past, present, and future. However, like Nora's *lieux*, Tokyo is in a constant process of change, which, for Hino, is best captured by depictions of decay and ruin. In Hino's decaying urban landscape and fraying Möbius strips of memory, we are left with uneven snatches of the past to cling to—partly recalled and largely imagined. That decay can result in complete obliteration, a preservation of ruin in an ossified form, or, as I suspect Hino wanted us to think of it, as the necessary starting point for an ongoing process of reimagining new and renewed futures from the *yakeato* of our urban surroundings.

NOTES

1. There is little academic scholarship on the historical evolution of the island of Yumenoshima. For a good journalistic summary of this material, see "Tōkyō, Yumenoshima" 2013.

2. This chapter was completed during a period at the International Research Center for Japanese Studies (Nichibunken) in Kyoto, funded by the Arts and Humanities Research Council's International Placement Scheme. All translations from the Japanese are mine, unless otherwise indicated.

3. The Geijutsu Senshō is a group of annual prizes awarded by the Japanese government's Agency for Cultural Affairs in a range of categories, including theatre, film, music, dance, literature, broadcasting, popular arts, promotion of the arts, criticism, and media arts. The prizes were originally established as the Geinō Senshō in 1950; the current name was adopted in 1956. They are among the earliest and most prestigious artistic prizes awarded in Japan. Individual prizes are given for both the most outstanding example of the art form and for an emerging proponent of the genre. For a full list of historical recipients of the prize, see the Agency for Cultural Affairs website: http://www.bunka.go.jp/seisaku/geijutsubunka/jutenshien/geijutsuka/sensho/

WORKS CITED

Adriasola, Ignacio. 2015. "Megalopolis and Wasteland: Peripheral Geographies of Tokyo (1961/1971)." *Positions: Asia Critique* 23 (2): 201–29.
Andō Yūichi. 2012. "Hino Keizō ron—'Yume no shima' ni miru sengo" (On Hino Keizō–The Postwar in 'Isle of Dreams'). *Nihon Bungaku Bunka* 12: 73–85.
Barthes, Roland. 1982 [1970]. *Empire of Signs*. Translated by Richard Howard. New York: Hill and Wang.
Collins, Susan. 2007. "Introduction: 1940 Tokyo and Asian Olympics in the Olympic Movement." *The International Journal of the History of Sport* 24 (8): 955–76.
Dodd, Stephen. 2004. *Writing Home: Representations of the Native Place in Modern Japanese Literature*. Cambridge, MA: Harvard University Asia Center.
Dusinberre, Martin and Daniel P. Aldrich. 2011. "Hatoko Comes Home: Civil Society and Nuclear Power in Japan." *Journal of Asian Studies* 70 (3): 683–705.
Faulkner, William. 1951. *Requiem for a Nun*. New York: Random House.
Fedman, David and Cary Karacas. 2014. "The Optics of Urban Ruination: Toward an Archaeological Approach to the Photography of the Japan Air Raids." *Journal of Urban History* 40 (5): 959–84.
Gordon, Andrew. 2015. "Making Sense of the Lost Decades: Workplaces and Schools, Men and Women, Young and Old, Rich and Poor." In *Examining Japan's Lost Decades*, edited by Yoichi Funabashi and Barak Kushner, 77–100. New York: Routledge.
Hein, Laura. 2004. *Reasonable Men Powerful Words: Political Culture and Expertise in Twentieth Century Japan*. Washington, D.C.: Woodrow Wilson Center Press.
Hijiya-Kirschnereit, Irmela. 1996. *Rituals of Self-Revelation: Shishōsetsu as Literary Genre and Socio-Cultural Phenomenon*. Cambridge, MA: Harvard University Press.
Hino Keizō. 1967. *Sonzai no geijutsu: haikyo o koeru mono* ("The Art of Existence: Beyond the Ruins"). Tokyo: Nanbokusha.
———. 1985. *Yume no shima* [*Isle of Dreams*]. Tokyo: Kōdansha.
———. 2010. *Isle of Dreams*. Translated by Charles de Wolf. Champaign, IL: Dalkey Archive Press.
Itagaki Ryūta, Chon Jiyon and Iwasaki Minoru. 2011. *Higashi Ajia no kioku no ba* ("East Asia's *lieux de memoire*"). Tokyo: Kawade Shōbō.
Jinnai Hidenobu. 1988. *Watashi no Tōkyōgaku* ("My Tokyo Studies"). Tokyo: Nihon Keizai Hyōronsha.
Kanno Akimasa. 1987. "Toshi no kakaseru monogatari: Hino Keizō 'Yume no shima' o megutte" ("A Narrative of the City: On Hino Keizō's *Yume no shima*"). *Gunzō* 42 (4): 210–25.
Kojima Nobuo, Akiyama Shun and Katō Norihiro. 1985. "Dai-hyakujūrokukai Sōsaku gappyō" ("The 106th Joint Critique"). *Gunzō* 40 (8): 293–324.
Kuehr, Ruediger. 1996. "Dreamland of Waste: Tokyo's Waste Management in Times of Land Shortage." *Global Environmental Change* 6 (2): 173–75.
Kuhn, Annette. 2010. "Memory Texts and Memory Work: Performances of Memory in and with Visual Media." *Memory Studies* 3 (4): 298–313.
Mackie, Vera. 2002. "Embodiment, Citizenship and Social Policy in Contemporary Japan." In *Family and Social Policy in Japan: Anthropological Approaches*, edited by Roger Goodman, 200–229. New York: Cambridge University Press.
Matsushita Hiroyuki. 1997. "Hino Keizō 'Yume no shima' ron—'haikyo' no jendā kuritiiku" ("On Hino Keizō's 'Yume no shima'—A Gender Critique of 'the Ruin'"). *Shōwa Bungaku Kenkyū* ("Research on Shōwa Literature") 35: 119–29.
Nora, Pierre. 1989 [1984]. "Between Memory and History: Les Lieux de Mémoire." Translated by Marc Roudebush. *Representations* 26: 7–24.
Orr, James J. 2001. *The Victim as Hero: Ideologies of Peace and National Identity in Postwar Japan*. Honolulu: University of Hawai'i Press.
Pendleton, Mark and Jamie Coates. 2018 (Forthcoming). "Thinking from the Yamanote: Space, Place and Mobility in Tokyo's Past and Present." *Japan Forum* 30 (2), DOI: 10.1080/09555803.2017.1353532.

Radstone, Susannah. 2005. "Reconceiving Binaries: The Limits of Memory." *History Workshop Journal* 59 (1): 134–50.
Rosenbaum, Roman. 2011. "Legacies of the Asia-Pacific War: The *Yakeato* (Burnt-Out Ruins) Generation." In *Legacies of the Asia-Pacific War: The Yakeato Generation*, edited by Roman Rosenbaum and Yasuko Claremont, 3–23. New York: Routledge.
Rosenbaum, Roman and Yasuko Claremont, eds. 2011. *Legacies of the Asia-Pacific War: The Yakeato Generation.* New York: Routledge.
Sano Mitsuko. 1985. "Shōtaiseki: Hino Keizō san" (The Guest Seat: Hino Keizō). *Sandē Mainichi* ("Sunday Mainichi"), December 1, 138.
Satō Izumi. 2004. "Nioi no aru posutomodan e: Hino Keizo 'Yume no shima' to rinkaifukutoshin kaihatsu" ("Towards a Postmodernism of Odours: Hino Keizo's *Isle of Dreams* and the Development of Tokyo's Waterfront"). *Bungaku* ("Literature") 5 (5): 136–62.
———. 2011. "Tōkyowan jinkōtō umetatechi no kūkyo. Hino Keizō 'Yume no shima' to posutomodan bigaku" ("The Emptiness of the Reclaimed Land on Tokyo Bay's Artificial Islands: Hino Keizo's *Isle of Dreams* and Postmodern Aesthetics). *Ajia Yūgaku* ("Asia Exchanges") 143: 44–52.
Seidensticker, Edward. 1983. *Low City, High City: Tokyo from Edo to the Earthquake*, London: Allen Lane.
Strecher, Matthew C. 1998. "Beyond 'Pure' Literature: Mimesis, Formula, and the Postmodern in the Fiction of Murakami Haruki." *Journal of Asian Studies* 57 (2): 354–78.
Thornber, Karen Laura. 2012. *Ecoambiguity: Environmental Crises and East Asian Literatures.* Ann Arbor: University of Michigan Press.
"Tōkyō, Yumenoshima—namae no yurai wa kaisuiyokujō kūkō keikaku mo" ("Tokyo, Yume no shima: Name and Origin Stem from Sea Baths and Airport Plans"). 2013. *Nihon Keizai Shinbun*, November 15, accessed 17 September 2015. http://www.nikkei.com/article/DGXNASFK13038_U3A111C1000000/.
Tokyo Metropolitan Government Waste Landfill Site. 2016. Tokyo: Landfill Site Management Office, Bureau of Environment, Tokyo Metropolitan Government, accessed 24 November 2016, https://www.kankyo.metro.tokyo.jp/resource/attachement/englishpamphlet.pdf
Yamanouchi Shōshi. 2009. "*Gendai Bungaku* shijō no Hino Keizō" ("The Hino Keizō of 'Contemporary Literature'"). *Kindai bungaku shiron* ("Essays on Modern Literature") 47, 43–52.
Yoneyama, Lisa. 1999. *Hiroshima Traces: Time, Space and the Dialectics of Memory.* Berkeley, Los Angeles and London: University of California Press.
"'Yume no shima' ni sumu hitobito–metarikku animizumu no sekai" ("The People who Inhabit 'Yume no shima'–the World of Metallic Animism"). 1987. *Suntory Quarterly* 8 (3): 27.

Chapter Four

Mapping Environments of Memory, Nostalgia, and Emotions in "Tokyo Spatial (Auto)biographies"

Evelyn Schulz

> To sum it up in simple words, this book expresses in a condensed way my feelings towards Tokyo, among them devotedness, attraction, sorrow, extreme patience, anger, pleasure, and laughter. The period I am writing about extends from 1964—the year of the Tokyo Olympics—to the year 2001.

These lines are from Kobayashi Nobuhiko's *Shōwa no Tōkyō, Heisei no Tōkyō* ("Tokyo in the Shōwa Period, Tokyo in the Heisei Period" 2002, 249), a collection of autobiographical essays about his life in Tokyo.[1] For Kobayashi, writing about Tokyo is a very personal and emotional act. Weaving his life story into historical narratives focused on Tokyo, Kobayashi frequently employs expressions belonging to the semantic field of memory, such as *kaisō* (retrospection), *omoide* (memory, recollection), and what is perhaps a more formal or scholarly term: *kioku* (memory).

The intertwining of Tokyo history with Kobayashi's memory-infused life story makes "Tokyo in the Shōwa Period, Tokyo in the Heisei Period" a representative example of a "Tokyo spatial (auto)biography." I introduce this term to draw attention to works that are based on a close linkage between transformations that have taken place within Tokyo urban space and a writer's memories about her or his life there. The parentheses around "auto" indicate that the works in question can be either an autobiography in the narrow sense of the word or a work in which Tokyo's modern history is conveyed through the medium of a particular person's biography. Spatial (auto)biographies retell Tokyo's eventful history and document its continuously changing cityscape and living environments from an individual's point of view. Such writings contribute to the ongoing mapping and remapping of Tokyo in fields that include literature, film, theater, photography, and the fine arts. How the contradictions and conflicts that have accompanied Japan's rapid modernization and globalization have played out in Tokyo is a common theme in the novels, short stories, poetry, and other forms that make up the body of Tokyo literature. In addition, a large quantity of descriptive writings about Tokyo has come into being—a category in which I include spatial (auto)biographies.

Spatial (auto)biographies reflect growing interest in the relationship between time and space in literature and the arts, and the impact of modernity and globalization on urban space. They help readers master the city's palimpsest-like nature. The overall framework of Tokyo spatial (auto)biographies is the formation and consolidation of the Japanese nation-state—symbolized and embodied by its capital, Tokyo. The economic and social processes of modernization and globalization form the long-term context underlying changes in Tokyo's cityscape and urban fabric. History and memory in all their manifestations and appearances have been triggered not only by modernism in architecture and progress-driven and growth-oriented urban planning but also by catastrophes such as the earthquake of 1923 and the large-scale American firebombing in the last two years of the Second World War. The speedy postwar reconstruction and the large-scale construction projects completed in the run-up to the 1964 Tokyo Olympics mark another decisive break in the history of Tokyo. The building boom of the bubble economy in the 1980s and the bursting of the bubble in the early 1990s signify another turning point. And, since the early twenty-first century, an inner-city redevelopment boom has accelerated the gentrification of urban space and the city's transformation from low-rise to high-rise.

There is more to the story, of course. While framing Tokyo's history within a narrative of progress, speed, and growth, and the erasure of the old in favor of the new, we cannot ignore increasing economic and social disparities, a slowdown in growth, and an ageing population. Such juxtapositions of immensely diverse and even contradictory trends are all taking place within the complex mega-urban system called Tokyo.

Such events and developments have stimulated the writing of Tokyo from a personal perspective. A common literary device for examining Tokyo's transformations in space-related (auto)biographical writings is sentimental depictions of spaces and places, customs, and traditions that are seen as having shaped Tokyo's particular character and atmosphere—and, importantly, are in danger of being erased or have already disappeared. In many instances, feelings of disconnection from the past are combined with a longing for spaces and places that maintain a sense of continuity with the past. Such locations are usually unpretentious, small-scale, "everyday" parts of the city, where the transformations—from modernization, growth, and prosperity to decline, destruction, and erasure—can be traced and explored on foot. In scaling Tokyo down to the living environment of a single person, the megacity is split into manageable pieces and, thus, can be restored to human scale. Spatial (auto)biographies, therefore, offer thought-provoking insights into the question of how life narratives are situated within and inscribed into Tokyo's multilayered landscape of remembering and forgetting. Spatial (auto)biographies are not unique to Japan. There are, for example, Orhan Pamuk's *İstanbul: Hatıralar ve Şehir* (2003, trans. *Istanbul: Memories and the City*, 2005) and Teju Cole's *Open City* (2011), which is based on the author's life in New York. Both works contain characteristic elements of the genre. However, a decisive difference in the case of Japan is that there exists an unparalleled large number and variety of space-related writings on Tokyo.

In this chapter, I analyze three examples of Tokyo spatial (auto)biographies. The first is a Tokyo tetralogy by Kobayashi Nobuhiko (b. 1932), comprising *Shisetsu Tōkyō hanjōki* ("An Account of Tokyo's Prosperity: A Personal Interpretation," 1984), *Shisetsu Tōkyō hōrōki* ("Wandering Through Tokyo: A Personal Account," 1992), *Shōwa no Tōkyō, Heisei no Tōkyō* ("Tokyo in the Shōwa Period, Tokyo in the Heisei Period," 2002), and *Watashi no Tōkyō chizu* ("My Tokyo Map," 2013). The second example is *Tōkyō no ryūgi: Zeitaku na machiaruki* ("Tokyo Style: Lavish Neighborhood Walks," 2008) by Fukuda Kazuya (b. 1960), and the third is *Yoshimoto Takaaki no Tōkyō* ("Yoshimoto Takaaki's Tokyo," 2005) by Ishizeki Zenjirō (b. 1945). Kobayashi, Fukuda, and Ishizeki have all published numerous, mainly essayistic, works on various topics, but they are not well known outside of Japan. Even though their work has yet to be translated, a goal here is to disseminate some of their ideas to a wider readership.

The purpose of this chapter is to give a representative overview of the wide range of Tokyo spatial (auto)biographies. I have chosen examples that illustrate the diversity of the form in terms of style and content. At the same time, all of these works share common features that define them as spatial (auto)biographies—the primary one of which is an intense interplay between an individual's life in Tokyo and memories that both incorporate and generate interpretations of Tokyo's way into modernity. The writers walk through a small-scale area and reflect on the passage of time. In mapping the city with life stories, spatial (auto)biographies shed light on the tensions, conflicts, and challenges triggered by Tokyo's history. They provide access to its manifold local histories, cultures, and topographies from an individual's perspective. I make reference to Mikhail Bakhtin's loosely defined concept of the chronotope in arguing that transformations of urban space, topography, and culture are brought into play in spatial (auto)biographies as pivotal moments of (auto)biographical identity (Bachtin [Bakhtin] 2008 [1975]). In what follows, I am particularly interested in the way Tokyo's chronotope is conceptualized through an individual's life story.

By way of exploring the tensions, emotions, and memories connected with and inscribed into certain spaces and places in Tokyo, I begin by identifying major characteristics of the locations that are the subject matter of the works on which I will focus. I will then outline key features of Tokyo spatial (auto)biographies, before moving on to an investigation of the specific examples I have selected.

SMALL-SCALE NEIGHBORHOODS AS POROUS SITES OF MEMORY, NOSTALGIA, AND EMOTION

Narratives of Tokyo frequently center on the tension that arises from a critique of the increasing acceleration in the pace of urban life and the city's fast growth. A sense of ongoing amnesia and oblivion is coupled with nostalgic evocations of small-scale, low-rise, and slow-paced sectors of "everyday" Tokyo. Over time, many such localities have given way to modern, high-rise buildings. Those that remain have been given high mnemonic value and are regarded as archives of local history—places where urban memory is inscribed.

Archetypal examples of fast-paced, high-rise areas are Shinjuku, Roppongi, and Shibuya. Tokyo's best-known low-rise districts are Asakusa, Ueno, and Yanaka—part of the Shitamachi, Tokyo's old downtown area, which, by the 1980s, had become a site of frequent evocations of the city's vernacular past and local character. Since then, the Shitamachi has evolved into a space of communal memory and cultural identity, and nostalgia has become commodified. Several Shitamachi districts are widely celebrated as being a *genius loci* of Tokyo—which is to say, they are seen as auratic and beautiful places with authentic environments possessing a unique atmosphere, places thought to express the essential character and spirit of the city (Norberg-Schulz 1980; Suzuki 2009). Most of these areas have been affected by redevelopment, gentrification, and commodification. Thus, they epitomize Tokyo's vanishing past as well as its continuous growth and acceleration through an ongoing cycle of erasure and rebuilding.

There are various reasons why small-scale districts are viewed as archives of Tokyo's local histories—districts that, with reference to Pierre Nora's concept of *lieux de mémoire* ("sites of memory"), have become key locations for remembrance of the past (1998). The most important reasons include their layout, urban fabric, and vernacular architecture, which are molded by "a language of form, space, and sensation shaped by the local history of habitation" (Sand 2013, 2). These districts are perceived as expressing Tokyo's particular vernacular, evoking feelings of familiarity and closeness. Many of these districts are *machi*—local communities and neighborhoods that represent the smallest administrative unit in Japanese cities.

The Yanaka Ginza. *Evelyn Schulz*.

Even today, many *machi* still consist of a grid of so-called *roji*, narrow, jointly-used lanes that run between houses and have long characterized traditional neighborhoods. Usually, these lanes are so narrow and winding that they can only be used by pedestrians. Often they come to a dead end. Common features include cramped spaces, mixed use, a strong sense of local community and social cohesion—with a majority of residents from families long established in the neighborhood. To this day, they are sites of informal encounters.

Even though the terms *roji* or *roji ura* ("backstreet") refer only to some characteristic elements of these neighborhoods, such as narrow lanes and collectively-used yards, they have come to be synonymous with Tokyo's vernacular in general. *Roji* represent spaces to live and meet. They are spaces where all generations can find their place in the community and where a deceleration in the pace of life is possible. *Roji* give residents spaces of calm and relaxation. They give children playmates in the neighborhood and offer older people friends with whom they can converse. Homes, businesses, and, sometimes, workplaces are close enough together so that the tasks of everyday life can be managed on foot. In many cases, the boundary between public and private space is barely evident. In recent years, *roji* and *roji*-like districts have been rediscovered for their potential to offer sustainable solutions for living together and for revitalizing local communities. While the majority of such districts gave way to modern building projects over the course of the twentieth century, those that remain provide a clue to a way of living that benefits from proximity to neighbors and areas of collective use, and are seen as sites of resistance to monumental Tokyo and its modernist urban fabric (Radović, Jager, and Beyerle 2008; Radović and Boontharm 2012; Schulz 2013).

An essential characteristic of these small-scale districts is "porosity," a term that serves as a programmatic theme in Walter Benjamin's essay on Naples (1924/25). Porosity describes the permeability of architecture and design in urban space (Benjamin and Lacis 1980, 309–10). Benjamin observed that many different elements of Naples are porous, meaning that its spaces are rich with the intermingling of public and private, exterior and interior, past and present (Farrar 2011, 731). Insofar as it implies a state of openness to all prevalent currents of historical experience, porosity has positive effects on both social life and memory politics (Müller Farguell 2006, 626–27). The concept of porosity is becoming increasing relevant in contemporary urban discourse. It is used to describe how the functional spaces of modern urbanity, often perceived as cold and deserted, threaten long-established vernacular environments. Even when they reveal signs of decay and decomposition, these "historical" vernacular environments have proven to be more flexible, sustainable, and able to facilitate human interaction than those designed more recently (Sennett 2016).

The more the vernacular architecture and cityscape of Tokyo's traditional neighborhoods disappear, the more the remaining ones evoke nostalgic feelings and longings—and the more mnemonic value is given to them. This process is also reflected in literature, film, television dramas, and photographs. Films directed by Ozu Yasujirō, such as *Tōkyō monogatari* (1953, trans. *Tokyo Story*), are good examples. In *Tokyo Story* and other Ozu films, these vernacular environments take center stage in the discourse of modern urban family and social life. The setting of the long-running film series *Otoko wa tsurai yo* ("It's Tough Being a Man," forty-eight installments of which were released between 1969 and 1995) is a Shitamachi district that displays all facets of intimate neighborly relations.

A more recent example is the award-winning series *San-chōme no yūhi* ("Sunset on Third Street") directed by Yamazaki Takashi (b. 1963). It consists of three films, *Always : Sanchōme no yūhi* ("Always: Sunset on Third Street," 2005), *Always: Zoku Sanchōme no yūhi* ("Always: Sunset on Third Street 2," 2007) and *Always: Sanchōme no yūhi '64* ("Always: Sunset on Third Street in '64," 2012). The settings are a 1960s Shitamachi district. The location is visually dominated by Tokyo Tower, the epitome of urban modernity in the 1960s, and is marked by a traditional lifestyle of neighborly closeness, intimacy, and—on the downside—mutual social monitoring. In focusing on the social and emotional qualities of these urban environments, books of photographs such as *Tōkyō kieta machikado* ("Street Corners of Tokyo That Have Disappeared," 1999) and *Shōwa no fūkei* ("Shōwa Landscapes," 2007) are infused with nostalgia.

Another approach is to conceptualize such districts as spaces of alterity. For instance, Takabe Uichi (b. 1950) explores in *Shifūzoku: Ueno kaiwai haikai nisshi* ("Personal Habits and Customs: Diary of Wandering around in the Vicinity of Ueno," 2002) and *Fūzoku mutan: Machi no soko o aruku* ("Dream Stories of Habits and Customs: Walking the Bottom of the City," 2007) downward trends in Shitamachi areas linked to the decline in economic prosperity in post-bubble Tokyo. These reportage-like works depict Ueno as a space of disappearing traditional culture and lifestyle—which then become the focus of nostalgic longing. Also, it is a space where the presence of foreign workers and homeless people disrupts the hegemonic narrative of modern Japan as a homogeneous society based on growth and prosperity.

In general, artistic depictions of Tokyo's vernacular—in works of literature, film, and photography—frequently highlight the shortcomings, contradictions, and losses created by Tokyo's rapid growth and transformation. It is also common practice that a writer and a photographer work together to critically interpret Tokyo's path to modernity by combining text with pictures. Examples include *Tōkyō* ("Tokyo," 2008) by the writer Tsubouchi Yūzō (b. 1958) and the photographer Kitajima Keizō (b. 1954) and Kobayashi's "An Account of Tokyo's Prosperity: A Personal Interpretation" and Ishizeki's "Yoshimoto Takaaki's Tokyo," in both of which the renowned photographer Araki Nobuyoshi (b.1940) was involved.

All of the writers, directors, and photographers mentioned above share similar approaches to Tokyo's vernacular environments. They thus contribute to the shaping of a dominant pattern in the depiction of Tokyo. Tokyo's small-scale areas—their lanes, alleyways, and narrow courtyards—are depicted as porous sites of modernity in Walter Benjamin's sense of the word, spaces in which there is a ceaseless and indefinable intermingling of public and private, exterior and interior, past and present. In the following section, I will show how Tokyo spatial (auto)biographies reflect this model of depiction.

FEATURES OF "TOKYO SPATIAL (AUTO)BIOGRAPHIES"

Over the last decade, the so-called spatial turn has strengthened our understanding of the fluidity and volatility of space, which no longer is treated "as obvious, as self evident and not really in need of further examination" (Crang 2005, 199), but rather as socially constructed—which is to say, produced by social interaction. Social life is "both space-forming and space-contingent; [as] a producer and a product of spatiality" (Soja 1989, 129). This approach has also gained importance in literary studies and is helpful for discussing the issues raised in this chapter. One of the main characteristics of biographical and autobiographical writings is their chronological structure. Although space is an essential dimension of almost any kind of writing, it is only recently that—given the impact of the spatial turn—attention is paid to the spatial aspects of (auto)biographical narratives (Arnold and Sofaer 2008).

Among scholars focusing specifically on Japan, there seems to be a growing awareness of the role of space and place in autobiographical writing and other genres of factual literature. "Environmental autobiography," a term coined by landscape architect and human geographer Clare Cooper Marcus (b. 1934) in the late 1970s, refers to a memoir that puts particular emphasis on the relationship between the individual and the environment (Cooper Marcus 1979). The term "environmental autobiography" was translated as *kankyōteki jijoden* in the Japanese edition of Cooper Marcus's treatise (Kūpā Mākasu 2013). The notion of "environmental autobiography," however, captures only some aspects of "Tokyo spatial (auto)biographies," which take as their subject matter one specific urban environment.

Other Japanese terms used to describe works in which Tokyo is seen and explored through the lens of personal experience and perception are *yūranki* (record of sightseeing) and *machiaruki* (urban walking). For example, Sakazaki Shigemori (b. 1942) published three books that, in a sense, serve as guides to this literary field. They are *Tōkyō yūranki* ("Record of Sightseeing in Tokyo," 2002), *Ichiyō kara hajimeru Tōkyō machiaruki* ("Walks through Tokyo's Districts: Beginning with [Higuchi] Ichiyō," 2004), and *Tōkyō dokusho: Shōshō zōenteki shinjō ni yoru* ("Tokyo Reader: Through Some of the Emotional Aspects of Landscapes," 2008). Sakazaki's focus is on short summaries of published writing (including several autobiographies) on Tokyo. He stops short of analyzing the works or offering a definition of the genre.

Research done by Tsuchida Mitsufumi (1926–2011), in particular his *Tōkyō kiroku bungaku jiten: Meiji gannen—Shōwa 20 nen* ("Encyclopedia of Documentary Literature about Tokyo: The First Year of Meiji—The Twentieth Year of Shōwa," 1994) is very instructive for understanding the cultural and social functions of Tokyo spatial (auto)biographies. Although Tsuchida focuses on "documentary literature" (*kiroku bungaku*) published between 1868 and 1945, his key ideas can also be applied to later works. Tsuchida points out that, compared to "novels" (*shōsetsu*), works of documentary literature depict Tokyo in more concrete and detailed ways—in Tsuchida's words, in "real time" (*riarutaimu*) (1994, ii). Looked at this way, "documentary literature" can be regarded as an umbrella term for "spatial (auto)biographies."

It is difficult to say when exactly the practice of writing about Tokyo from an individual's point of view began. Early examples are *Tōkyō no sanjūnen* (1917, trans. *Thirty Years in Tokyo*, 1987) by Tayama Katai

(1872–1930) and *Watashi no mitaru Tōkyō* ("Tokyo as I Saw It," 1921) by Kimura Shōhachi (1893–1958).[2] Later on, more and more works appeared with the word "I" (*watashi, watakushi, boku*) in the title, such as *Boku no Tōkyō chizu* ("My Map of Tokyo," 1936) by Satō Hachirō (1903–1973) and *Watakushi no Tōkyō chizu* ("My Map of Tokyo," 1949) by Sata Ineko (1904–1998). Both works have been reprinted, indicating a renewed interest in this kind of writing (Satō 2005; Sata 1989). Newer examples are *Boku no Tōkyō chizu* ("My Map of Tokyo," 1985) by Yasuoka Shōtarō (1920–2013), *Watashi no naka no Tōkyō* ("The Tokyo inside Me," 1978) by Noguchi Fujio (1911–1993), and the three works by Kobayashi Nobuhiko.[3] With the exception of Sata Ineko, all of the authors mentioned above are male. Indeed, it is very hard to find spatial (auto)biographies written by female authors. One reason might be that "documentary literature" originates from historical and topographical Chinese writings that were introduced to Japan from the eighth century onward and mainly were written by men. Perhaps this element of the tradition still continues today.

Tokyo writing, like the examples just given, mainly explores unspectacular, small-scale locations of everyday, private life. It is also concerned with the transformations—from modernization to erasure—inscribed in the city. In line with Walter Benjamin's notion of porosity, one could say that porous spaces of private and public life enter the realms of history and collective memory through a literary mapping of Tokyo. The memories center on how such places once were by looking at the lives associated with them. The "stuff" of memory includes smells, sounds, and even certain foods. In inscribing a small-scale, local Tokyo onto the incessantly expanding global megacity, such works tackle the master narrative of nation building, progress, and growth.

The primary reason for the quest by writers to place individual memories outside of the framework of modern and global Tokyo is to counter the memory politics of the Japanese nation-state:

> The very specificity of recalling a particular neighborhood, alleyway, or old shop that some literary figure of the past had once frequented positioned the author and the work outside narratives of the nation. These local nostalgias, tied to particular places rather than to the ideological fusion of blood and soil, were thus free from the demand to find redemption in the past, free to dwell in reflection—and, it should be said, free also to be cultivated in idle uselessness. (Sand 2013, 22)

In scaling down Tokyo and splitting it into manageable pieces, spatial (auto)biographies offer interpretations of Tokyo's history comprised of individual experiences. According to historian Frank Ankersmit, history concerns everyone and "becomes a kind of metropolis where each individual has to find one's own way" (1996, 204–6). This approach to history is also reflected in the fact that in all of these works the narrator explores Tokyo at street-level by walking—thus offering to the reader the very personal perspective of a city dweller. In this context, Walter Benjamin's thoughts about the flâneur are useful for analyzing how present and past are set in relation to each other from an individual's point of view. Walking is a means for digging into Tokyo's past and its memories, unveiling a palimpsest of entangled local, national, and global histories. In blurring the border between memory and city life, walking serves as a nostalgic act. Walking enables the discovery of locations in Tokyo that maintain a sense of continuity with the past and where a sense of belonging and authenticity is tangible. Since walking is slow-paced, locally limited movement, it represents—at least for the moments while walking—an alternative to modernity's addiction to speed and acceleration (Schulz 2012).

That said, modernity's fascination with motion and speed is based on a dialectic of acceleration and deceleration. A yearning for slowness and stillness can therefore be considered as a form of resistance. Walking is not only one of mankind's fundamental modes of relating to the environment and of creating a sense of place, but also a spatial practice of slowing down. In strolling around the city and relating their impressions and memories, the writers of spatial (auto)biographies inscribe meaning into the places they visit through the lens of their own life history or, when writing about another person, that person's biography. This kind of quest for memories of the past is a performative act.

The modern model for spatial (auto)biographical writing is found in the work of Nagai Kafū (1879–1959). For Kafū, exploring traces of the past was indispensable for understanding the present. In this, he was inspired by Baudelaire's flâneur and Edo-period traditions of guidebook literature and topographical writings (Schulz 2012, 187–90). He dedicated a great deal of his life to documenting the spatial, social, and cultural conflicts inherent in the Edo-Tokyo transformation and has recently been rediscovered and even reinvented as a critical chronicler of Tokyo (Schulz 2011, 139–64). Many authors, among them Kobayashi Nobuhiko and Fukuda Kazuya, refer to Kafū.

THREE EXAMPLES OF "TOKYO SPATIAL (AUTO)BIOGRAPHIES"

Kobayashi Nobuhiko's Tokyo Tetralogy: Writing Tokyo as Autobiography

Kobayashi Nobuhiko is best known as a writer of essays on a variety of film and literary topics. His work includes a tetralogy focusing on his Tokyo experience. "My Tokyo Map" is the most recent installment in his longstanding project to document the changing city (2013, 196). Kobayashi's attempt to inscribe his life story into the ever-changing landscape of Tokyo in the four volumes written so far gives readers an interesting look at Tokyo from the point of view of a person who has spent his entire life there. Although Kobayashi's tetralogy covers the period from the 1960s until 2013, he focuses on the economic high-growth period of the 1960s and 1970s and the early, post-bubble 1990s. Except for "Tokyo in the Shōwa Period, Tokyo in the Heisei Period," all of the titles in the set allude to earlier works of autobiographical and topographical writings on Tokyo.

"An Account of Tokyo's Prosperity: A Personal Interpretation" (1984) refers to the series of so-called *hanjōki* ("accounts of prosperity"), a type of guidebook literature. *Hanjō* ("prosperity") is an expression used in reference to urban success. The earliest *hanjōki* is the *Edo hanjōki* ("Report on the Prosperity of Edo," 1832–36) by Terakado Seiken (1796–1868). It was written in classical Chinese (*kanbun*). Terakado described the fading of Edo culture in the wake of unrest and upheaval in the years before the so-called opening of the country in the 1850s, and made satirical comments on the Confucian bureaucracy and its desperate attempts to keep control over the rapidly changing society.

The prototype of the modern *hanjōki* is *Tōkyō shin hanjōki* ("New Report on the Prosperity of Tokyo," 1874) by Hattori Bushō (1842–1908). Hattori portrays Tokyo in the period after the advent of Westernization and modernization brought about by the Meiji reforms. The opening of the country in the 1850s, which led to the Meiji Restoration in 1868, marks the beginning of Japan's modernization. With the Restoration, the Emperor moved from Kyoto to Edo, which then was renamed Tokyo and became Japan's capital. In the following decades, fundamental reforms were undertaken to transform Japan from a feudal state into a modern, Western-style nation state. Tokyo's status and function as Japan's capital made it the site of intensive, ongoing processes of modernization, nation building, and globalization. People's perception of Japan's modernization was mainly shaped by their Tokyo experience. The Meiji reforms initiated Tokyo's tremendous growth and also its transformation into a symbol of the new Japanese nation. Under the guidance of foreign architects, public buildings such as banks, schools, theaters, libraries, and ministries were built in Western neoclassical style. Tokyo also became a showcase to display the latest fashions and inventions that were imported from the West and were deployed to demonstrate Japan's modernity.

Hattori describes a city that is full of possibilities and opportunities as well as contrasts and contradictions. His *hanjōki* testifies to the tremendous speed of Tokyo's modernization and the asynchronicities of social and cultural developments it created. It became a bestseller and a model for succeeding *hanjōki*, such as *Tōto shin hanjōki* ("New Report on the Prosperity of the Eastern Metropolis," 1918) by the social thinker Yamaguchi Koken

(1883–1920), which highlights the downsides of Tokyo's rapid industrialization—among them, increasing environmental pollution and the poor living conditions of the many workers who arrived from outside of the city. The subsequent well-known *Dai Tōkyō hanjōki* ("Report on the Prosperity of Greater Tokyo," 1928) is a two-volume collection of essays by eighteen authors, among them Akutagawa Ryūnosuke (1892–1927), Izumi Kyōka (1873–1939) and Kitahara Hakushū (1885–1942), which reflect on the rebuilding of Tokyo after the disastrous earthquake of 1923. Each essay contains illustrations by a famous painter such as Kishida Ryūsei (1891–1929) and Yamamoto Kanae (1882–1946). In the postwar period of rapid reconstruction and growth, Kimura Shōhachi's *Tōkyō hanjōki* ("Report on the Prosperity of Tokyo," 1958) takes up the issues raised in preceding *hanjōki* from an autobiographical perspective and critically reflects on the modern history of Tokyo and Japan overall. Kobayashi's "An Account of Tokyo's Prosperity: A Personal Interpretation" can be considered a continuation of this kind of writing, with emphasis on a more personal, if not directly autobiographical, approach to Tokyo.

Despite the similar titles of these works, they differ in structure, content, and style. What all of them have in common is that they critically examine a city in a period of rapid transition. The premodern urban fabric underwent significant change as new social structures and lifestyles were adopted and disseminated. The word "prosperity" is mainly used ironically or even in a negative sense, given the many references to the undesirable consequences of Japan's policy of modernization (Schulz 2003; 2004).

Similar to the "Report on the Prosperity of Greater Tokyo" and Kimura's "Report on the Prosperity of Tokyo," which both contain drawings that depict Tokyo landscapes and scenes of everyday life in the city, Kobayashi's work is illustrated with photographs by Araki Nobuyoshi. Araki's images enrich Kobayashi's "An Account of Tokyo's Prosperity" by using visual means to illustrate the complex spatial and temporal realities of Tokyo. The photographs complement Kobayashi's words by depicting scenes of everyday life in Tokyo's small-scale neighborhoods and documenting the transformation from a low-rise to high-rise city.

The title of Kobayashi's second work on Tokyo, "Wandering Through Tokyo: A Personal Account" (1992), alludes to the well-known *Hōrōki* (1928, trans. *Diary of a Vagabond*, 1997) by Hayashi Fumiko (1903–1952), a novelist and poet, who became renowned for her feminist critique of Japanese society and a role model for many female writers. *Diary of a Vagabond* is an autobiographical, literary semi-narrative about Hayashi's poor living conditions in the mid-1920s. Kobayashi's *Hōrōki* is a critical account of Tokyo's transformation from the 1960s until the post-bubble period. "Tokyo in the Shōwa Period, Tokyo in the Heisei Period" is a collection of essays about his life in Tokyo. In the afterword of "My Tokyo Map," Kobayashi states that he regards "My Tokyo Map" as a continuation of his tetralogy. He further notes that his project of mapping Tokyo using stories from his life was inspired by Satō Hachirō's 1936 "My Map of Tokyo" and Sata Ineko's 1949 "My Map of Tokyo" (2013, 196–97).

Kobayashi was born in Nihonbashi, a district markedly shaped by Tokyo's transformation from a low-rise to high-rise city and its growing role as the nation's capital and a global urban center. The way Nihonbashi has changed over the course of the twentieth century is representative of many parts of Tokyo. During the Edo period, Nihonbashi and its surroundings were known for their waterways and bridges. It was an area where people strolled along the canals and rivers or used boats for transportation. This way of life was frequently depicted in literature and the arts. From the late seventeenth century onward, the area became densely populated and developed into a commercial center. After the Meiji Restoration, Nihonbashi emerged as Japan's main financial district, and has subsequently been redesigned and transformed several times.

A decisive event in the history of Nihonbashi was the construction of an expressway over the famous bridge of the same name in the early 1960s. The expressway not only covered Nihonbashi Bridge but also obscured the famous view of Mount Fuji from the bridge, which was a prominent subject in Edo-period woodblock prints. The expressway was one of the ambitious large-scale construction projects carried out in the run-up to the 1964 Tokyo Olympic Games. In "My Tokyo Map" Kobayashi devoted the chapter "Only the Bridge Has Remained—Nihonbashi" to the transformations and restructurings of Nihonbashi (2013, 120–28).

Kobayashi uses literal and figurative itineraries through areas related to both his life and Tokyo's history to structure his recollections. Major events to which he refers include the Pacific War, reconstruction during the postwar period, the 1964 Tokyo Olympics, the bubble economy of the late 1980s, the bursting of the bubble in the early 1990s, and, finally, the redevelopment boom taking place since the early twenty-first century. Each of these affected Tokyo differently, shaping its history and leaving traces in its topography.

In this respect, the tables of contents in the works that make up the tetralogy are very informative. Except for "Tokyo in the Shōwa Period, Tokyo in the Heisei Period," all of the works contain chapters devoted to well-known Tokyo wards and districts, such as Asakusa, Nihonbashi, Ginza, Shinjuku, Harajuku, and Roppongi. The systematic arrangement of urban space by means of administrative units gives, at first glance, the impression that Kobayashi's writings are simple guidebooks. However, because Kobayashi's depictions are shaped by his personal experiences and memories of his life in Tokyo, they represent individual narratives of Tokyo.

Each area treated by Kobayashi stands for a particular aspect or episode in the history of Tokyo's transformation into a fast-paced modern and global city. Asakusa, Yanaka, and Tsukudajima, among other areas, contain the remains of low-rise, traditional Tokyo—a cityscape in danger of being erased by high-rise apartment and office buildings, as is happening around the city. Shinjuku and Roppongi, in contrast, represent the ever-changing, high-rise megacity with its limitless consumption and high-pressure lifestyle. Shinjuku and Roppongi exemplify what is most modern and new in the city and point to the financial investment in and development of urban space, which lays the foundation for Tokyo's continuous growth.

Kobayashi's strolls through Tokyo are like journeys of remembrance. In mapping Tokyo with memories laid down before its metamorphosis into a global city, Kobayashi's recollections hint at Tokyo's multiple temporal registers. In "My Map of Tokyo" expressions such as "to come to mind" (*omoiukabu*), "memory" (*kioku*), "metamorphosis" (*henbō*), and "to remain" (*nokoru*) are often used. Kobayashi's recollections frequently scrutinize present-day images of particular areas. In a chapter on the Omotesandō district, for example, Kobayashi evokes scenes of destruction and death as he relates his wartime memories:

> When I think about the firebomb attacks on Tokyo, the huge firebomb attacks on the Shitamachi on March 10, 1945, come to mind almost immediately. I also cannot forget the huge firebomb attacks on Yamanote that immediately followed on May 5th. One can say that, due to the huge firebomb attacks on Yamanote, areas such as Aoyama, Akasaka, Roppongi, and Omotesandō—in other words, today's Minato and Shibuya Wards—became victims of indiscriminate bombings by the U.S. army. The scale was probably even larger. It is said that 37,000 people died, a number that, compared to the several hundred-thousand people who died in the firebomb attacks on the Shitamachi, appears rather small. However, as the actual numbers are not clear, they are not reliable. (2013, 34)

Nowadays, Aoyama, Akasaka, Roppongi, and Omotesandō are known for luxury shops selling world-famous brands and expensive lifestyle goods appealing to the global consumer. In describing the extensive wartime destruction, Kobayashi uses memories of the war to map these areas where remnants of the past are now entirely absent.

The final chapter of "My Tokyo Map" is titled "Tokyo is still under construction" (*Tōkyō wa mada fushinchū*). This is an allusion to Mori Ōgai's (1862–1922) famous novel "Under Reconstruction" (*Fushinchū*, 1910) about an unhappy relationship (1994 [1910], 148–53). From 1884 to 1888, Ōgai studied medicine and bacteriology in Germany, eventually becoming surgeon general of the Imperial Japanese Army. During his stay in Germany he developed a strong interest in European literature and started to translate German literature and philosophical works into Japanese. He also began writing essays and novels. After his return to Japan in 1888, Ōgai became one of the most influential representatives of modern Japanese literature. "Under Construction" is thought to be based on Ōgai's unhappy love affair with a German girl during his stay in Berlin. However, the underlying context of Ōgai's story is the inexorable cycle of Tokyo's expansion, demolition, and construction, representing Japan's general situation at the time. As Kobayashi has written, "Because Tokyo is incessantly changing, there is no precise image of Tokyo. Of course, this has been the case since the Meiji period. No matter how much time passes, there is no objection to calling this 'under construction'" (2013, 190).

In writing the story of his life in relation to major events and developments along Tokyo's path to modernity, Kobayashi composed a history of the city in four volumes. He organizes Tokyo into an interwoven collection of narratives. In their spatial and temporal specificity, his itineraries mark out the trajectory of his own life. By inscribing memory, affection, and emotion into places and locations that have changed or even disappeared, his writings can be considered attempts to reclaim both urban territory and remembrance about it.

Fukuda Kazuya's "Tokyo Style: Lavish Neighborhood Walks": Mapping Tokyo with Culinary Nostalgias and Local Specialties

A professor of literature at Keiō University and a prolific author with strong nationalist tendencies, Fukuda Kazuya was born in the Tabata area in Kita Ward of Tokyo in 1960. He served as intellectual sidekick to Ishihara Shintarō (b. 1932), the former right-wing governor of Tokyo. Fukuda's writings cover a wide range of topics, from historical and cultural studies to literary essays. He received the Mishima Yukio Prize for *Nippon no kakyō* ("Japan's Homeland," 1993), a prestigious literary award presented annually in memory of the writer Mishima Yukio (1925 1970). "Tokyo Style: Lavish Neighborhood Walks" first appeared as a series in the men's lifestyle magazine *GQ Japan*, and in 2008 it was published as a book. In this work, Tokyo is organized around real or imagined walking tours through small-scale Shitamachi neighborhoods. In contrast to Ishizeki and Kobayashi, who consider these quarters as important sites of both their own lives and Tokyo's history, Fukuda is particularly interested in the area's culinary associations with the past.

In Japanese culture, food plays an important role in the construction of national and local identities. Japan's slow-food boom of recent years has contributed to a growing interest in local food products. The concepts of *meibutsu* ("local specialty") and *meisho* ("famous place") have an important role to play here. *Meisho* are topographically or culturally and historically important landmarks, such as shrines and temples, bridges, street corners, and gardens. Known as *utamakura* ("pillow words"), *meisho* are also used in poetry. Throughout most of the history of Japanese literature, it was common practice to celebrate special locations in nature as well as in villages and cities, and to give them the status of a mnemonic site.

Traditional *meisho* were most frequently linked with the old Japanese capitals of Nara and Kyoto. From its founding in the early seventeenth century, Edo was a city of newcomers. A vast range of guidebook literature on Edo evolved, addressing the need for information about the growing and changing city. Edo's *meisho* came into being as the city's population swelled and its popular culture developed and thrived. Though most *meisho* were originally related to temples and shrines, their religious nature was rather marginal and they were best known to local people as market streets and entertainment districts with restaurants, theaters, sideshows, and brothels. Such thriving places of gathering, leisure, and informality are called *sakariba*. Both *meisho* and *sakariba* embody social practices that are closely linked to particular localities. As sociologist Yoshimi Shun'ya has written, "*Sakariba* is a uniquely Japanese word which means the place in the city where people customarily gather and enjoy theaters, movies, exhibitions, shopping, eating some special kinds of food, drinking, and many other cultural interactions. It is a centripetal point of urban culture and a main stage of Japanese urban life" (2001, 89).

There are many Tokyo walking guides focusing on the culinary specialties of an area and introducing local restaurants that offer customers a taste of the past. Examples are *Edo sanpo–Tōkyō sanpo: kiriezu kochizu de tanoshimu, taishin Tōkyō chizu de aruku hyaku no machi to michi* ("Edo Walks Tokyo Walks: Having Fun with Old Maps, Walking with the Newest Maps of Tokyo Through a Hundred Quarters and Lanes," 2005) and *Edo Tōkyō: Aji no sanpomichi: arukiajiwau rekishi gaido* ("Edo Tokyo: Hiking Paths of Taste: A Historical Guide to Tasty Walks," 2011). The book cover of the latter invites readers "to eat, to buy, to have fun." In both examples, Tokyo is depicted as a culinary space, the history of which can be explored sensually by eating traditional-style food in little restaurants in compact, but lively, *sakariba*-like quarters.

At first glance Fukuda's "Tokyo Style" calls to mind such guidebooks, although a closer look reveals that it is far more than just an introduction to cozy Edo-style restaurants and bars. In the preface, Fukuda mentions that he was inspired by Nagai Kafū when going out for walks to gather materials for his book. He was particularly inspired by Kafū's masterpiece *Bokutō kidan* (1937, trans. *A Strange Tale from East of the River,* 1972), a novel composed of layered narratives that shows literary influences from the Edo period, early twentieth-century France, classical China, and modern Japan. Fukuda was particularly impressed by the novel's setting, the red-light district of Tamanoi on the east bank of the Sumida River, and the overall nostalgic atmosphere created by Kafū. In the 1930s Tamanoi consisted of a maze of alleyways and *roji*, and seemed a place apart from modern Tokyo. Here, *roji* were narrow cul-de-sacs forming the entrance to small brothels.

Fukuda also refers to Kimura Shōhachi, who not only drew the illustrations for *A Strange Tale from East of the River* but is also known as one of the preeminent writers following in Kafū's footsteps (2008, 3–5). Kimura wrote lengthy essays on Tokyo. In them, he takes the position of a walker and explores Tokyo from the inhabitant's viewpoint. This perspective allows him to tie together Tokyo's history with personal memories as he reflects on the passage of time embodied in the transformation of the locations he describes. In referring to Kafū and Kimura, Fukuda seems to identify with their way of writing about Tokyo. Kafū's writing became an important model for mapping a Tokyo of small-scale localities that exemplify the dichotomy between bright sites of modernity and their dim counter-sites. A similar foregrounding of alleyways can be seen in recent publications in which carefully restored and well-kept backstreets are juxtaposed with rundown and cluttered narrow spaces between buildings—showing that *roji* can even be urban wastelands (Satō 2005, 110–11). Another example is *Nagori no Tōkyō* ("Remnants of Tokyo," 2009) by writer and photographer Kataoka Yoshio (b. 1939), who has written numerous books on Tokyo. "Remnants of Tokyo" portrays small-scale structures in Tokyo that evoke the beauty of *aware*, the melancholic aesthetic of loss and nostalgia.

In this regard, the photography on the cover of "Tokyo Style" is instructive. It shows Fukuda in front of a run-down wooden house, which exudes an atmosphere of *aware*. The picture bears striking similarities to Kafū's self-portraits in sketches and photographs. Just as Kafū used to take photographs on his walks with a Rollei camera, Fukuda hangs an old-style analog camera around his neck to make it seem that he, too, is taking photographs as he strolls along. Against expectations, however, "Tokyo Style" doesn't contain any illustrations, neither photographs nor maps or any other kind of image. The picture on the cover of the book is an expression of Fukuda's intention to guide the reader through his favorite locations in Tokyo. These include, above all, restaurants and bars in traditional, *sakariba*-like neighborhoods.

For Fukuda, exploratory walks in such areas function as an escape (*tōhi*) from bustling, global Tokyo with its towers of glass and concrete (2008, 4, 7, 143). Therein lies the meaning of "lavish walks." "Tokyo Style" consists of three main chapters: "Walking Sake—I like it Very Much: Drinking, Walking, Eating and Drinking;" "Tokyo Now and Then: What Does It Mean to Be a Neighborhood Kid?;" and "My One and Only Restaurants, My One and Only People: Contemporary Out-of-the-way Destinations." In the foreword to his famous essay *Hiyorigeta: Ichimei Tōkyō sansakuki* ("Fairweather Clogs: A Report of Walks through Tokyo," 1914), Kafū praised the advantages of going out for a walk (1992–95, 111–12). Similarly, in the first chapter of "Tokyo Style," Fukuda extols the benefits of walking in the city.

His point is that people should slow down and enjoy Tokyo's unique atmosphere as they walk from one restaurant or bar to the next (2008, 14–17). He introduces various cuisines available in Tokyo, among them traditional Japanese food such as *tonkatsu* (a Japanese type of schnitzel) and *oden* (a stew-like dish consisting of various ingredients such as potato, boiled egg, and chicken). His recommendations extend to Chinese food, beer bars, and *izakaya* (Japanese-style pubs).

Fukuda reflects on what constitutes a city. Tokyo provides diverse possibilities, as there are many places that still retain a significant amount of traditional character:

> Tokyo has changed to a large extent, but there is also a Tokyo that doesn't change. [. . .] Another facet of the city is that there are alleyways (*roji*). From the outset, in the ample countryside there is no room for establishing *roji*. Only when people are crowding, joining together and separating, when there is a coming and going and prosperity and affluence are calling for shadow, neighborhoods (*machi*) emerge. (53–54)

For Fukuda, urban life centers on small districts and alleyways. His premise is that to go out to one of the many restaurants and bars is a good way to explore their distinctive culture and atmosphere. Compared to Kobayashi, who systematically arranges urban space according to administrative units, Fukuda's mapping of Tokyo appears sporadic and inconsistent. This is also reflected in his book's table of contents. Only some of the headings within the chapter titled "Tokyo Now and Then: What Does It Mean to Be a Neighborhood Kid?" contain names of well-known areas such as Nihonbashi, Ginza, Shibuya, and Shinjuku—all of which have witnessed tremendous change and are frequently treated in spatial (auto)biographies and other descriptive writings about Tokyo. In this chapter, Fukuda refers to some of the changes these areas have experienced since the 1920s and provides information about their history. He turns his attention to the alleyways and *machi* and encourages the reader to seek them out on their walks. He mentions little shops and tiny restaurants that form the core of these backstreet *sakariba* (60–148).

Like Kobayashi, Fukuda depicts Tokyo in an associative and anecdotal manner, a writing style characteristic of the Japanese essayistic (*zuihitsu*) tradition. Compared with Kobayashi's works, however, Fukuda's is much more associative. This becomes obvious in the third chapter, "My One and Only Restaurants, My One and Only People." While wandering around, whether literally or figuratively, he jumps from one theme to another. Observations and memories, facts and data are all lightly strung together. He refers to artists and public figures, such as the photographer Tanaka Chōtoku (b. 1947), the publisher, film producer, and screenwriter Kadokawa Haruki (b. 1942), and the literary critic Etō Jun (1932–1999), who all knew Tokyo very well (151–54).

Ishizeki Zenjirō's "Yoshimoto Takaaki's Tokyo": Exploring Tokyo's Transformation through Changing Living Arrangements

Ishizeki Zenjirō, who writes on various cultural and literary topics, was born in Ibaraki Prefecture and moved to Tokyo in the 1960s. After studying literature, he began working as an editor at a publishing house. From the late 1960s onwards, he wrote about Kobayashi Hideo (1902–1983), Dazai Osamu (1909–1948), and Yoshimoto Takaaki (1924–2012)—all of them celebrated writers who addressed key issues of modern Japan. The main concern of all three was the impact of Western modernity on Japan and issues relating to national and cultural identity. To date, Ishizeki has written two books about Yoshimoto, "Yoshimoto Takaaki's Tokyo" and *Yoshimoto Takaaki no kokyō* ("Yoshimoto Takaaki's Native Home"), which was published the year Yoshimoto died.

Yoshimoto's life and writings are very well suited to exploring Tokyo's and Japan's path to modernity. Dedicated to investigating the social, political, and cultural contradictions and conflicts of postwar Japan, Yoshimoto became a major intellectual voice of his generation. He also composed poems and essays, among them *Haikei no kioku* ("Recollections of Settings," 1994), a collection of autobiographical writings. Yoshimoto's name is closely linked to the protest movement against the renewal of the U.S.-Japan Mutual Security Treaty and to the emergence of New Left activism in Tokyo during the 1960s. The "Treaty of Mutual Cooperation and Security Between the United States and Japan," also known in Japan as *Anpo jōyaku* or *Anpo*, was an important component of the postwar world order. Its precursor was signed in 1952 following the signing of the Treaty of Peace with Japan in San Francisco and was amended in 1960. The treaty was a major encroachment on Japan's national autonomy. It permitted the United States to act for the sake of maintaining peace in East Asia, granted extraterritorial rights for U.S. military exercises on Japanese soil, and placed Japan under the protection of the so-called American nuclear umbrella. The amendment of the treaty brought about intense conflicts, protests, and turmoil in Japan, which lasted, exacerbated by the Vietnam War and subsequent student uprisings, until the early 1970s. The debates centered on the question of which path towards modernity Japan should pursue, involving issues of the democratization of society and discussions of the pros and cons of Japan's rapid economic growth. Another issue was Japan's military alliance with the United States. Yoshimoto supported the protest movement against the 1960 Anpo treaty as an expression of the contradictions of the postwar order. In taking a critical and independent stance towards state authorities, as well as academic institutions, Yoshimoto gained a reputation as one of the most important public intellectuals in postwar Japan. He combined political and philosophical thinking with a restless life, which helped make him a celebrated figure.

Yoshimoto's life and work are deeply intertwined with Tokyo. He moved eleven times within the city. Among the Tokyo locations where he lived are his birthplace Tsukishima, a neighborhood in Chūō ("Central") Ward, Kami-Chiba in Katsushika Ward, Tabata in Kita Ward, Sendagi and Yanaka, two neighborhoods in the vicinity of Ueno, and Komagome in Toshima Ward. As a child, he resided in a *nagaya*, a traditional type of townhouse; in the 1940s, he and his wife occupied a tiny and cramped apartment in Kami-Chiba; and, after the birth of their two daughters in the 1960s, the family moved into a small house in Sendagi. All of these places are small-scale neighborhoods characterized by an average living standard. None of them would be considered the kind of modern and upscale area where well-off people might prefer to live.

Yoshimoto experienced firsthand times of tremendous growth and prosperity as well as large-scale destruction and life-threatening shortage. In his childhood, he witnessed Tokyo's rapid reconstruction after the 1923 earthquake. Growing into adulthood, he first faced Tokyo's destruction during the war years of 1944 and 1945 and then its fast-paced rebuilding and industrialization in the postwar period. In the 1980s, Yoshimoto witnessed the building boom of the bubble economy and its aftermath in the early 1990s. He experienced the globalization of the Japanese economy, which gave Tokyo the status of a "world city." In the 1980s an unparalleled construction boom left its mark from central Tokyo to the city's farthest edges, proof of Tokyo's growing importance in the national and global economy. Since then, countless redevelopment projects have continued to transform Tokyo's urban fabric, leading to increasing gentrification.

There are quite a number of publications, in addition to Ishizeki's, in which Tokyo's history is told by means of mapping the city with the biography of a renowned novelist and scenes from the person's writings. Examples are Matsuyama Iwao's (b. 1945) *Ranpo to Tōkyō* ("Ranpo and Tokyo," 1984), Tomita Hitoshi's (b. 1946) *"Ranpo 'Tōkyō chizu'"* ("Ranpo's 'Map of Tokyo,'" 1997), Takeda Katsuhiko's (b. 1929) *Sōseki no Tōkyō* ("Sōseki's Tokyo," 1997–2000), Kondō Nobuyuki's (b. 1931) *Tanizaki Jun'ichirō Tōkyō chizu* ("Tanizaki Jun'ichirō's Map of Tokyo," 1998), and Kawamoto Saburō's (b. 1944) *Kafū to Tōkyō* ("Kafū and Tokyo," 1996). Each publication explores Tokyo from its own unique angle. Edogawa Ranpo (1884–1965) was a writer of detective fiction, and, as might be expected, investigations of Ranpo's Tokyo take the reader into uncanny and mysterious sites of the city. Novelists Natsume Sōseki (1867–1916) and Tanizaki Jun'ichirō (1886–1965) reflected on the ambiguities inherent in Japan's modernization and its impact on Tokyo. Sōseki spent most of his life in Tokyo; Tanizaki was born in Tokyo and lived there until 1923.[4] Sōseki and Tanizaki were attentive observers of Tokyo's growth and expansion, the social and cultural impact of the huge domestic migration into the city, and the breathtaking speed in which modernization took place. Nagai Kafū, too, spent most of his life in Tokyo. He wrote numerous literary works documenting the spatial, social, and cultural conflicts inherent in the Edo-Tokyo transformation.

At first glance, "Yoshimoto Takaaki's Tokyo" seems to be in line with such publications. The work comprises five chapters, each investigating an important phase in Yoshimoto's life, such as his family background and university years, his wartime and postwar experiences, and his rise to prominence during the 1960s and 1970s. Ishizeki's account cuts off in 2005, the year of the book's publication. However, there are substantial differences between the works focusing on the Tokyo of the writers mentioned above and Ishizeki's volume on Yoshimoto's Tokyo. The former are all based on close readings of literary titles set in Tokyo, with the goal of examining how Tokyo is presented in these works and how they relate to the writer's life in the city. Ishizeki's work, in contrast, evokes a more intimate atmosphere stemming from Ishizeki's own interest in Yoshimoto. Ishizeki knew Yoshimoto personally, meeting him twice for walks through Tokyo to gather material for the book. The first tour led through Tsukishima, Yoshimoto's birthplace, with the second stroll covering a much wider radius. Accompanied by photographer Araki Nobuyoshi, they wandered through areas where Yoshimoto had actually lived (Ishizeki 2005, 258–59).

What historical, cultural, and topographical layers of Tokyo can be uncovered by inscribing Yoshimoto's life into the city? What narratives of Tokyo can be traced in Yoshimoto's living environments? How is Ishizeki's life story framed within an overall narrative of Tokyo's transformation? In the afterword to "Yoshimoto Takaaki's Tokyo," Ishizeki sketches out the reasons he wrote Yoshimoto's biography as a "life history" (*seikatsushi*). His stated intention was to document Yoshimoto's life by separating his ordinary life from his professional one (Ibid., 259). In exploring Yoshimoto's living environments, Ishizeki rewrites Tokyo's history by describing different forms of housing and the diversity of living conditions from the 1930s until the early twenty-first century—the period of time covered by "Yoshimoto Takaaki's Tokyo."

Ishizeki's investigation of Yoshimoto's Tokyo focuses on two main themes. One is Tokyo's rapid growth and transformation from low-rise to high-rise that took place during Yoshimoto's lifetime. The other is Yoshimoto's restless life in Tokyo. Ishizeki intertwines biographical information about Yoshimoto with material gleaned through archival research about the places where Yoshimoto lived. In complementing descriptions of places with quotations from Yoshimoto's works and conversations between Ishizeki and Yoshimoto during their walks, "Yoshimoto Takaaki's Tokyo" provides vivid images of Yoshimoto's various living environments. Maps of the areas and floor plans of the houses in which Yoshimoto lived, along with photographs of his family and their places of residence, deliver realistic impressions of living conditions in Tokyo over time. Yoshimoto's experiences correlate with the various stages of Tokyo's transformation from low-rise to high-rise and with the erasure of the old and the arrival of the new.

The photograph on the cover of "Yoshimoto Takaaki's Tokyo" was taken by Araki. It highlights the sharp contrast between high-rise condominiums and low-rise houses in Tsukishima. Tsukishima plays an important role in Yoshimoto's life and in the way Ishizeki structures the book. Ishizeki frames his account by including reflections on the changes that took place in Tsukishima over the course of Yoshimoto's life in the first chapter and in the epilogue (Ibid., 13–56; 217–26). Tsukishima is an emblematic and even primordial area for understanding the fundamental conflicts inherent in Tokyo's rapid transformation. Architectural historian Jinnai Hidenobu summarized this complex process as the reshaping of the city from the "Edo on water" (*mizu no Edo*) into "the Tokyo on land" (*riku no Tokyo*) (1995, 107). Jinnai's point is that Edo's transportation routes, which had originally been based on a network of moats, canals, and rivers, were filled in or gradually replaced by railway lines and streets that were later built over with highways. Many of Tokyo's waterways were straightened out and their banks reinforced. Tokyo's cityscape was further altered through the replacement of simple low-rise houses with, in many cases, expensive high-rise buildings in order to accommodate the rapidly growing population. These are exactly the developments that took place in Tsukishima and its surrounding districts. Thus, it is an area that can be considered a microcosm of the overall transformation of Tokyo.

Located in the immediate vicinity of Tsukudajima, a natural island that used to be a fishing village, Tsukishima is an island made from reclaimed land in the Sumida River estuary. Its history dates back to the seventeenth century. Reclamation work finished in 1893, when both islands were joined together by landfill and took their current form. Until well into the twentieth century, Tsukudajima's inhabitants had mainly made their living from fishing, thus leading lives unlike most residents of Tokyo. For the most part, Tsukudajima escaped damage in the 1923 earthquake and during the war. However, Tokyo's reconstruction during the postwar period and its growth in the decades since then have posed threats to the island on two fronts: from the construction of high-rise buildings with expensive apartments and from increasing industrial pollution caused by plants located by the Sumida River and the Tokyo Bay. While the first led to gentrification, the second caused the fish population to decrease—taking with it local culture and ways of life.

Starting with architect Tange Kenzō's (1913–2005) famous 1960 plan for Tokyo—a spectacular vision of a megastructure in Tokyo Bay, by which a new physical order was to be imposed on the city—Tokyo Bay and its surroundings have become a unique experimental ground for new concepts of urban planning and architecture. Although Tange's plan was never realized, it inspired many construction projects. Since then, Tokyo's waterfront has gradually been pushed further outwards, with more land being reclaimed for large-scale urban developments. The northern part of Tsukishima was redeveloped in the 1990s and has subsequently been built-up with Okawabata River City 21, an amalgam of several large construction projects and high-rise buildings. Soon after, the high-rise office and residential complex Harumi Island Triton Square opened next to it.

Tsukishima and Tsukudajima are now surrounded by exclusive high-rise condominiums, offering a vivid contrast to the old wooden houses and back alleys that have survived various calamities and make up what remains of a local, close-knit community. Along with Yanaka, Nezu, Sendagi, and Asakusa, Tsukishima is one of the few places in Tokyo where one can still get a feel for Tokyo's historical urban fabric. Tsukishima's skyline, formed by the historical Sumiyoshi Shrine and the modern high-rise buildings, is a study in contrasts in an area that clearly reflects the ongoing reshaping of Tokyo—one of the major subtexts of which is the widening gap between the new-rich and the old- and new-poor.

A view from Tsukudajima. *Evelyn Schulz.*

In documenting Yoshimoto's life in Tokyo and framing it within the narrative of Tsukishima, Ishizeki links the biography of an individual with Tokyo's transformation. There are other writers who also illustrate Tokyo's transformation using the example of Tsukishima. Yomota Inuhiko (b. 1953), a well-known film historian, lived in a traditional townhouse in Tsukishima from 1988 until 1994. In 1992 he published *Tsukishima monogatari* ("Stories of Tsukishima"), a collection of autobiographical essays. In the early 2000s, he returned to Tsukishima to investigate the ongoing changes there and to write about them. In 2007 he published *Tsukishima monogatari futatabi* ("Tsukishima Stories Revisited," 2007), a collection of nostalgia-filled autobiographical essays.

CONCLUSION AND OUTLOOK

Tokyo spatial (auto)biographies depict the city from the point of view of an individual. Urban space is conceived of as a subjective experience. I focused on very different works in order to give a sense of the wide range of content, structure, and approach to Tokyo contained in this category of writing. Spatial (auto)biographies closely interweave impressions and memories by combining texts with photographs, drawings, and maps, which often make reference to earlier depictions of Edo and Tokyo. They highlight the affective dimensions of places and spaces from various perspectives, thus producing very personal impressions and images of Tokyo. Spatial (auto)biographies provide insights into how people relate to Tokyo and how they make their own "native" Tokyo.

Spatial (auto)biographies are the product of literal and figurative peripatetic, slow-paced wanderings interspersed with narratives of Tokyo's history as well as commentary on how the city has internalized modernity and globalization. The itineraries point out zones and areas in which asynchronicities of social and cultural developments and the resulting conflicts become visible and tangible. The overall context of these works is the grand narrative of nation-building, modernization, and globalization—and resistance to it. As long as Tokyo's development is triggered by cycles of destruction and reconstruction, renewal and growth, or, in other words, by rapid economic, social, and cultural change, the desire to inscribe memories of one's own life into Tokyo urban space—as seen in spatial (auto)biographies—will probably continue. It is interesting to note that, although Japan's globalization is an important reference point in these writings, specific depictions of global Tokyo and of Tokyo's relationship with the rest of the world are rather scarce.

As attachment to place have become problematic in this gigantic megacity, spatial (auto)biographies offer the reader explorative journeys through neighborhoods of Tokyo where a sense of "hometown" can still be found. The personal style and the clear and straightforward language in most of these works help make the experience of Tokyo comprehensible and tangible. One possible explanation for the great popularity of such writing in Japan is that many readers share similar experiences and impressions. The wide variations in the works reflect the fact that almost any life narrative can be inscribed into the space of Tokyo. Each work is in and of itself a re-creation of Tokyo. Tokyo spatial (auto)biographies are a sizable and diverse body of writing worthy of increased recognition and study outside of Japan.

NOTES

1. All translations from texts not yet published in English translation are by Evelyn Schulz.
2. For the English translation of Tayama's work, see Tayama 1987.
3. A revised edition of *Shisetsu Tōkyō hanjōki* was published in 1992. This edition contains an additional chapter titled "Hachi-nen nochi" ("Eight Years Later"). In it, Kobayashi reflects on the changes and transformations that took place in Tokyo since the book's first edition came out in 1984 (see Kobayashi and Araki 1992, 289–312). Araki added new photographs in order to document the changes and transformations.
4. The earthquake of September 1923, which destroyed Tanizaki's house in Yokohama, prompted him to move to Kyoto.

WORKS CITED

Ankersmit, Frank R. 1996. "Die postmoderne 'Privatisierung' der Vergangenheit," in *Der Sinn des Historischen: Geschichtsphilosophische Debatten*, edited by Helga Nagl-Docekal, 201–34. Frankfurt am Main: Fischer Taschenbuch Verlag.
Arnold, Dana and Joanna R. Sofaer, eds. 2008. *Biographies and Space: Placing the Subject in Art and Architecture*. New York: Routledge.
Bachtin, Michail M. [Bakhtin, Mikhail]. 2008 [1975]. *Chronotopos*. Translated by Michael Dewey. Frankfurt am Main: Suhrkamp.
Benjamin, Walter and Asja Lacis. 1980 [1972]. "Neapel." In *Walter Benjamin: Gesammelte Schriften*, edited by Rolf Tiedemann and Hermann Schweppenhäuser, IV.1, edited by Tillman Rexroth, 307–16. Frankfurt am Main: Suhrkamp.
Cooper Marcus, Clare. 1979. *Environmental Autobiography* (Working Paper, 301). Berkeley: Institute of Urban and Regional Development, University of California.
Crang, Mike. 2005. "Time Space." In *Spaces of Geographical Thought: Deconstructing Human Geography's Binaries*, edited by Paul Cloke and Ron Johnston, 199–217. London: Sage.
Hayashi Fumiko. 1997. "Diary of a Vagabond." In *Be a Woman: Hayashi Fumiko and Modern Japanese Women's Literature,* edited and translated by Joan Ericson, 123–214. Honolulu: University of Hawai'i Press.
Farrar, Margaret E. 2011. "Amnesia, Nostalgia, and the Politics of Place Memory," *Political Research Quarterly*, 64(4): 723–35.
Fukuda Kazuya. 2008. *Tōkyō no ryūgi: Zeitaku na machiaruki* ("Tokyo Style: Lavish Neighborhood Walks"). Tokyo: Kōbunsha.
Ishizeki Zenjirō. 2005. *Yoshimoto Takaaki no Tōkyō* ("Yoshimoto Takaaki's Tokyo"). Tokyo: Sakuhinsha.
Jinnai Hidenobu. 1995. *Tokyo: A Spatial Anthropology*. Berkeley: University of California Press.

Kobayashi Nobuhiko. 1992. *Shisetsu Tōkyō hōrōki* ("Wandering Through Tokyo: A Personal Account"). Tokyo: Chikuma Shobō.

———. 2002. *Shōwa no Tōkyō. Heisei no Tōkyō* ("Tokyo in the Shōwa Period, Tokyo in the Heisei Period"). Tokyo: Chikuma Shobō.

———. 2013. *Watashi no Tōkyō chizu = My Tokyo Map*. Tokyo: Chikuma Shobō.

Kobayashi Nobuhiko and Araki Tsunetada [Nobuyoshi]. 1984. *Shisetsu Tōkyō hanjōki* ("An Account of Tokyo's Prosperity: A Personal Interpretation"). Tokyo: Chūō Kōronsha.

———. 1992. *Shinpan–Shisetsu Tōkyō hanjōki* ("New Edition–An Account of Tokyo's Prosperity: A Personal Interpretation"). Tokyo: Chūō Kōronsha.

Kūpā Mākasu, Kurea [Cooper Marcus, Clare]. 2013."Kankyōteki jijoden ("Environmental Autobiography"). Translated by Nagahashi Tamesuke. *Ritsumeikan sangyō shakai ronshū* 49 (1): 145–53.

Mori Ōgai. 1994 [1910]. "Under Reconstruction" *[Fushinchū].*" Translated by Ivan Morris. In *Youth and other stories*, edited by J. Thomas Rimer, 148–53. Honolulu: University of Hawai'i Press.

Müller Farguell, Roger W. 2006. "Städtebilder, Reisebilder, Denkbilder," in *Benjamin-Handbuch: Leben, Werk, Wirkung*, edited by Burkhardt Lindner, 626–42. Stuttgart: Metzler.

Nagai Kafū. 1992–95 [1914]. *Hiyorigeta* ("Fairweather Clogs"). In *Kafū zenshū* 11, 109–89. Tokyo: Iwanami Shoten.

Nora, Pierre. 1998. *Zwischen Geschichte und Gedächtnis*. Translated by Wolfgang Kaiser. Frankfurt am Main: Suhrkamp.

Norberg-Schulz, Christian. 1980. *Genius Loci: Towards a Phenomenology of Architecture*. New York: Rizzoli International Publications.

Radović, Darko and Davisi Boontharm, eds. 2012. *Small Tokyo*. Tokyo: Flick Studio.

Radović, Darko, Heide Jager, and Ammon Beyerle. 2008. *Another Tokyo: Nezu and Yanaka, Places and Practices of Urban Resistance*. Tokyo: Center for Sustainable Urban Regeneration, University of Tokyo.

Sand, Jordan. 2013. *Tokyo Vernacular: Common Spaces, Local Histories, Found Objects*. Berkeley: University of California Press.

Sata Ineko. 1989. *Watakushi no Tōkyō chizu* ("My Map of Tokyo"). Tokyo: Kōdansha.

Satō Hachirō. 2005. *Boku no Tōkyō chizu* ("My Map of Tokyo"). Tokyo: Netto Musashino.

Schulz, Evelyn. 2003. "Narratives of Counter-Modernity: Urban Spaces and Mnemonic Sites in the *Tōkyō hanjō ki*." *European Journal of East Asian Studies* 2 (1): 117–151.

———. 2004. *Stadt-Diskurse in den 'Aufzeichnungen über das Prosperieren von Tōkyō' (Tōkyō hanjō ki): Eine Gattung der topographischen Literatur Japans und ihre Bilder von Tōkyō (1832–1958)*. Munich: iudicium.

———. 2011. "Nagai Kafū's Reflections on Urban Beauty in *Hiyorigeta*: Reappraising Tokyo's Back Alleys and Waterways." *Review of Asian and Pacific Studies* (Center for Asian and Pacific Studies, Seikei University, Tokyo) 36: 139–64.

———. 2012. "Walking the City: Spatial and Temporal Configurations of the Urban Spectator in Writings on Tokyo." In *Urban Spaces in Japan: Social and Cultural Perspectives*, edited by Christoph Bruman and Evelyn Schulz, 184–202. New York: Routledge.

———. 2013. "Beyond Modernism." In *Future Living: Collective Housing in Japan*, edited by Claudia Hildner, 11–26. Basel: Birkhäuser.

Sennett, Richard. 2016. *The Public Realm*. Accessed June 27. https://www.richardsennett.com/site/senn/templates/general2.aspx?pageid=16&cc=gb.

Soja, Edward W. 1989. *Postmodern Geographies: The Reassertion of Space in Critical Social Theory*. London: Verso.

Suzuki Hiroyuki. 2009. *Tōkyō no chirei (geniusu roki)* ("Tokyo's Sense of Place (Genius Loci)"). Tokyo: Chikuma Shobō.

Tayama Katai. 1987. *Literary Life in Tokyo 1885–1915: Tayama Katai's Memoirs (Thirty Years in Tokyo)*. Translated by Kenneth G. Henshall. Leiden: Brill Academic Publishers.

Tsuchida Mitsufumi. 1994. *Tōkyō kiroku bungaku jiten: Meiji gannen–Shōwa 20 nen* ("Encyclopedia of Documentary Literature about Tokyo: The First Year of Meiji—The Twentieth Year of Shōwa"). Tokyo: Kashiwa Shobō.

Yoshimi Shun'ya. 2001. "Urbanization and Cultural Change in Modern Japan: The Case of Tokyo." In *Cultural Studies and Japan*, edited by Steffi Richter and Annette Schad-Seifert, 89–101. Leipzig: Leipziger Universitätsverlag.

Chapter Five

Held Hostage to History

Okuda Hideo's "Olympic Ransom"

Bruce Suttmeier

Should the history of a city include its brushes with disaster? Should the story of its past contain near-catastrophes that would have brought about wildly different futures? Should memory maintain what might be called catastrophic counterfactuals—those epoch-altering events that come close to occurring—if only to acknowledge their enormous unrealized significance? Or, to pose the question more narrowly: what if the grandest of Japan's postwar spectacles, the opening ceremony of the 1964 Tokyo Summer Olympics, had narrowly escaped a domestic terrorist attack? What if that ceremony on October 10, 1964—taking place in a stadium filled with 75,000 spectators, dignitaries, heads of state (including the Emperor himself)—had nearly suffered a massive explosion emerging from the Olympic torch? What if a world audience numbering in the tens of millions, watching the first-ever live Olympic broadcast sent simultaneously via relay satellites to television sets in Japan, North America, and Europe, had witnessed such a spectacularly dramatic assault as it unfolded? Would knowledge of that close call alter our understanding of Japan's postwar—its embrace of pacifistic policies, its rejection of wartime radicalism, its image as a first-world, supremely competent, safe society?

The scenario might seem a mere thought experiment, an alternate-reality thriller in an airport bookstore, but what is termed counterfactual scholarship has drawn increased academic attention in the last decade, leading to "a veritable explosion of counterfactual research in history" (Lebow 2010, 6) and becoming "an important trend in contemporary historiography" (Rosenfeld 2014, 451). This approach to scholarship insists that history scrutinize its deterministic reliance on linear causation, making "absolutely explicit the logic connecting antecedent and consequent, and the assumptions on which all the chains of causation they consider are based" (Lebow 2010, 28). As one scholar notes, "I do not use counterfactuals to make the case for alternative worlds, but use the construction of those worlds to probe the causes and contingency of the world we know" (Ibid., 6).

Such weighty ideas find entertaining expression in Okuda Hideo's sprawling *Orinpikku no minoshirokin* ("Olympic Ransom," 2008a, 2008b), a two-volume novel recounting a fictional terrorist plot to disrupt the opening ceremony of the 1964 Games. The narrative, crudely summarized as a cat-and-mouse thriller featuring the young bomber and the police, describes a long, dramatic chase through Olympics-era Tokyo until eventually, by the novel's end, all parties converge on National Stadium and we watch a lone figure, pursued by police, explosives in hand, furtively approaching the Olympic flame.

The story, in content and in tone, could be considered a departure from other best-selling works by Okuda (b. 1956). His novels often appear darkly comic, full of odd, harmless characters living far outside contemporary norms of social, economic, and sexual respectability. His 2005 work *Rarapipo* (trans. *Lala Pipo*, 2008c), one of his two novels available in English, follows six individuals whose experiences increasingly interconnect as they seek sexual titillation (along with less erotic forms of human connection) in Tokyo's smutty underbelly. Okuda is best known in Japan for his linked stories, collected in three novels, concerning the fictional psychiatrist Irabu Ichirō, a medical practitioner whose obsessions and eccentricities often overshadow those of his patients. The first in the series, *In za pūru* (2002, trans. *In the Pool*, 2006), the only one available in English, finds the eccentric Dr. Irabu and his disaffected, exhibitionist nurse, Mayumi, treating six patients, from a high school boy with a cell-phone addiction to a recently divorced, middle-aged man afflicted with a permanent erection. The second book of the series, *Kūchu buranko* ("Trapeze," 2004), whose featured patients include a yakuza underboss so scared of needles that he can no longer use chopsticks, won the prestigious Naoki Prize, which honors the year's best work in popular literature. Several of his works, including *In za pūru*, *Lalapipo*, and *Orinpikku no minoshirokin*, have been made into films.

"Olympic Ransom" may contain little of the overt and comic smuttiness of the other works, but it shares with them an astute understanding of social space and a complex playfulness in articulating that space through its narrative structure. My chapter discusses how to assess the novel's staging of remembrance, how to gauge, so to speak, its epistemological poking at established history. Simply put, I ask what an invented tale of postwar history can reveal about early twenty-first-century attitudes toward memory. To do this I focus on the stark juxtaposition that animates the novel: a scrupulous attention to recorded history and an improbable, even absurd, narrative supplement to that history. On the one hand, the novel works extraordinarily hard to demonstrate a commitment to historical accuracy. Each chapter unfolds on a single day and obsessively records events that occurred in the city, from the weather and traffic to news items both momentous and mundane. Okuda's appendix lists dozens of monographs, histories, and memoirs he used as research for the novel, as if to impress upon readers his efforts at historical precision. Yet, on the other hand, the novel's predominant theme is how events get bypassed by history, how even the most momentous of moments can go unnoticed and forgotten. Again and again, the press, beat cops, crime bosses, and myriad spectators are all present as the plot unfolds and yet all fail to make much sense of what they see. All fail to recognize and record what happens as moments for public remembrance.

We should be wary of reading this theme too literally, though, since the narrative offers far more than a conspiracy-laden lesson in how power orchestrates history. We should be wary, as well, of reducing the narrative to a simple historiographical truism: that the past is forever yielding fresh insights through new sources and new discoveries. Even a more generously nuanced reading—that the book extends the postcolonial project of inscribing heretofore-invisible subjects into history—does not quite capture the critique of remembrance within the work. Rather, I read the novel as dramatizing the production of historical knowledge, a process taking place not through a straight-line signification of historical traces, but through an assertion of the past's radical plurality, an acknowledgment that events, governed as they are by historical contingency, are better understood by folding speculation itself into understanding, thereby expanding the boundaries of future remembrance.

I do this by examining two crucial moments near the end of the novel, one set on Tokyo's Yumenoshima ("Dream Island"), the other at National Stadium (Kokuritsu Kyōgijō), each illustrating the complex staging and fraught consequences of contemporary memory practices. Okuda's novel rides a wave of late twentieth- and early twenty-first-century nostalgia for the newly emerging postwar city, a city on the eve of the 1964 Olympics. But this sentimentality toward the years of the Shōwa thirties (1955–1964) exists alongside a less prominent, more critical strain of memory, one that centers on the social, environmental, and political costs of the Olympics. It is one that grows increasingly visible as Japan embarks on another Olympic adventure, the Tokyo Games of 2020, a Games best known for its early missteps, a Games that is sure to spur increasing dips into the archives of memory, seeking both what is there and what is missing.[1]

EXPLOSIVE NARRATIVES

"Olympic Ransom" begins at dusk on August 22, 1964, at a Tokyo fireworks display that, beyond being a summer celebration, is serving as a police security rehearsal for the upcoming Olympic Games. During the colorful display, a nearby house belonging to the head of Olympic security bursts into flames, the target of a homemade bomb planted in the back of the home. A letter to police headquarters a few days later insists that officials cancel the Opening Ceremonies and stop all preparation for the Games—or additional "fireworks" will follow. This is but the first of several acts of "domestic terrorism" perpetrated by the central character of the story, Shimazaki Kunio, a Tokyo University graduate from Akita Prefecture, radicalized a month earlier after learning the real reason for his older brother's death: a heroin overdose after years of excruciating, debilitating work on Olympic construction sites. Shimazaki himself gets work at the construction sites for the summer, ostensibly to honor his brother's memory and "to be nearer," both physically and spiritually, to the working class (Okuda 2008a, 153–54).[2]

When another construction coworker dies weeks later, Shimazaki's anger turns toward the Olympics more directly. It is an event celebrated on the back of workers, he fumes, a "distraction from reality" (Ibid., 365). With the help of explosives stolen from a work site, he and an older compatriot named Murata begin their series of bombings. Shimazaki demands hundreds of millions of yen, threatening a spectacular, embarrassing disruption of the Games. The sprawling story increasingly unfolds as a thriller, with each chapter focused on the actions and thoughts of a different character. Half of the chapters follow Shimazaki, while others follow police officials, journalists, and students. Shimazaki barely avoids capture again and again as he moves around the city, relocating from his apartment in the Nishikata neighborhood of Bunkyō Ward in north-central Tokyo to the construction workers' bunkhouse in far-south Haneda, near the airport, and from the clandestine confines of student dorms on the University of Tokyo's Hongō campus to a seedy room above a pachinko parlor in Edogawa Ward on Tokyo's eastern edge.

The action culminates on the afternoon of Saturday, September 10th, with the Opening Ceremony at National Stadium. Shimazaki surreptitiously enters the stands and, as the Emperor's address reverberates over the loudspeaker, he draws closer and closer to the Olympic Cauldron, dynamite in one hand, a lighter in the other. Police officers chase him through the stands, finally surrounding him as he nears the entrance to the soon-to-be-lit torch. The bomber and his primary pursuer, Inspector Ochiai Masao, stare at each other across the sea of unsuspecting spectators—Shimazaki contemptuously fingering the dynamite, and Ochiai nervously gripping his gun. Their long-awaited confrontation sets up the work's final pages, which, in deference to the deferral and delay typical of the thriller genre, I discuss later in the chapter.[3]

THE STINK OF THE PAST

Late in the novel, amid an ever-expanding manhunt, Shimazaki calls police headquarters from his latest and last hideout in the city. He instructs the listening officers how to deliver the ransom and abruptly hangs up, leaving police to hurriedly review the tape of his call, eager for clues to his whereabouts. The recording reveals the distinctive sound of seagulls in the background. Precincts bordering Tokyo Bay, already ordered to watch all public phones, are put on stepped-up patrols. "This is hardly a helpful clue," one officer says, frowning: "Ōi, Shinagawa, Tsukishima, Tsukiji, Fukagawa . . ."—reeling off the names of just a few of the hundreds of places along the bay where Shimazaki could be (Ibid., 325).

The frantic search of the bay shore, pulling in officers from every precinct in Tokyo, fails to find Shimazaki and Murata, since their hiding place on Yumenoshima, in the northwest corner of Tokyo Bay, seems an uninhabitable section of the city, an inconceivable spot for someone to hide.[4] Today, Yumenoshima, or "Reclaimed Land Site #14" (14-gō Umetatechi), as it was originally known, houses a "multipurpose park" with sports fields, a tropical greenhouse, and a large yacht marina. It is slated to host archery and equestrian events for the 2020 Olympics. But to anyone familiar with Tokyo urban history, Yumenoshima signifies an egregious folly in Japan's push for Olympic-era modernity.

The artificial island was first proposed in the 1930s as the site of Tokyo's new municipal airfield. Dredging on the ambitious project, to build the "world's largest airport," began in 1939 ("Tōkyō Yumenoshima" 2013). Wartime shortages halted construction just two years later, and the space lay half-completed for the remainder of the war. Following defeat, the prewar airport proposal morphed into a postwar plan for a beach resort. Dubbed "Tokyo's Hawaii" and given a name that means "Dream Island," Yumenoshima opened in 1947, only to close three years later due to financial mismanagement and typhoon damage. Finally in 1957, the artificial landmass assumed its most enduringly infamous form: as garbage dump. Built originally using millions of tons of the city's own waste sandwiched between layers of construction-displaced soil, the 4578-hectare island opened as a garbage dump in 1957, accepting over ten million tons of garbage in its ten-year life as a landfill (Ibid.).

The old dump is best remembered when, for a few sweltering weeks in late June and early July 1965, less than a year after the Olympics were held, the skies above Tokyo blackened and a plague of flies descended upon the wards east of the Sumida River. The source of the infestation was soon traced back to Yumenoshima. When an aerial spraying of insecticide at the end of June seemed only to hasten their spread, hundreds of members of Japan's Self-Defense Forces and municipal firemen descended on the island with flame-throwers, incinerating the flies and leaving the island, in Edward Seidensticker's colorful phrase, "a cinder on which not even flies could live" (1990, 260). It was not a new problem. Just two months before Murata and Shimazaki's fictional stay on the island in September 1964, newspapers reported bursts of spontaneous combustion amid the garbage and explosions of methane gas exacerbated by the record-high heat. Fires from these explosions burned over five thousand square meters of the landfill (*Shōwa nimannichi no zenkiroku* 1990, 70).[5] Yumenoshima and, by extension, the so-called great garbage war (*Tōkyō gomi sensō*) would emerge into view every so often for the next few years, until the closing of the landfill in 1967 and the opening, over ten years later, of "Dream Island Park" (Yumenoshima Kōen), with its sports stadiums and green spaces available to a still-wary public (Itō 1982, 2–3).

During their overnight stay on Yumenoshima, Shimazaki and Murata experience the island not as an uninhabitable, dangerous site, but as a safe, privileged space, one that affords unparalleled views of the city. For these two temporary inhabitants, the garbage piles yield not insect swarms or methane explosions—common occurrences on the island in the mid-sixties—but, instead, offer much-needed items for daily life. Their only significant mention of the huge trash piles has Murata "returning from the middle of the garbage . . . smiling, in high spirits" and carrying armfuls of shoeboxes. He wears a pair of black wingtips found amid the trash that "with a little spit and some polishing had begun to gleam" (Okuda 2008b, 327). "What's your size, kid? What color you want?" he asks Shimazaki, and passes him the box with requested size 26 white shoes. Shimazaki opens the box, smelling the "new rubber sole and canvas uppers," and puts one on. "It fits perfectly," he says, "like Cinderella's glass slipper" (Ibid.). The find is especially fortuitous, given that Shimazaki had fled their last hideout in his stocking feet, two minutes ahead of the police. At the conclusion of the chapter, Shimazaki

> laced up his brand-new shoes and they set off. Not a soul was in sight. The wind was pushing clouds across the sky and the sun was beginning to shine. Tokyo Tower, earlier obscured by mist, was now clearly in view. Scraps of paper danced in the wind. . . . The blue sky was awash in white with flocks of sea birds as far as the eye could see. . . . Their cries echoed around the area. Shimazaki spread his arms wide and felt as if his body was able to float. (Ibid., 330)

How might we explain a rendering so at odds with the historical record? Why not make Yumenoshima a garbage-choked, insect-infested, inhospitable site, as the sources from the sixties attest, and force the characters to endure what any visitor to the island would have endured? Why not present Yumenoshima as it has been presented elsewhere, most memorably in Hino Keizō's novel *Yume no Shima* (1985, trans. *Isle of Dreams*, 2010) where "the stench of rot hung in the air, blending with the smell of the sea" (2010 [1985], 46)? Hino's main character, Sakai Shōzō, noting the methane gas bubbling and gurgling up around him, "feels the wriggling movement, the breath, the body temperature of Tokyo, as it ceaselessly filled the vacuum of the bay" (Ibid.). Compare this to Shimazaki, "immersed in Dream Island's panoramic views" as the morning mist begins to lift.

> He couldn't guess how wide the island was. All the Olympic track events could be held all at once here. To the west, he could dimly make out Tokyo Tower.[6] On his right was the recently completed Hotel New Otani.[7] The sea breezes felt pleasant. All he could hear were the cries of the seagulls and the roar of jet engines. (Okuda 2008b, 326)

Unlike Hino's narrator, darkly noting the island's menacing, hazardous nature, Shimazaki describes the floating garbage dump as a safe and scenic refuge, an idyllic rendering that transforms it into a place providing security, shelter, and material comfort. One might attribute his ease amid the garbage to his status in a modernizing Tokyo, for he, too, is being cast off as the country single-mindedly makes preparations for the Olympics. Perhaps it is no wonder that the garbage, recognizing a figure of similar fate, welcomes him.

Such a thematic rationale, however, fails to comport with the mimetic imperative that runs so strongly throughout the novel. Even though the novel constructs a counterfactual, hidden Olympic history of terrorist threats and police cover-ups, it constantly seeks what might be called a period-specific verisimilitude. The narrative is dotted with cultural signifiers of Olympic-era Tokyo: Beatles songs,[8] the new bullet train,[9] elevated highways which cut across and transformed the city,[10] and Miyuki-zoku fashion—the short-lived penchant for madras plaids and penny loafers, a style embraced by "loitering youths" who were deemed rebellious and delinquent by nervous authorities.[11] Documented historical events, from the mundane (rain on August 20, the first to fall on the parched city in over a month) to the grand (the meticulously detailed accounting of the Opening Ceremony of the Olympics), are woven among the fictionalized incidents. These efforts at historical authenticity play out, as well, in the work's geographical precision, where drives around Tokyo unfold as a detailed street-by-street accounting of every turn, with each element of the rapidly evolving streetscape observed out of a car window. The novel's opening lines provide an excellent example:

> From Yoyogi Hatsudai he headed south on Yamanote Avenue, turned left at the Tomigaya intersection, and there, straight ahead as he headed down an incline were a series of low green hills stretching out before him. The gentle curve of their slopes resembled a glamorous woman beckoning him to bed. He turned right at the bottom of the hill and accelerated over the fresh pavement as if cruising down a highway. He could see to his left the NHK radio tower, recently relocated from the Uchisaiwaichō neighborhood. He felt a strong wave of pleasure as he viewed new office buildings under construction, surrounded by greenery. He turned left at the Udagawachō intersection and pressed the gas pedal to the floor to climb the steep slope. The roof of the nearly complete Yoyogi National Gymnasium, set against the looming sky of the late August summer, increasingly displayed the majestic sweep of a dragon's head. (Ibid., 3)

Many novels will position their characters in a fine-grained geographical space, orienting readers through place-specific signifiers and street-level landmarks. But the meticulous recitation here (and elsewhere in the book) of intersections, avenues, and neighborhoods goes far beyond the functions of any literary establishing-shot. Indeed, the scene serves as a virtual tour of prominent Olympic sites in 1964 Tokyo. In his brand-new, red Honda S600 sports car, Tadashi and his girlfriend Midori (both minor characters) first pass by Yoyogi Park, the site of the nearly completed Olympic Village, which was, until late 1963, the site of an American military housing complex. They notice the new NHK broadcast center (built, in part, to support the demands of Olympic television coverage) and view the famously sweeping roofline of Tange Kenzō's Yoyogi National Gymnasium (Kokuritsu Yoyogi Kyōgijō), the site of swimming and diving events. In addition to driving by these and other prominent examples of Olympic-era construction, the two admire the newly widened surface roads and newly erected elevated highways constituting their route. Tadashi turns onto Aoyama Avenue (Aoyama-dōri), and

> the large eight-lane road spread out before his eyes. With its road-widening project now complete, Aoyama Avenue resembled an airport runway, an uninterrupted stretch extending for several blocks. The streetcar that had run from Shibuya to Kita-Aoyama 1-chome had been removed a year ago, and the pockmarked asphalt had been smoothed. "Geta-haki apartments," the multi-storied residential buildings built atop ground-floor businesses, had sprung up on both sides of the street. (Ibid., 7)[12]

As Tadashi nears the Akasaka Prince Hotel, where he and Midori plan to use the rooftop pool, he sees in front of him the elevated Metropolitan Expressway 4 (Shuto Kōsoku Yon-gō Sen), opened just twenty-two days earlier on August 1. He thinks to himself, this scene was one of his favorites. Miyake slope (Miyake-zaka) was up ahead, along with the newly finished elevated interchange. And perched high above was Metropolitan Expressway 4, like the Milky Way itself, sublimely stretching out across the sky. How beautiful were all these roads, winding in all directions. . . . This is a city of the future, he thought. (Ibid., 8)

The drive to the hotel pool unfolds as a catalog of the changes that had vastly altered Tokyo in the years leading up to the Olympics. Terms like "geta-haki apartments" are glossed for the potentially uninformed younger reader. Sites familiar to twenty-first century Tokyoites, like the eight-lane Aoyama Avenue and the elevated highway system, are described in the breathless, astonished prose common in periodicals of the day.[13] Aoyama Avenue, a well-known mecca for high-end shopping, was, in the late 1950s, only twenty-two meters wide, about half its current width, and was largely two-story shop fronts. In the early 1960s, given its position connecting the center of the city to Shibuya (and the Olympic venues situated there), it was dubbed Olympic Tokyo's "Main Street" (*Mein Sutoriito*) and designated part of the "Olympic roads" (*Orinpikku dōro*) construction project. Officials widened the avenue to forty meters, tearing down buildings on both sides of the street and ripping up the streetcar line, an endeavor that cost over twenty-one billion yen. It was the most expensive transportation project, meter for meter, in the huge Olympic budget.[14]

We see in Tadashi's wide-eyed praise of the Metropolitan Expressway the enthusiasm that greeted the new high-speed roadways. The thirty-two-kilometer elevated highway system—stretching from near Haneda Airport in the south, into the center of the city, and out to Olympic venues in the west—soared high above the city and symbolized the growing prowess of domestic engineering. It also seemed to offer a near-utopian solution to the city's famous traffic problems. With the city's population growing by three-hundred-thousand per year and new cars entering its roads at an annual rate of fifty-thousand, newspapers in the early 1960s spoke endlessly of the "traffic paralysis" (*kōtsū mahi*) that threatened both the success of the Games and the long-term viability of the city. Letters to the editor regularly complained of commutes from the airport to downtown taking nearly three hours, which made the promises given when the highway opened all the more enticing and unbelievable: a ride from Haneda Airport to central Tokyo "in a mere twelve minutes" ("Tōkyō kaizō" 1963, 17). Throughout this passage, and, indeed, throughout the entire novel, the profusion of named sites and spaces serves as a signifier of precision and authority, of fidelity to a documented reality, not just of topographic space but, implicitly, of cultural and national history itself.

The very structure of the novel registers its meticulous attention to Tokyo and the city's historical record. Each of the fifty-six chapters is marked with a specific date, the earliest being Chapter 4 (July 13, 1964: Monday), the latest being Chapter 56 (October 11, 1964: Sunday), the day after the opening ceremonies. The chronology is often non-linear. To give one of many examples, August 30 (Chapter 3) precedes July 13 (Chapter 4), but this only highlights the book's demand that events be ordered and that the most audacious flights of fictional fancy be set within a rigorously arranged timeline of the documented past. The precise chronological accounting suggests a scrupulous attentiveness to the historical record, as if the speculative outrageousness of the alternate history requires an equally strong attention to actual events.

Why, then, with the care Okuda gives to mapping the city and tethering actual events to a fictional frame, does a historically resonant site like Yumenoshima receive such an unconventional (and ahistorical) representation? The reason, I contend, has to do with how the novel's signification of time and place functions largely through an indexical realism, a deployment of period details that serves as a discursive shorthand for historicity. What matters in this rendering are the visible, material signifiers of the city, the surface manifestations of this particular moment in Japan's past. In this sense, the staging of history in "Olympic Ransom" is not unlike many contemporary dramatizations of the recent past, insofar as it strives for verisimilitude through an accretion of visual signposts for remembrance. It also follows dominant modes of evoking nostalgic memory in 1990s and 2000s Japan, where, as Jordan Sand puts it, museum audiences and filmgoers alike expected representations of the postwar past "to conjure the images and feelings of urban life in the Shōwa thirties" (2013, 133). Sand invokes Yamazaki Takashi's wildly popular 2005 film *Ōruweizu: Sanchōme no yūhi* ("Always: Sunset on Third Street") and its gauzy, romanticized reproduction of "an imaginary Tokyo street in the year 1958," proclaiming it "the most successful evocation of Shōwa nostalgia in visual media." In succinctly summarizing the film's popular and critical success, Sand notes that the "star of the movie, in essence, was the set," one in which filmmakers painstakingly "invested as much in accurate reconstruction as any museum" (Ibid., 136). The movie exemplified a collapsing of national history into private nostalgia, insofar as a generalizable, domesticated past, composed of "artifacts and carefully reconstructed settings," often encouraged the individual's enjoyment of mass-mediated memories over any historian's narrative constructions (Ibid.).

How then to understand the narrative's rendering of Yumenoshima, which appears to exemplify, even parody, such staging? The scenographic props are in place, most notably the mountains of trash. But missing are the messiness of the site, the methane eruptions, and the sensory assault of rotting garbage on hot September days. What are missing, in fact, are the somatic experiences that, by dint of their intrusion into everyday life, pushed their way into 1960s national politics. That such experiences, and by extension the nationalized history they enabled, are missing here speaks to Okuda's use of history more generally. What we get, one might say, are scenes largely sanitized of the stink of the past, scenes that can simultaneously be a complete and utter fiction while also maintaining a near fanatical fidelity to the historical record.

ATTENDING TO THE PAGEANTRY OF HISTORY

While the scenes on Yumenoshima stage a history stripped of embodied experience, subsequent scenes at Olympic Stadium, the book's penultimate set piece stretching over several chapters, dramatize a more expansive version of this historical elision, thus presenting a more complex scripting of historical events. The episode unfolds at the Olympic Stadium on the afternoon of Saturday, September 10. Shimazaki, entry ticket in hand and disguised first as a mendicant monk and then as a bus driver, is chased by police detective Ochiai Masao, starting from a remote parking lot, through an underground tunnel, and then up a series of stairs and into the stadium. As the chase continues into the stands, the Emperor's opening address reverberates over the loudspeakers, followed by the Olympic Fanfare, the raising of the Olympic flag, and, then suddenly, three deafening bursts. The detective's "heart stops" and he whirls around, only to notice the ceremonial cannons and the thousands of brightly colored balloons released into the autumn sky (Okuda 2008b, 371). Almost immediately "a thunderous roar rose as the Olympic torch-bearer entered the stadium, the white smoke visible at the north gate" (Ibid., 372). Amid the noise and commotion, Shimazaki melts into the crowd. "Ochiai scanned the crowded stands, looking for Shimazaki. He suddenly saw a man climbing the stairs, strikingly conspicuous at that instant as the only head not turned toward the field" (Ibid.). The chase continues, with Shimazaki heading toward the torch stand, his path traced through each successive section of stadium seats—from section 40, to section 39, to section 38, as he gets closer and closer to the cauldron. As he nears section 36, the entrance to the torch stand, another policeman appears above him, blocking his path. "Stop or I'll shoot!" the policeman shouts. A wave of cheering erupts around them as Sakai Yoshinori, the Olympic torch bearer, reaches the torch stand and lights the flame. "Put your hands up now or we'll shoot!" yells Ochiai, his voice nearly drowned out by the loudspeaker. "In the name of all the competitors, I promise that we . . ." Out on the field, the gymnast Ono Takashi, his right hand raised high, recites the Olympic Oath. Shimazaki grips a stick of dynamite in his left hand. "Please move away," he says in a soft voice, "move away or I'll light it" (Ibid., 374). With his right hand, he pulls a lighter from his pocket. Ochiai aims his gun and pulls the trigger. "A dry pop rang out and the bullet struck Shimazaki in the chest . . . he slumped to the ground, the dynamite falling to the ground and rolling away" (Ibid.). Ochiai rushes to Shimazaki's side and wraps him in his jacket, then picks up his unconscious body and heads toward a waiting ambulance.

> Shadows flickered from something overhead. The crowd instinctively craned their necks and looked up. It was doves, several thousand of them, released into the skies of Tokyo, followed by strains of the Japanese national anthem, *His Imperial Majesty's Reign*, sung by 75,000 spectators. Shimazaki was laid out on a stretcher. His face was pale. Ochiai couldn't determine if he was breathing or if he had a pulse. The minute they set him in the ambulance it sped off. The rumble of jets echoed in the east. The assembled crowd was rooted in place, wondering what was to come. Five fighter jets appeared in tight formation. An ear-splitting explosion rippled across the stadium and surrounding park. The jets traced a graceful looping curve and broke formation. From the rear of their fuselages, they began to release smoke, each one forming a large ring in the sky. Ochiai silently stared at the scene. In less than a minute, the five Olympic rings were floating in the clear blue sky. Waves of applause and cheers reverberated from the stands. A single impression flashed in his mind: Japan is quite a country (*mattaku Nihon wa taishita kuni da*). (Ibid., 375)

With its breathless pacing, its high-wire historical stakes, and its absurdist staging of Shimazaki's single-minded dash toward the Olympic cauldron, the narrative invites vicarious pleasure in this dramatic pursuit. Analogously, it also displays the pleasure of the stadium audience, ostensibly cheering the national ceremony performed on the field, but, by dint of narrative focus, cheering each stage of the chase as well. How else can we reasonably interpret the roars of approval as police surround Shimazaki, as he is ordered "hands up" when the athletes themselves raise their hands for the Olympic Oath, and, most farcically, as several thousand doves are released when Shimazaki falls from a bullet to the chest? The staging positions Shimazaki as a kind of athlete, competing before the crowd, asked to submit to an Oath pledging allegiance to the Games. He is offered the sanctioned, nationalized script to follow, and, with his refusal, is subdued by official forces and removed from the field, all to the cheers of his countrymen. The narrative places him on the Olympic stage and thrills as his radical attempt to disrupt proceedings is thwarted and punished.

This framing suggests that we interpret his removal as an erasure of the past's radical potential, as an allegory of amnesia. Shimazaki, the center of this work's sprawling counter-history, enters the stadium intent on shattering the economic and political triumphalism of the Games and exploding (quite literally) the reductive narratives of inevitability accompanying Japan's modernizing path. These narratives of the Olympic era, as Jordan Sand and others have shown, are overwhelmingly inscribed in early twenty-first-century popular memory as "a time of innocence and optimism, when citizens were bound by a sense of national purpose and faith in progress, but life was still rooted in traditional communities" (2013, 128). Throughout the scene at the stadium, Shimazaki's doomed fantasy of resistance is on full display, visible to the nearly seventy-five thousand people in attendance and, yet, no one in the crowd seems to notice any of this action, not the chase, not the shooting, not the hastily removed body. It is certainly tempting to see this scene as a demonstration of memory's blind spots, of how the past, unfolding as multiple, often competing, narratives, coalesces into a unified spectacle insisting on attention and absorption, an imposed pageantry with the capacity to assimilate and neutralize acts of resistance.

COUNTER-HISTORY: AN INVITATION TO INTERPRETATION

To accept this reading is to overlook the work of the fictional narrative itself, which stages in meticulously wrought detail not only what happened, but also what could have happened. The counter-history is conventionally characterized as a thought experiment in narrative form, an historical exercise built on fictional suppositions that resist or even overturn standard narratives of the past. Its commonly understood function is to critically cleave the most hardened of historical truths, and, as in exemplary examples like Philip Dick's *The Man in the High Castle* (1963) or Philip Roth's *The Plot against America* (2004), to expose political and social certainties to speculative inquiry. We can supplement this characterization of the genre, seeing its function not as mere opposition to dominant systems of understanding past and present worlds, but as a mode of historical understanding itself. The story's terrorist plot can serve not just as a narrative proxy for long-latent opposition to Olympic orthodoxies, but also as an invitation to interpretation, an exegetical exercise.

Viewed this way, Shimazaki's fictional narrative is less a radicalizing addendum to the Olympic past than it is an allegory of that past's radical plurality, an allegory that exposes an epistemic feature of all such events: that they exceed, by definition, the available interpretations. As the stadium's blindness to Shimazaki's efforts makes clear, attention to the historical field entails a process of exclusion, "of rendering parts of a perceptual field unperceived" (Crary 1999, 24–25). The implications of this exclusion require that we consider the ways attention is solicited and structured, affixed and dispersed, whether in historical experiences themselves or in the narratives by which those experiences are remembered. Counter-history both insists on and assists in remedying that exclusion, encouraging and enabling us to look away from the field of historical truths where forces and institutions structure attention and, instead, toward the stands where fellow citizens abide. To borrow the felicitous phrasing of New Historicism, counter-history allows us "to dwell in history's dead-ends" and, by extension, to attend to and recognize discarded, discredited experiences in the past as possible seeds of future historical understanding (Gallagher and Greenblat 2000, 55). It might also allow us to dwell in the historical contingencies present in these moments, allowing the radical plurality of the past to surface through fictional interventions.

WEDDING HISTORY TO MEMORY

We might look to another historical pageant, staged five years earlier in the streets of Tokyo, to illustrate how even the most visible, most arresting of moments can wind up in history's dead ends, unrecognized and overlooked in the event's recounting. On the afternoon of April 10, 1959, the royal carriage carrying newly married Crown Prince Akihito and his bride, the commoner Shōda Michiko, pulled onto the streets of Tokyo. Over half a million spectators lined the parade route, with "over fifteen million watching the extended coverage on television," beginning with the 6:00 a.m. live footage of the bride leaving her home and ending with the post-midnight replay of the day's events. Viewers watched on average an astounding "ten hours and thirty-five minutes of coverage" (Watanabe 1989, 23). The "Ceremony of the Century," as it was dubbed, had dominated news reports for months, an extraordinary mobilization of national attention driven through a kind of collaboration, a negotiation between institutions shaping and supporting middle-class desires, and a public, newly possessed of leisure time and disposable income, who sought to satisfy these desires. The event's popularity emerged through a political and economic marketplace keen to produce images of romance and glamor, and a national polity, still scarred from military defeat and colonial loss, eager to embrace the Imperial Family through the idioms of romance, glamor and, most significantly, celebrity.

But, just after 2:30 p.m., as the royal carriage crossed into the square outside of the Imperial Palace, a young man emerged from the crowd. He ran into the street, throwing rocks and screaming at the couple. He managed to grab hold of the open-air, horse-drawn carriage and pull himself far up its side. His head and chest rose above the side door, giving him a clear view of the cowering, startled princess. The carriage briefly sped up and police quickly piled on the young man, wrestling him to the ground in the middle of the street.[15] The royal procession then continued as before, the couple waving to the crowds and the crowds cheering in response.

The episode was caught on camera and some of it was broadcast during the live coverage. It is a startling, arresting moment, captured by television cameras and seen by millions of viewers. However, as the sociologist Yoshimi Shun'ya points out, it was effectively "removed as a media image." It was "ignored . . . except for a very small number of weekly magazines," and "[t]elevision and newspapers both made absolutely no mention of it" (2000b, 271).[16] Such elision continues to this day, with scholarly and popular accounts almost never including it in their narratives.[17] It is telling that I learned of the incident first through fiction, in Ōe Kenzaburō's (b. 1935) novella *Sebuntīn* (1961, trans. *Seventeen*, 1996), where the young terrorist narrator, obsessively following news of the royal marriage, describes "seeing the youngster throwing stones on television" (1996, 86).[18]

It is easy to see why contemporary coverage and subsequent accounts would not absorb the jarring scene. The wedding, overwhelmingly presented in the mass media through apolitical, romanticized discourses, offered little space to make sense of such an attack. Since the brief and unsuccessful assault caused no injuries, it was easy to dismiss the man's motives as solipsistic delusions, not publically shared concerns. Surely, ethics informed the public elision of the scene as well. Should the attack be available for re-view, many wondered, if doing so might encourage other would-be terrorists seeking publicity or hoping to inspire anarchic violence? Expunging the image comes with costs as well. What, for instance, are the historical consequences of making such an image unavailable for re-view, particularly an image of such potential significance, an image that illustrates the Imperial Household's unsettling place in the postwar period? Might visibility be particularly crucial when that image itself speaks to national forgetfulness, when its very absence signifies the amnesia that allows a "symbolic emperor system" to be distanced from the burdens of its wartime past? And, finally, can fiction, with its suspect epistemology, be a sufficient mode for summoning such moments? What happens when the production of historical knowledge relies on a poetical and imaginative signification, not on a reference to the real, for its legitimizing force?

THE ENDS OF MEMORY

At the end of "Olympic Ransom," a character who has surreptitiously learned of the bombings turns to Suga Masaru and asks "It's over, isn't it? . . . [The bomber] has been caught, hasn't he?" Suga, whose father is overseeing all Olympic security, has an outsized interest in the case. He is a senior official in the Ministry of Finance and his own family's home was the first to be bombed six weeks (and over eight hundred pages) earlier. Investigators and officials had managed to keep the escalating string of explosions out of the press, even when the bomber threatened the Olympic Opening Ceremony. With the Olympics safely underway, the threat, the character assumes, is over. Pausing for several seconds, Suga smiles and answers, "What bomber? I don't know what you're talking about." "Well," the character replies, "it's ended then, thank heaven." "Listen," Suga responds bluntly, "it's not that anything's ended, it's that there was nothing from the very beginning" (Okuda 2008b, 385).

It is a suggestive response, either a complete disavowal that the bombings ever happened or, less rigidly parsed, a mere dismissal of events, an assertion that whatever happened holds no historical significance, that it merits no claim for future remembrance, and that it is, in a word, forgettable. This complex, sprawling story of domestic terrorism *could* have happened as described and simply left no trace in the historical record. The alleged experiences of Tokyo in the novel, its bombings and chases, its frustrated cops and befuddled bystanders, are mis-inscribed or unrecorded by authorities, attributed to gas leaks or construction accidents, dismissed as moments of no consequence and not worth remembering. Except, of course, that in staging such events in 1964 Tokyo, the novel both recounts and records these moments, albeit as imaginative history, as a fictional intervention in the postwar past.

In recounting and recording these moments in such painstaking and precise detail, "Olympic Ransom" underscores the state of memory in twenty-first-century Japan. Okuda's fictional narrative focuses on the everyday, on the minute details of place and personal experience. It articulates with calendric precision a history of national events intersecting with individual lives. Such a formulation of Olympic-era memory in one sense narrows the political range of remembered events. To borrow Jordan Sand's eloquent formulation,

> This "Shōwa thirties boom" shows the way that the potentially homogenizing effect of everydayness as a foundation for politics permits it to be simultaneously privatized—narrowed to the domestic sphere and to private memory—and nationalized—used as the basis for coercing memory into the mold of supposedly common national experience. (2013, 144)

In another sense, as Sand himself articulates, this focus provides "the materials for staking out new political turf" (Ibid.), challenging the insistence by those in power, like Suga Masaru, that "there was nothing from the very beginning." The novel's mimetic fixation makes available for re-viewing the "unrealized potentialities of the historical past," in philosopher Paul Ricoeur's phrasing (quoted in Lebow 2010, 277). By creating a meticulously chronicled counter-history of Tokyo during its Olympic summer, and by weaving into actual events a "hidden thread" of postwar history, the novel coaxes its audience to turn from rigid mimesis, from the model of a containable, representable world, and take seriously, if only through fictional speculation, the contingency of the recognizable past.

"Olympic Ransom" ends with two young women, minor characters in the story, heading off to the first women's volleyball game, laughing and marveling at the sheer size of the huge elevated expressway above. After the unnoticed shooting in the stadium and the brisk removal of Shimazaki's injured body, the story quickly returns in its final pages to a sanctioned historical narrative, free from the destabilizing presence of a past encumbered by contingency and potential and by the weight of epistemic uncertainty. The fictional narrative has, throughout its eight-hundred-plus pages, exposed this uncertainty and, by so doing, has introduced into remembrance a more exhaustive, radically speculative rendering.

NOTES

1. For a useful example of how the 2020 Olympics are spurring visible reexamination of the 1964 Games, see Whiting 2014.
2. Unless otherwise noted, all English translations are my own.
3. It is significant, if not surprising, that, although the book spends about half of its chapters focused on Shimazaki, fostering sympathy (or at least pity) for his radicalized path, the 2013 made-for-television movie version centers on (and sympathizes with) Inspector Ochiai Masao. This change in focus pushes the narrative toward a more standard police-procedural structure, showing the intrepid officer (complete with flashbacks to his childhood during World War II-era Tokyo) as he struggles to stop Shimazaki's senseless string of bombings.
4. Indeed, the idea to head to Dream Island comes from a taxi driver who, when Shimazaki archly notes that he is a bank robber looking for someplace without cops, the cabbie jokingly responds, "How about going to Dream Island?" (Okuda 2008b, 312).
5. Even decades after the dump's decommissioning, all open flames (including smoking by players on the new golf courses) were prohibited for fear of gas explosion. See Itō 1982, 2–3.
6. Tokyo Tower, to the immediate west of Shiba Park (Shiba Kōen) in Minato Ward, was built in 1958 as a communications tower for television (and soon after, radio) broadcasting. Three hundred and thirty-three meters tall, thirteen meters taller than its stylistic twin, the Eiffel Tower, Tokyo Tower was the tallest freestanding structure in the world the year it was built. Its observation deck is popular with tourists. With its distinctive "international orange" and white paint colors, Tokyo Tower has long served as a symbol of postwar Japan, perhaps most memorably in monster movies like *Mosura* (1961), where the giant larval Mothra destroyed much of the tower and built a cocoon at its base.
7. The Hotel New Otani was built in the run-up to the Tokyo Olympics, requested by the government in response to the perceived shortage of hotel space for visitors. As James Kirkup wrote after his visit to Japan in 1965, "From the monorail or the expressway, one's first overall view of Tokyo is of a sprawling, squat city. There were no skyscrapers until the Hotel New Otani, with its revolving circular restaurant sixteen floors up, was opened just in time for the Olympics in September 1964" (1966, 9). Kirkup's comments highlight that, until building height codes were lifted in 1963, all buildings in Tokyo were restricted to under thirty-one meters. The first major structure to exceed that limit was the Hotel New Otani at five times this limit—one hundred fifty-six meters (seventeen stories, the top floor housing the revolving restaurant) ("Nakunaru biru" 1963, 45). The hotel's idiosyncratic and futuristic presence on the horizon is used to dramatic effect in the 1967 James Bond film, *You Only Live Twice*, when the hotel serves as the Japanese headquarters of the villainous SPECTRE organization.
8. The group's popularity in Japan, beginning in late 1963 and early 1964, reached a fever pitch during their 1966 Asia tour after the release of the album *Rubber Soul*, a tour during

which they performed at the Nippon Budōkan Hall, the site of judo matches and several demonstration sports during the Olympics. See Beat Takeshi and Hidaka Kotarō, et. al. 2005, 95–98.

9. The bullet train (or *shinkansen*) began service on October 1, 1964, just ten days before the Opening Ceremony. Its initial route ran between Tokyo and Osaka, cutting total travel time from over six and a half hours using the existing express trains to about four hours. See Hood 2006, 27–28.

10. With the 1959 decision to bring the Olympics to Tokyo, the city famously embarked on a massive project to tear down and reconstruct huge portions of its built and natural environment. No portion of this project altered Tokyo more than the radically repurposed streets and new highways that arose before the Games. "Huge elevated expressways, some over forty meters high, began winding their way through the city in the early 1960s, dwarfing nearby buildings, shadowing parks and canals, and towering over large swaths of public spaces." The elevated highway system promised "a near-utopian solution" to the city's world-famous traffic woes and were part of larger utopian city plans proposed during the era. See Suttmeier 2016, 210–12.

11. After pleas and warnings by authorities to stop loitering in the Ginza failed to deter the Miyuki-zoku adherents, police amassed in the district on September 19, 1964, just weeks before the Olympics, and detained two hundred kids in their Oxford shirts and three-button jackets. As David Marx put it, "the Miyuki tribe disappeared from Ginza for the rest of the year, and . . . not a single foreigner returned home with lurid tales of misbehaving Japanese teenagers in shrunken cotton trousers" (2015, xi).

12. Geta-haki apartments (*geta haki apāto*) were defined, as the text explains, as multi-storied residential apartment buildings that had businesses (often retail stores, restaurants, or parking lots) in allotted spaces on the ground floor. The image of a Japanese wooden clog (*geta*) was used because the apportioned, visually divided space on the first floor resembled the stilt support-teeth of the footwear. The term was coined and gained prominence in the 1960s. See Yonekawa 2002, 297.

13. Reporters and writers described the drive on the newly opened highways as "a roller coaster . . . racing through river beds, climbing up elevated grades, passing through tunnels, turning right, turning left, going up, going down" (Kawazoe 1964, 104). As one effusive reporter put it, "Racing atop the beautiful pavement (*utsukushii hosō*), you can't believe this was once a dirty ditch (*dobugawa*)" ("Tōkyō kaizō" 1963, 17). Likewise, the newly widened Aoyama-dōri was, according to the poet Saitō Shigeta (1916–2006, a native of the area), now one of the "most pleasant drives in the city" (Saitō 1966, 84).

14. The project to widen Aoyama Avenue extended over 8,199 meters, which comes to 2.67 million yen per meter, about 90% of which was for acquiring land and compensating landowners on either side of the road. The bullet train, by comparison, was on average a "mere" 687,658 yen per meter (380 billion yen for 552 kilometers). Total spending on transportation projects (including new subway lines) consumed about 75% of the city's total one-trillion-yen cost for its five-year Olympic overhaul. See "Itchō-en no 'orinpikku seisen'" 1964, 37 and Suttmeier 2016, 212.

15. Many of these details come from Okamura (1988, 149) and the British Pathé footage on Youtube (footage largely unavailable until posted in 2014).

16. The incident, happening early in television's history in Japan, suggests that the allure of the unexpected, disturbing image—an allure that was soon to dominate televisual presentation—was not yet so utterly irresistible.

17. This includes such well-regarded studies that describe in detail the 1959 wedding by scholars clearly familiar with the stone-throwing incident, such as Ken Ruoff's *The People's Emperor* (2003) and Yoshimi Shun'ya's "The Cultural Politics of the Mass-mediated Emperor System in Japan" (2000a).

18. For more on this story and the historical event it describes, see my "Assassination on the Small Screen." As I note in the article, to this day the story's second half, "The Political Youth Dies," originally published in the journal *Bungakkai*, remains difficult to find, absent from Ōe's collected works (it has never been reprinted in any form) (Suttmeier 2008, 77). In fact, many

Japanese library collections have reported it missing, likely torn from the original journal by right-wing sympathizers intent on silencing it further. See Komori 2002, 92.

WORKS CITED

Beat Takeshi and Hidaka Kotaro, et. al. 2005. *Rokujū nendai: "Moeru Tōkyō" o aruku* ("Walking in 1960s Tokyo: A City Aflame"). Tokyo: JTB Publishing.
British Pathé. 2014 "Japanese Royal Wedding." Youtube video, 1:37, from a ceremony televised on April 10, 1959. Accessed 15 December 2015. https://www.youtube.com/watch?v=JPIBGRwRDx0.
Crary, Jonathan. 1999. *Suspensions of Perception: Attention, Spectacle, and Modern Culture.* Cambridge: The MIT Press.
Gallagher, Catherine and Stephen Greenblatt. 2000. *Practicing New Historicism.* Chicago: University of Chicago Press.
Hino Keizō. 2010 [1985]. *Isle of Dreams* [*Yume no shima*]. Translated by Charles De Wolf. Champaign, IL: Dalkey Archive Press.
Hood, Christopher. 2006. *From Bullet Train to Symbol of Modern Japan.* New York: Routledge.
"Itchō-en no 'orinpikku seisen'" ("The one trillion yen 'holy war'"). 1964. *Shūkan Yomiuri* ("The Yomiuri Weekly") 23(41): 34–41.
Itō Yoshiichi. 1982. *Edo no yume no shima* ("Edo's Dream Island"). Tokyo: Yoshikawa Kōbunkan.
Kawazoe Noboru. 1964. "Orinpikku shisetsu o hyōsuru" ("Assessing the Olympic Facilities"). *Asahi Jānaru* ("Asahi Journal") 6(34): 102–7.
Kirkup, James. 1966. *Tokyo.* London: Pheonix House.
Komori Yōichi. 2002. *Rekishi ninshii to shōsetsu: Ōe Kenzaburō ron* ("Historical Consciousness and the Novel: On Ōe Kenzaburō"). Tokyo: Kōdansha.
Lebow, Richard Ned. 2010. *Forbidden Fruit: Counterfactuals and International Relations.* Princeton: Princeton University Press.
Marx, W. David. 2015. *Ametora: How Japan Saved American Style.* New York: Basic Books.
"Nakunaru biru no takasa seigen" ("The Disappearing Height Limits"). 1963. *Asahi Jānaru* ("Asahi Journal") 5(12): 45.
Ōe Kenzaburō. 1996. *Seventeen and J: Two Novels.* Translated by Luk van Haute. New York: Blue Moon Books.
Okamura Reimei. 1988. *Terebi no shakai shi* ("A Social History of Television"). Tokyo: Asahi Sensho 361.
Okuda Hideo. 2004. *Kūchū Burankō* ("Trapeze"). Tokyo: Bungei Shunjū.
———. 2006. *In the Pool.* Translated by Giles Murray. Berkeley: Stone Bridge Press.
———. 2008a. *Orinpikku no minoshirokin: jō* ("Olympic Ransom: Volume 1"). Tokyo: Kadokawa Bunko.
———. 2008b. *Orinpikku no minoshirokin: ge* ("Olympic Ransom: Volume 2"). Tokyo: Kadokawa Bunko.
———. 2008c. *Lala Pipo.* Translated by Marc Adler. New York: Vertical Press.
Rosenfeld, Gabriel D. 2014. "Whither 'What If' History?" Review of *Altered Pasts: Counterfactuals in History* by Richard Evans. *History and Theory* 53 (October): 451–76.
Ruoff, Ken. 2003. *The People's Emperor: Democracy and the Japanese Monarch, 1945–1995.* Cambridge: Harvard East Asian Monographs 221.
Saitō Shigeta. 1966. "Aoyama dōri kaiwai: 1" ("The Neighborhood of Aoyama Avenue"). *Tanka Kenkyū* 23(7): 84–87.
Sand, Jordan. 2013. *Tokyo Vernacular: Common Spaces, Local Histories, Found Objects.* Berkeley: University of California Press.
Seidensticker, Edward. 1990. *Tokyo Rising: The City since the Great Earthquake.* New York: Knopf.
Shōwa nimannichi no zenkiroku ("Shōwa Day by Day"), Vol. 13: *Tōkyō Orinpikku to Shinkansen* ("The Tokyo Olympics and the Bullet Train"). 1990. Tokyo: Kōdansha.

Suttmeier, Bruce. 2008. "Assassination on the Small Screen: Images and Writing in Ōe Kenzaburō." *Mosaic* 41(2): 75–92.

———. 2016. "On the Road in Olympic-Era Tokyo." In *Cartographic Japan*, edited by Karen Wigen, et.al., 210–13. Chicago: University of Chicago Press.

"Tōkyō kaizō" ("Tokyo Renovation"). 1963. *Asahi Gurafu* ("Asahi Picture News") 10 May: 16–27.

"Tōkyō Yumenoshima: namae no yurai wa kaisuiyokujō kūkō keikaku mo" ("Tokyo Dream Island: A Name Originating from Beach Resort and Airport Plans"). 2013. *Nikkei Shinbun*. November 15. Accessed 11 January 2016. http://www.nikkei.com/article/DGXNASFK13038_U3A111C1000000/

Watanabe Midori. 1989 *Gendai terebi hōsōgaku: genjō kara no messēji* ("A Study of Contemporary Television Broadcasting: The Message from the Scene"). Tokyo: Waseda Daigaku Shuppanbu.

Whiting, Robert. 2014, 24 October. "Negative Impact of the 1964 Olympics Profound." *Japan Times*. Accessed 11 January 2016. http://www.japantimes.co.jp/sports/2014/10/24/olympics/negative-impact-1964-olympics-profound/#.Vp1jJzaDDzK

Yonekawa Akihiko, ed. 2002. *Meiji Taishō Shōwa no shingo ryū kōgo jiten* ("A Dictionary of Neologisms and Buzzwords of the Meiji, Taishō and Shōwa eras"). Tokyo: Sanseidō.

Yoshimi Shun'ya. 2000a. "The Cultural Politics of the Mass-mediated Emperor System in Japan." In *Without Guarantees: In Honour of Stuart Hall*, edited by Stuart Hall, Paul Gilroy, et al., 395–415. London: Verso.

———. 2000b. "Media ibento to shite no 'go-kekkon'" ("'The Royal Wedding' as Media Event"). In *Sengo Nihon no media ibento: 1945–1960 nen* ("Postwar Japan's Media Events, 1945–1960"), edited by Tsuganesawa Toshihiro, 268–87. Tokyo: Sekai Shisōsha.

Chapter Six

The Tokyo Cityscape, Sites of Memory, and Hou Hsiao-Hsien's *Café Lumière*

Barbara E. Thornbury

In director Hou Hsiao-Hsien's film *Kōhī jikō* (2003, trans. *Café Lumière*), the character named Hajime (played by actor Asano Tadanobu, b. 1973) is an amateur urban archivist, a hobbyist with professional-grade equipment who in his spare time records the everyday soundscape of the Tokyo rail system. Listening intently through his headset, he points his microphone into the cacophony of arriving and departing trains, the incessant loop of live and recorded announcements, the voices and footsteps of travelers in motion, the loudspeaker melodies that serve as auditory timers counting down the moments until train doors close, and the myriad other sounds that make up the acoustic mix of Tokyo in transit. When Yōko (played by singer-actress Hitoto Yō, b. 1976) asks Hajime why he makes the recordings, he says that every time he goes out with his equipment the sounds he hears are different—and he finds that interesting. Laughing, he adds that maybe one day his archive will be useful to the authorities in an investigation. As Hajime implicitly recognizes, his compilation of sounds is not just the record of one man's passage through the city. It is also part of the city's collective memory.

What makes *Café Lumière* a particularly compelling film is the way in which Hou constructs the Tokyo cityscape as an interlocking set of *lieux de mémoire*, to borrow the phrasing of historian Pierre Nora (b. 1931). Presented from the point of view of Yōko, a young freelance writer, the sites of memory resonate individually and collectively, culturally and historically. In specific geographic terms, they include the aging north-central neighborhoods whose residents, Yōko among them, are served by the slow-moving, quaintly antiquated Toden Arakawa streetcar line that traces an arc between Waseda Station in Shinjuku Ward and Minowabashi Station in Arakawa

Ward.¹ Yōko rents a tiny, old-fashioned apartment (with its tatami mats, dark wood trim, and windows and shutters that noisily clatter when slid open and shut) near historic Kishibojin (sometimes rendered as Kishimojin) Temple—itself not far from Zōshigaya cemetery, the memorial grounds of numerous well-known figures such as the literary luminaries Natsume Sōseki (1867–1916) and Nagai Kafū (1879–1959).

Jinbōchō, a center-city area of university campuses and publishing houses in Chiyoda Ward, is another important site of memory in the film. Especially before the advent of the online book market, the district was prized by scholars and readers across the spectrum of academic specialties and intellectual interests for its large concentration of used-book stores. The remaining generations-old stores, such as the one Hajime owns and runs, are a repository of the past that provides Yōko with access to needed resources for her research. Homey and long-established Jinbōchō cafés, like the one named Erika in the film, also provide regular customers like Yōko with a sense of grounded belongingness-in-the-city as well as opportunities to develop and sustain vital social and professional connections with people they meet there.

Sites of memory also include the Ginza, the sector at the heart of the city in Chūō Ward that epitomizes high-end Tokyo style. However, Yōko looks past the chic and expensive stores and restaurants as, map and camera in hand, she searches for traces of a past that tell the life story of composer-poet Jiang Wenye (1910–1983), the current focus of her research and writing. Born in colonial Taiwan, Jiang moved to Japan at the age of thirteen to attend school. Later, while pursuing advanced training in electrical engineering at a technology institute, he also studied music part time at Tokyo Music School (Tōkyō Ongaku Gakkō), which later merged with Tokyo School of Fine Arts (Tōkyō Bijutsu Gakkō) to form Tokyo University of the Arts (Tōkyō Geijutsu Daigaku), as it is known today. Music, along with poetry, became his main life's work.² In Japan he rose to musical prominence, first as a singer and then as a composer, only to fade from the memory of succeeding generations—a situation Yōko seeks to reverse through her work.³ Her quest for details relating to Jiang's Tokyo biography encompasses two other sites of memory. One is the bucolic environs of Senzoku-ike Park—named for the scenic pond enjoyed by strollers and boaters—in Ōta Ward, located in the city's southern quadrant. The other, on Tokyo's west side in Suginami Ward, is Kōenji, Tokyo's self-styled "coolest neighborhood"—with its dozens of animation studios and the many small shops and restaurants that line its streets.

Hou (b. 1947), a world-renowned director from Taiwan, made *Café Lumière* in response to a commission he was awarded by the film division of entertainment conglomerate Shōchiku Company, Ltd. to produce a work commemorating the centennial birth year of Ozu Yasujirō (1903–1963).⁴ A longtime admirer of Ozu, one of the twentieth-century's most influential directors whose well-known filmography includes *Banshun* (1949, trans. *Late Spring*) and *Tokyo monogatari* (1953, trans. *Tokyo Story*), Hou cinematically envisions the twenty-first-century Tokyo of *Café Lumière* as a locus where new kinds of dynamic and compassionate interpersonal relationships can be forged from fragments of memories made whole. Those memory fragments are dramatized in narrative threads concerning Yōko's childhood past, her relationship with and subsequent rejection of the man who is the father of her as yet unborn child, and her research into the life of Jiang Wenye—an aspect of the storyline that, in linking the film to the history of Japan's colonial occupation of Taiwan (1895–1945), is amplified by the real-world Taiwanese identities of actress Hitoto Yō, the actress Yo Kimiko (b. 1956) (who takes the role of Yōko's stepmother in the film), and Hou himself.[5]

The selection of Hou to celebrate the memory of Ozu was an investment with multiple returns. Although *Café Lumière* did not garner the "best film" Golden Lion award for which it was nominated at the 2004 Venice Film Festival, it gave Shōchiku (Ozu's own studio) a chance to demonstrate the great Japanese director's border-crossing influence. Embarking on a project with Hou also helped Shōchiku lend a hand to efforts aimed at strengthening Japan's cultural ties with its regional neighbor, while at the same time raising the company's own global profile. Hou was a safe choice, so to speak, given his known admiration for Ozu as well as the fact that his work already contained ample evidence of his warm feelings toward Japan. As Tonglin Lu notes in connection with Hou's 1989 film *Beiqing chengshi* (trans. *A City of Sadness*), a Golden Lion award-winner, "even Japanese interpreters were shocked by the degree of idealization of Japanese culture in the film's representation of every detail related to Japan: music, cherry flowers, and swords" (Lu 2011, 769).[6] In the late 1980s and early 1990s, Hou, a central figure in Taiwan's New Cinema movement, had "started the trend of positively representing the Japanese colonial period" (Ibid.).[7] Although Hou is based in Taiwan, *Café Lumière* is "from Japan" (a prerequisite for texts discussed in this volume of essays), insofar as it was commissioned by a Japanese studio for domestic Japanese audiences, the language spoken by the actors is Japanese, and the story takes place in Japan and is written from the viewpoint of characters who were born, grew up, and live in Japan.[8] Moreover, it is an important "Tokyo" film that adroitly pays homage to Ozu.[9]

The focus of this chapter is on what French historian Pierre Nora calls *lieux de mémoire*—sites of memory—such as those through which Hou constructs the urban imaginary of Tokyo in *Café Lumière*. The concept of *lieux de mémoire* derives from the monumental seven-volume compendium of essays titled *Les Lieux de Mémoire* that was produced under Nora's direction and brought out by Éditions Gallimard in France between 1984 and 1992. A three-volume English-language edition of the work was published under the title *Realms of Memory: Rethinking the French Past* by Columbia University Press between 1996 and 1998. In his introduction, Nora defines *lieux de mémoire* as "moments of history [that] are plucked out of the flow of history, then returned to it—no longer quite alive but not yet entirely dead, like shells left on the shore when the sea of living memory has receded" (1996 [1984], 7).

Sites of memory (also variously translated as "realms" and "places" of memory)[10] may literally be geographically distinct locations—like Hou's depiction in *Café Lumière* of Kishibojin, Jinbōchō, and the Ginza (along with Kōenji and Senzoku-ike Park), on which I center my discussion. They can also take many other forms—from scholarly compilations (such as dictionaries) to commemorative events and monuments. *Café Lumière* in and of itself counts as a *lieu de mémoire*, its opening frame telling viewers in boldly written *kanji* characters that the film commemorates the hundredth anniversary of Ozu's birth. The extended soundtrack of pieces by Jiang Wenye and the narrative thread of Yōko's research project on the composer also position the film as a *lieu de mémoire*. Although Nora's *Les Lieux de Mémoire* takes France as its subject matter, its analysis can be applied to any society (including Japan's) that is "fundamentally absorbed by its own transformation and renewal . . . [a society that] values the new over the old, youth over old age, the future over the past" (1996 [1984], 6).[11]

Through the developing emotional intimacy between the characters Yōko and Hajime, *Café Lumière* offers the possibility of fusing together discrete sites of memory within Tokyo by way of satisfying what Hou sees as a yearning in Japan, as elsewhere, for recapturing the embrace of what Nora calls *milieux de mémoire*, "settings in which memory is a real part of everyday experience" (1996 [1984], 1).[12] Hou cinematically gives concrete spatial expression to *milieux de mémoire* (thus asserting their conceptual importance) by scrupulously using for location shots old and established Tokyo businesses that were all ongoing when the film was made. These include, as comprehensively summarized in the entry on *Café Lumière* in *Eiga de Tōkyō sanpo* ("A Stroll through Tokyo in Film") (Marubatsu Purodakushon 2006, 115), Hajime's bookstore and Café Erika in Jinbōchō, the café where Hajime and Yōko relax as they seek clues to Jiang's past in the Ginza, the bookstore that Jiang frequented in Kōenji, and the restaurant in the Senzoku-ike Park neighborhood where Yōko meets Jiang's widow. This is in addition to the large percentage of Tokyo footage recorded within and outside of moving trains as well as that recorded in and of various streetscapes around the city.[13]

"The processes of cinema specify representations of the city, refract memory, and shape perspectives of history that engender the formulation and reading of social space—re-generating processes of spectatorship—and thereby changing a society's cultural vocabulary," as Allan Siegel has noted

(2003, 137). In the three sections that follow, I frame my discussion of *Café Lumière*'s Tokyo cityscape in terms of memory and childhood, memory and adulthood, and memory and history. With the aim of situating Hou's film within the broader context of cinematic representations of Tokyo urban space viewed from the perspective of memory, I then conclude the chapter by bringing into the discussion Kitano Takeshi's (b. 1947) film *Kikujirō no natsu* (1999, trans. *Kikujiro*).[14] *Kikujiro*, like *Café Lumière*, visualizes Tokyo as a locus where new kinds of dynamic and compassionate relationships can arise from fragments of memories made whole. The *lieu de mémoire* cityscape of *Kikujiro* is bounded by the Asakusa neighborhood—which more than any other single locale today embodies the real and figurative old downtown (Shitamachi) area that is a primary defining element of Tokyo urban memory.

KISHIBOJIN: MEMORY AND CHILDHOOD

At the very beginning of *Café Lumière*, in the seconds before the printed message proclaiming the film a commemoration of Ozu's birth fades away, the viewer becomes aware of the sound of a moving train. Then, as the light of an early morning in Tokyo illuminates the screen, a single-carriage Toden Arakawa streetcar steadily moves along its tracks from left to right. The screen then darkens and once more lights up—this time to a mid-day brightness. Yōko is in her Kishibojin apartment, hanging up a basketful of freshly washed laundry. She has just returned home from a trip to Taiwan. The birthplace of Jiang Wenye, it is also the residence of the man who is the father of the baby she is carrying. If there is one thing that Yōko values, it is her autonomy. She is determined to give birth to the baby, but it will be on her own terms, part of the life she has made for herself in Tokyo. She rejects permanent partnership with the man in Taiwan for his lack of independence, epitomized by what she sees as his overly close attachment to his mother.

The quiet residential neighborhood of Kishibojin—which takes its name from the famous old Kishibojin Buddhist temple that sits at its center among tall, shady zelkova trees—is a primary site of memory in *Café Lumière*. Generations of Tokyo residents and visitors (including, in the film, Yōko's stepmother) go there to pray for the safe delivery of newborns and the health of children. Although Hou does not include a shot of the temple (the closest he gets is footage of the nearby Kishibojin-mae streetcar stop), reference to it suggests the survival of a deeply rooted "folk" belief that a gently protective being stands watch over young lives.[15] By way of suggesting that Hajime has already begun to perform that very function for Yōko and her baby, Hou shows him toward the end of the film warmly gazing down at the seated Yōko as she sleeps while riding a train. The scene is made all the more poignant in that Yōko is unaware of Hajime's presence. He just happens to get on the same train she is taking.

In the film, Kishibojin is the location of Yōko's small, old-style apartment, where the slow but steady Toden Arakawa streetcar gives her access to the rest of Tokyo and the world beyond. In contrast to the warp speed of city life that defines Shinjuku, Shibuya, and the rest of Tokyo's commercial, financial, and political power centers, memory is allowed to breathe in the area around Kishibojin. It is a place where trends and fashions do not seem to matter too much. Yōko, for whom urban mobility is key, thrives there among a population of older people who ride the streetcar with her and make their way along the sidewalks at their own comfortable pace—and whose presence Hou unhurriedly records in the film. Along with its namesake temple, many viewers familiar with Tokyo will readily associate the Kishibojin area with Zōshigaya, the landmark cemetery that was established by city ordinance in 1874. In the film, Kishibojin is a spatial nexus between preparing for new lives to come (Yōko's baby) and memorializing those who have passed away (from the real-life Ozu and Jiang Wenye to the fictional deceased characters to whom tribute is also paid in the film[16]).

Kishibojin Temple. *Barbara E. Thornbury.*

Kishibojin is also spatially associated with Yōko's childhood past. Dreams of a baby being stolen away have been haunting Yōko, dreams that seem to emerge from her own experience as a small child: one day her mother suddenly walked out, leaving Yōko and her father behind. In sharing

Toden Arakawa streetcar at Kishibojin-mae Station. *Barbara E. Thornbury.*

these dreams with Hajime, she is able to stitch together fragments of childhood memories. And, in the process of doing so, she draws closer to him, thus by the end of the film opening up the possibility that—with his companionship and help—she can attain the emotionally and psychologically satisfying life that she wants as a Tokyo woman and mother.

The spatial association between Kishibojin and Yōko's childhood past conceptually extends to an interlude at her childhood home northwest of Tokyo that occurs early in the film. One of Yōko's first tasks after her return from Taiwan is to spend a few days with her father (played by actor Kobayashi Nenji, b. 1941) and stepmother (actress Yo Kimiko) in the small countryside town of Yoshii in Gunma Prefecture. (In this segment of the film, too, Hou shoots scenes on location.) It is the season of Obon, a Buddhist summer festival of remembrance, a time when Japanese people return to their "roots"—to the family homes where they were born and grew up. Connections are re-established and memories are shared as families come together to clean the gravestones of relatives who have passed on and to leave offerings, such as fresh flowers, at the gravesites. Arriving at the house after her father picks her up at the train station, Yōko eases back into home life—lazily flopping down on the floor, caressing the family cat, inquiring what her stepmother is making for dinner, and the next day taking a bicycle ride in the soft summer rain to see the small, worn-down station where she used to catch the train to school and to give a word of greeting to the old pet cat that still lives on in the stationmaster's office. Nostalgia infuses this segment of the film: Yōko's life is now defined by her work, circle of friends, and residence in Tokyo, but she still values ties to and memories of her *furusato*—her "original" home.

The association between "mother" and *furusato*, as Jennifer Robertson has written, is "so tenacious that social critic Matsumoto Ken'ichi insists that the two words are synonymous" (1991, 20). Just as Pierre Nora argues that *milieux de mémoire* no longer exist, having been replaced by *lieux de mémoire*, Matsumoto similarly maintained that, with rapid urbanization and "the concomitant predominance of urban nuclear families, 'mother' no longer symbolizes the countryside (*inaka*), the farm village, the land and soil, or rice"—and went so far as to assert that "both *furusato* and 'mother' [have become] 'dead words' (*shigo*)" (Ibid).[17] And, just as *Café Lumière* hints at the possibility of recapturing the embrace of *milieux de mémoire*, so too does Hou literally breathe new life into "mother" in the figure of Yōko's stepmother.

Temporarily transitioning from life in her Kishibojin apartment to life in her childhood home, Yōko gets up in the middle of the night from an extended nap, the cumulative fatigue of a busy professional career and pregnancy causing her to sleep through her welcome-home dinner. Her stepmother wakes to reheat the dishes that she carefully prepared for Yōko's homecoming and to keep her company while she eats. It is in this scene that Yōko confides that she is pregnant. She has no intention of marrying the father of the baby, she says, adding that she is confident that she will be able to raise the child on her own in Tokyo. Like any good mother, the older woman worries that Yōko does not fully appreciate the challenges that lie ahead. Her concerns are practical but loving. Later in the film, when she and Yōko's father go to Tokyo to attend the funeral of a business associate to whom the father owes a heavy debt of gratitude, they visit Yōko at her Kishibojin apartment. The stepmother brings along a pot of the homemade beef and potato stew that Yōko craves, and it is she who prefaces the time spent in Yōko's apartment with a visit to Kishibojin Temple. Both gestures help re-equate "mother" and *furusato* within a web of individual and collective memory. In the course of the film, Hajime also enters the space of Kishibojin when, unbidden but obviously welcome, he helps care for Yōko in her apartment when she is not feeling well. Parallel to showing that the stepmother has assumed the role of "real" mother to Yōko, Hou likewise suggests that a thoughtful and affectionate man can potentially assume the role of "real" father to Yōko's baby—thus enriching the childhood memories of a person who has yet to be born—even though there are no actual biological ties.

JINBŌCHŌ: MEMORY AND ADULTHOOD

Just after returning to Tokyo from Taiwan and before setting out on her brief Obon-season family visit, Yōko stops at Hajime's bookstore in Jinbōchō. Her purpose is twofold: to pick up research materials that he obtained for her while she was away and to give him the *omiyage* gift that she brought back for him from Taiwan. The written form of the Japanese word *omiyage* uses two characters, one meaning "product" and the other meaning "place" (literally, the soil). Like the English word souvenir (from the French verb meaning "to remember"), an *omiyage* is an object of memory linked to the place from which it comes as well as to the traveler who purchased the object with thoughts (and memories) of the recipient in mind. In Japan, giving *omiyage* remains very much a ritualized act of connection and remembering.

In contrast to the relatively inexpensive box of sweets that usually suffices (such as the one Yōko brings back for her Kishibojin landlady), the *omiyage* for Hajime is extravagant: it is a handsome, old-style trainman's pocket watch. At this early point in the narrative, the relationship between Hajime and Yōko is friendly yet straightforwardly businesslike: she unhesitatingly pays for the research materials he gets for her and he unhesitatingly accepts the money. However, the pocket watch clearly signals Yōko's wish for a deepening of their relationship as friends. When Yōko gives him the gift, he correspondingly reacts with evident delight. To clarify the intended significance of Yōko's gesture, Hou has Hajime politely offer to reimburse her. No, she immediately says, it is a gift. More than just an *omiyage*, it is also a birthday present, she explains—marking the gesture as an even more personal one.

Hajime is Yōko's confidant as she tries to make sense of the dreams she has been having about a baby being stolen away. As such, he enables her to reassemble the fragments of her childhood memories so that she can make sense of them and move on with her life as an adult. Yōko's gift of a trainman's pocket watch serves as a key image in the film—a marker of time past and present. As Yōko tells Hajime, the item was made to commemorate the start of rail service in Taiwan (at the end of the nineteenth century). However, it is not an archaic timepiece. On her way to see Hajime in Jinbōchō, Yōko stands in a train car just behind the engineer's glassed-in booth. Peering into the enclosure as the train speeds along the tracks through central Tokyo, she can see the same sort of pocket watch in its proper place just to the right of the engineer on his control deck. It is a reliably analogue instrument in a digital world, a symbol of both age and endurance.

The trainman's pocket watch connects Hajime to the Tokyo rail system that fascinates him—so much so that he feels compelled to spend his free time travelling the system with microphone in hand recording the mix of sounds that constantly yet fleetingly vibrate the air around him. Simultaneously, the watch connects him to Yōko, the person who gave him the gift, as they move emotionally closer together through an unfolding present. In a subsequent scene, Hajime has his own gift for Yōko—a copy of Maurice Sendak's (1928–2012) *Outside Over There*. He thinks that the illustrated storybook (originally published in 1981) about a little girl whose baby sister is taken by goblins, may hold the key to Yōko's dreams. As soon as she sees the book, she realizes that she must have encountered it as a child. After her mother left home years earlier, the illustrations had implanted in the young and vulnerable Yōko images of a baby being stolen away—images which reappear in her dreams at a vulnerable time in her adult life.

Café Lumière evokes a strong sense of the real in its representation of Tokyo urban space. Hajime's bookstore in the film "is" Seishindō, one of Jinbōchō's actual surviving used-book stores. Hou's cinematographer Mark Lee Ping-Bing (b. 1954) captures a shot of the shop visibly bearing the name Seishindō, set against the backdrop of a lively Jinbōchō's street. Inside Hajime's store (as in Seishindō itself), the abundant materials on the shelves are neatly stacked and tagged. There is a sense of expectation, as if the materials are waiting for a researcher such as Yōko to appreciatively ferret out the stories of the past that they contain.

The Café Erika of the film in Jinbōchō is also a part of Tokyo's real cityscape: its business name in Japanese is Kōhī Erika ("Coffee [shop] Erika"). Located near Hajime's store in the film (and in actuality), it is a place that Yōko, a freelance writer without a fixed workspace outside of her apartment, has made her own. As she sits at her favorite table in a cozy corner by a window, the grandfatherly café proprietor brings her the glasses of hot milk that she requests. The polished dark wood of Café Erika's interior is suffused with layer upon layer of time's passage. This is where Yōko feels comfortable, at home in a place where many preceded her. The café provides the perfect setting for a freelance writer endeavoring to uncover aspects of a forgotten past. When Hou has Hajime telephone Yōko at Café Erika, the call is placed through the café's phone. Having Hajime reach her that way rather than contacting her on her cellphone enables him to say a few words of greeting to the proprietor, who readily summons Yōko to the phone at the shop's counter. Hou's point here is to underscore the social ties that bind a community of friends and associates within the big city.[18]

GINZA, KŌENJI, AND SENZOKU-IKE PARK: MEMORY AND HISTORY

In the 1930s Jiang Wenye became one of the leading figures in Japanese music. A student of renowned composer and conductor Yamada Kōsaku (1886–1965), Jiang garnered awards for composition four times between 1934 and 1937 in Japan's prestigious annual national music competition. The winning pieces included "Shirasagi e no gensō" (trans. "Fantasy for a White Egret") and "Jōnai no yoru" (trans. "A Night in the City") (Wang 2015, 200; see also Liu 2010, 233). Stepping onto the international stage, he won a prize for "Taiwan bukyoku" (trans. "Taiwan Dance") at the 1936 Berlin Olympics. In 1938 Jiang decided to leave Japan to take a position as a professor of music at a college in Beijing. As Liu Ching-chih writes of Jiang,

> It is difficult to infer what the true reason was that, at the height of his composing career, he resolutely left behind the material comforts of life in Tokyo, his high status in the musical world and his Japanese wife, and moved to Peking just as the Japanese invasion was intensifying. (2010, 235)

In China, where he remained until his death, Jiang suffered personally and professionally during his later years for views perceived as inconsistent with the ideology of the Chinese Communist Party. Never abandoning his trademark practice (developed after arriving in China) of employing traditional folk motifs in a musically innovative way, Jiang should be remembered, in Liu's estimation, as "a sparkling star in the firmament of new Chinese music" (Ibid., 243).

Yōko's research on Jiang takes her to three Tokyo locations—the Ginza, Kōenji, and Senzoku-ike Park. In the Ginza, long famous for its world-class shopping and dining, she is looking for what might remain of a music café where Jiang was known to spend time during his most musically productive years in Japan. The 1930s were an era when Ginza cafés were the height of urban sophistication. Music cafés were particularly popular, offering their customers hours of sonic riches—sometimes live, sometimes recorded—for the price of a glass of wine or a cup of coffee. Hajime joins Yōko in her quest. Stopping first at a coffee shop overlooking a Ginza-area station concourse, they examine a period map of the neighborhood that Hajime was able to find for Yōko.[19] The document is a signifier of time past: in the decades that have gone by since Jiang's time, continuous construction and reconstruction have transformed the Ginza, and maps have been redrawn. Yōko consults the café proprietor, an older man with a quiet warmth and a long memory, who is able to perform the feat of figuring out the coordinates of where the old music café used to be and giving her the walking directions she seeks. When Yōko and Hajime get to the location, they are not surprised to discover that a gleaming multistory building stands where the old café used to be. Undeterred, Yōko takes photos of the spot, as if to memorialize a past that she knows is there even if it cannot literally be seen. The scene precisely illustrates Jordan Sand's point that "preservation need not be about the material object itself . . . the historical site [being] a mental space as well as a physical one" (2013, 145).

Like the character Yōko in the film, Jiang also frequented the city's used-book stores. One of his favorites was Tomaru Shoten, which continues in business in the Kōenji neighborhood.[20] On a visit to the shop looking for further clues about Jiang's life in Tokyo, Yōko asks the middle-aged owner, whose father ran the place before him, if he happens to know anything about the composer who patronized the bookstore sixty or seventy years ago. Although the man says "no," the trip has been worthwhile. Tomaru Shoten, after all, still exists—as both a storehouse of the past contained in the materials stacked on its shelves and as a tangible site of memory with its own long history. On leaving the store, Yōko takes photos of the front entrance of the shop and its weathered sign. She also trains her camera lens on the neighborhood in which the store is situated—a part of the city that is now chockablock with funky restaurants, music joints, and shops offering imaginatively repurposed used clothes. Shots of the Kōenji street scene in *Café Lumière* capture the go-your-own-way Tokyo vibe that Hou expresses through the characters Yōko and Hajime.

Yōko's purpose in going to Senzoku-ike Park is to make direct contact with and probe the memories of individuals who knew Jiang well. In a pleasant sun-filled restaurant overlooking the park grounds, she meets with Jiang's former wife and their daughter.[21] It is a scene made all the more affecting by the fact that the women in the film are in reality Jiang's ex-wife and daughter. Together with Yōko they look through an album of photographs filled with images of a loving marriage—though one that ended when

Jiang decided to leave Japan to begin a new life in China. Hou is possibly suggesting that Yōko, who has decided to move on from a relationship with a man from Taiwan, may also be able to attain in Tokyo the kind of loving partnership depicted in the photos—but, in her case, a partnership (with Hajime) that can be indefinitely sustained.

In *Café Lumière*, memory and history are spatially expressed through Yōko's travels to and ensuing encounters in the Ginza, Kōenji, and Senzoku-ike Park. Thematically, memory and history are expressed in the narrative thread relating to Jiang Wenye, while also being personified in the rich composite overlay Hou achieves by casting the real-life singer-actress Hitoto Yō in the role of the character Yōko. She—both singer-actress and character—is a woman whose life story transcends the boundaries between Japan and Taiwan. Memory and history are additionally embodied in Hou himself as director of a made-in-Japan film.

In Hou's hands, *Café Lumière*, as a film made for Japanese audiences, is a call to Japan to take a fresh look at both its existing and its historical relationship with Taiwan. Hou's unequivocal point is that the present relationship between the two regional neighbors is like that of two fully independent and autonomous adults. The pregnant Yōko is free to reject her Taiwanese boyfriend, scorning him for being too closely tied to his mother. Yōko, whose dual identity is ever-present in the audience's mind, puts the highest value on self-reliance. It was an independent, self-reliant Yōko who in the past had gone to Taiwan to teach Japanese, leading her to meet the man in the first place. Although she rejects the man, she wants the baby. However, her stated intention of maintaining her work schedule, while also giving birth to and raising the baby on her own in Tokyo is admittedly an almost reckless assertion of independence. Hou drives home the point in scenes clearly showing that Yōko's pregnant body will no longer let her move as freely as she once did. If she is to retain her independent life in Tokyo, it is evident that she needs help. The source of that help will be Hajime, who has supplanted the man from Taiwan as the person with whom Yōko is already emotionally bound through the memories that she has confided in him.

At the same time, *Café Lumière* is a call for Japan to think back to its colonial past. While also making good on his promise to produce a film commemorating the life and work of Ozu—especially in sequences that recall the eminent Japanese director's artistry in delicately dramatizing the interactions that take place between adult children and their parents—Hou builds on his transnational reputation by boldly asserting that Taiwan's colonial past should also be remembered—and commemorated—in Japan (and globally) through the life of individuals such as Jiang Wenye. *Café Lumière* shares with other films by Hou (and his contemporaries in Taiwan) "a topography of haunted spaces and spectral glimmers, of restive pasts that invade the boundaries of the present . . . [where] memory competes with history"

(Ma 2010, 7). It is a topography that, translated into the vocabulary of Tokyo urban space, includes Kishibojin, Hajime's bookstore, Café Erika, the Ginza music café that Jiang once frequented but that no longer exists, the Kōenji bookstore where the owner no longer remembers the composer's presence there, and the Senzoku-ike Park restaurant where the elderly woman who was once Jiang's young wife shares with Yōko images of a marriage that ended only a few years after it began.

The trajectory of the film's storyline suggests that Hajime will supplant the man from Taiwan in Yōko's life—in part because he willingly joins her in her quest to learn about the life of the composer. Together, they are agents of memory. "With its defeat in the war," Yoshikuni Igarashi has written, "Japan lost not only its former colonies but also the memories of its colonial enterprises" (2000, 35). Jiang's presence in Japan in the 1930s—and perhaps his decision to leave Japan as well—relates directly to that colonial enterprise. Within a contemporary Taiwanese context, which informs Hou's directorial perspective, the colonial period is seen in quite a different way. Lu has noted that, rather than being a period to forget, it is a period to remember: "Japanese colonial history is an anchorage in the collective imagination, as most traditional and even modern values have melted into thin air in the midst of the mad circulation of global capital in East Asia since the late twentieth century" (2011, 764). Given the chance to work in Japan, Hou takes the opportunity to construct memories-as-anchorages there, too. He approaches the task in a gentle and understated way. The soundtrack of the film—piano music written by Jiang—is in effect the "living voice" of the composer. "The foundational narrative of postwar relations," as Igarashi further notes, "turned the attention of Japanese society away from the country's colonial past. Japan was protected from its own past, so to speak, in this Cold War political paradigm" (2000, 199). Hou opens up that past by melding Jiang's past with the present of Hitoto Yō/Yōko, herself a child of Japan and Taiwan in real life and, in the film, the mother-to-be of a child of Japan and Taiwan and the stepdaughter of an actress/character of Japan and Taiwan.

FILM, URBAN SPACE, AND MEMORY

In this concluding section I would like to position *Café Lumière* within the broader context of cinematic representations of Tokyo urban space viewed from the perspective of memory. I do so by also considering Kitano Takeshi's film *Kikujiro*—a slightly earlier work that shares a number of similarities with *Café Lumière*. The central characters of both films—Yōko in *Café Lumière* and Masao (played by actor Sekiguchi Yūsuke, b. 1989) in *Kikujiro*—were abandoned by their mother. The elementary-school-age Masao lives in Tokyo's Asakusa neighborhood with his grandmother (actress

Yoshiyuki Kazuko, b. 1935). A child of Tokyo's iconic old downtown—the Shitamachi—his paths to and from school and play crisscross the Sumida River and the grounds of Sensōji Temple—one of the most recognizable of Tokyo's historic landmarks.[22] Although well taken care of by his grandmother, Masao's spirits are deflated when he sees his friends taking off on trips with their parents and siblings as soon as school lets out for the summer. He is seemingly the only one left behind. His grandmother has repeatedly told him that his father died in an accident and his mother is away from the city because she is working to help support him. He spontaneously sets out to find his mother after, by chance, coming upon her Toyohashi, Aichi Prefecture, address among a stash of old photographs showing him as a baby in her arms. In a general sense, Yōko's trip to Yoshii in Gunma Prefecture similarly early in *Café Lumière* is also motivated by the wish to reunite with the mother who left her behind.

In contrast to the interlocking set of Tokyo *lieux de mémoire* of *Café Lumière*, the Asakusa neighborhood alone suffices in *Kikujiro*. Asakusa and the nearby environs of the Sumida River make up the entirety of Masao's everyday Tokyo world. It is the place from which he starts his journey outside of the city to find his mother and the place to which he returns at the end. Despite the spatial significance of Asakusa as a primary site of Tokyo urban memory, Kitano does not romanticize the place.[23] In the opening moments of the film, Masao and a friend change course on their way home from school when they see a group of bullies lying in wait for small boys like them. It is a scene that foreshadows what happens almost immediately after Masao sets out to find his mother: walking along Asakusa's streets with his summer-vacation schoolwork and a few possessions stuffed into his backpack, he becomes the target of older boys who descend on him to steal his money. The tough, but kindly neighbor (actress Kishimoto Kayoko, b. 1960) who rescues him from this predicament sympathizes with his quest and (optimistically) sends him off in the care of her blustering, ne'er-do-well husband Kikujirō (played by Kitano Takeshi himself).

In an essay on *Kikujiro*, Aaron Gerow writes that "Asakusa is a matriarchal space in the film since the main figures of authority we see are Masao's grandmother and Kikujirō's wife" (2007, 165). Gerow also argues that Kikujirō's wife is "yakuza"-like, in part because she readily lies to Masao's grandmother (saying that her husband has taken Masao to the seaside for a few days) rather than reveal the actual purpose of the journey (Ibid., 161). That may be true, but it is the kindly grandmother who has been lying to Masao all along. In the course of the trip, Masao discovers that his mother has in fact begun a new life with a husband and child—and will never return to him. In a society that continues to marginalize single mothers—even those cast into that state by widowhood—she was perhaps encouraged to believe that it would be easier for her to begin a new life if she were to leave Masao behind with her own mother, a woman who lovingly cares for the boy—and who presumably plans to tell him the truth one day.

In *Café Lumière*, Yōko describes her dreams to Hajime; in *Kikujiro*, Masao's dreams are vividly—and disturbingly—dramatized within the film's narrative. Although Masao's dreams are triggered by episodes that occur on his journey with the semi-comical and always-unpredictable Kikujirō, as with Yōko they ultimately arise from the pain of being abandoned by his mother.[24] He would never have undertaken the journey if he, still a child (albeit one who is basically able to negotiate the streets of Asakusa on his own), were in the care of his mother. Kikujirō is roughly analogous to Hajime insofar as he offers a new kind of dynamic and compassionate relationship to Masao—a father-like relationship that is amplified when he "recruits" three young guys they meet on the road. Playing the role of kindly (though temporary) older brothers, they help Masao recover his spirits after the shock of learning the truth about his mother. It is also Masao who in turn offers a new kind of dynamic and compassionate relationship to his traveling companion—as when the boy tenderly administers first aid to the injured Kikujirō after he gets into a violent confrontation with a group of thugs.

For Masao, fragments of memory are made whole by the time he returns to Asakusa. Unlike Yōko, for whom partnership with Hajime will potentially make possible the Tokyo life she wants, for Masao, the relationship with Kikujirō must necessarily remain a distant one. Even so, when Kikujirō bends down to momentarily hug the boy and says "let's go looking for your mother again sometime," it is a send-off that helps ensure Masao's growing self-reliance and independence in the city.[25] Masao is smiling when he heads home by himself—having just learned Kikujirō's name. Masao had begun by calling him *ojisan* ("Mister") and ended up calling him *ojichan* (a term equivalent to a more affectionate "Uncle"), but he does not know who Kikujirō is as an individual and is never likely to find out. Whether *ojisan*, *ojichan*, or Kikujirō, there is little chance that the older man and Masao will be part of each other's future lives. But, they have become part of each other's memories.

Both Hou and Kitano depict Tokyo urban space through sites of memory that resonate with Japan's historical past. "[W]e have come to read cities and buildings as palimpsests of space," Andreas Huyssen has written. "[A]n urban imaginary in its temporal reach may well put different things in one place: memories of what there was before, imagined alternatives to what there is. The strong marks of present space merge in the imaginary with traces of the past, erasures, losses, and heterotopias" (2003, 7). Hou invites audiences to look "outward" toward Taiwan in memories refracted through spaces ranging from Kishibojin and Jinbōchō to the Ginza, Kōenji, and Senzoku-ike Park. Kitano invites audiences to look "inward" to a Japan symbolized by Asakusa. Asakusa may be revered as the warm heart of traditional

Tokyo, but it is the home of individuals such as Kikujirō—people who, as the film amply demonstrates, lack the basic education, skills, and character traits needed to advance in the wider world. For them, Asakusa is a closed world. At the same time, it is the home of a child like Masao, who is already well on his way toward becoming a productive member of society. For him, Asakusa is an open world—as Tokyo in its entirety already is for Yōko. In *Café Lumière*, as in *Kikujiro*, Tokyo urban space is rendered through the city's *lieux de mémoire*—sites of collective memory where fragmented individual memories can potentially be made whole.

NOTES

1. In 2017, the Tokyo Metropolitan Government's Bureau of Transportation announced that the official nickname of the Toden Arakawa line was Tōkyō Sakura Toramu (Tokyo Sakura Tram, lit. "Tokyo Cherry Blossom Tram"). The nickname was to be used mainly for tourism marketing purposes. See https://www.kotsu.metro.tokyo.jp/eng/news/2017/20170428_7414.html.

2. One of Jiang's high school teachers was the writer Shimazaki Tōson (1872–1943), who "initiated [Jiang] into the realm of lyrical poetry" (Wang 2015, 217).

3. The Japanese pronunciation of Jiang Wenye's name is Kō Bun'ya. Because he is known internationally by his birth name, I use that here.

4. In a published conversation with his longtime collaborator, screenwriter Zhu Tianwen (b. 1956), Hou relates that Shōchiku originally envisioned a commemorative film for the centennial Ozu anniversary comprising segments contributed by several internationally renowned directors—among them, Hou, Abbas Kiarostami (1940–2016), and Wim Wenders (b. 1945). In the end, it was decided that a single director should make a film, and Hou was the director selected (Zhu and Hou 2016 [2004], 255).

5. Hitoto Yō, who took her mother's family name (Hitoto) after her father's death, was born in Tokyo to a Taiwanese father and Japanese mother. She spent her early childhood in Taiwan before moving back to Japan with her mother and sister. Prior to being cast in *Café Lumière*, her first film, she made her reputation as a popular singer. (See, for example, Zhu and Hou 2016 [2004], 260). Yokohama-born Yo Kimiko, who has a long résumé of work in film, is also the daughter of a Taiwanese father and Japanese mother.

6. Other films directed by Hou include *Hai Shang Hua* (1998, trans. *Flowers of Shanghai*), *Qianxi Manbo* (2001, trans. *Millennium Mambo*), winner of the Technical Grand Prize at the Venice Film Festival, and *Le Voyage du Ballon Rouge* (2008, trans. *Flight of the Red Balloon*), a French production. Hou received the Best Director Award at the 2015 Cannes Film Festival for *Nie Yinniang* (2015, trans. *The Assassin*).

7. Lu sees Taiwan's concern about the possibility of a Chinese military incursion as a main reason why "the repressed colonial history of Japan has reemerged in a new light in Taiwanese cinematic representations, offering a fantasy space to reformulate local Taiwanese identity" (2011, 766).

8. "In 2003, I served as one of the producers on Hou Hsiao-Hsien's *Café Lumière*, his first film shot entirely in Japan and in Japanese," Yamamoto Ichirō, a producer at Shōchiku has written (2014, 310). Soon after its release in Japan, *Café Lumière* was commercially distributed internationally. In the United States, the DVD rights were acquired by Genius Entertainment and Wellspring Media, divisions of Genius Products, Inc.

9. Reflecting on *Café Lumière*, Hou has described himself as "the eyes of the other" who can give audiences in Japan (and elsewhere) "a new perspective from which to comprehend Tokyo" (Zhu and Hou 2016 [2004], 269). In studying the film, I have also been interested in the way in which Hou "channels" Ozu in his portrayal of Yōko as simultaneously daughter, mother-to-be, and a woman determined to live life on her own terms in twenty-first-century

Tokyo. My essay "Re-imagining Ozu: Hou Hsiao-Hsien's *Café Lumière* and the Contemporary Tokyo Woman" (Thornbury 2010) looks at how *Café Lumière* reimagines Ozu's iconic family films in its portrayal of the contemporary Tokyo woman.

10. Even though the English-language edition of *Les Lieux de Mémoire* uses *Realms of Memory* in the title of the work (adding *Rethinking the French Past* as the subtitle), in the body of the work translator Arthur Goldhammer appears to prefer the English term "sites," and occasionally other words such as "places," for *lieux*. Translator Marc Roudebush also uses "sites of memory" in his earlier translation of Nora's introduction. See, for example, Nora 1989 [1984], 7.

11. In the foreword to *Realms of Memory*, Lawrence D. Kritzman writes that memory comprises "the variety of forms through which cultural communities imagine themselves in diverse representational modes. In this sense, as a critical category 'memory' distinguishes itself from history, which is regarded as an intellectual practice more deeply rooted in the evidence derived from the study of empirical reality." To quote Kritzman's list, *lieux de mémoire* include "geographical place or *locus*," "historical figures," "monuments and buildings," "literary and artistic objects," and "emblems, commemorations, and symbols." All "are the result of an imaginary process that codifies and represents the historical consciousness of 'quintessential France.'" In sum, Kritzman writes, Nora's project is a "cataloging of the memory places produced over time which depict the 'imaginary communities' binding national memory" (Kritzman 1996, ix and x.).

12. On the same page Nora writes that "*[l]ieux de mémoire* exist because there are no longer any *milieux de mémoire*."

13. Hou described his approach to filming scenes on location in Tokyo bookstores and cafés during normal business hours. He also described how he was able to record footage on Tokyo trains during their regular runs, despite not being able to obtain actual permission to do so from the rail lines (Zhu and Hou 2016 [2004], 267–69).

14. Kitano, a veteran actor and comedian who frequently appears on television and in the films that he directs, travels the same international film-festival circuit as Hou. Kitano won a Golden Lion award at the 1997 Venice Film Festival, for *Hanabi* (trans. *Fireworks*, 1997). *Kikujiro* had its world premiere as a nominee for the Palme D'Or prize at the 1999 Cannes Film Festival, where it took honors as "an audience favorite" (Davis 2001, 75, note 5).

15. As Paul Waley notes, "Kishibojin is one of those Japanese deities that embody some of the religious aura of their country of origin, India. She is a goddess of fertility. . . . People come from all over [Tokyo] with entreaties to Kishibojin to bring them offspring or to deliver their children safely or to bring them up in good health and wisdom" (1992, 180). The stately zelkova trees for which Kishibojin is also famous themselves have a noteworthy history: four of them, according to Waley, were planted in the sixteenth century (Ibid., 182).

16. The fictional deceased characters include Yōko's ancestors, whose graves she helps clean on a family visit during the season of Obon. They also include her father's revered former boss.

17. As Robertson notes in her bibliography, Matsumoto expressed these ideas in an *Asahi shimbun* article published on August 19, 1980. The article's title "Sengo sono seishin fūkei: Kotoba" was translated by Robertson as "The affective landscape of the postwar period: Words" (1991, 222).

18. The particular purpose of Hajime's phone call is for him to tell Yōko that he has found a book (*Outside Over There*) that may help shed light on the meaning of her dreams of a baby being taken away. Heading the short distance to Hajime's store, she has takeout coffee service from Café Erika delivered to him there. This is Yōko's second gift to Hajime since the start of the film, another indicator of her desire for a closer relationship with him.

19. The café where they stop is Momoya, which has since gone out of business. It was in Yūrakuchō, which abuts the Ginza.

20. For a photo of the exterior of Tomaru Shoten and film stills from the *Café Lumière* scene inside the actual bookstore, see Berra 2011, 66–67.

21. The name of the restaurant, which has since closed, was Terasu Jure.

22. The history of Sensōji, often referred to as the Asakusa Kannon Temple (because it is dedicated to the bodhisattva Kannon), goes back to the seventh century when two fishermen are

said to have found a golden statue of Kannon in the nearby Sumida River. The main hall, pagoda, and gates (including Kaminarimon, with its much-photographed giant red lantern) seen today are reconstructions of edifices that were destroyed by firebombs in 1945. The image of Sensōji as a prominent historic Tokyo landmark is a composite one that includes these structures along with the always bustling *nakamise* (the "inner" small-shop-lined street) that leads to the main hall from Kaminarimon gate. In the film, Masao's grandmother sells sweet-bean-filled figurine cakes (*ningyō-yaki*) in one of the *nakamise* shops. The centrality of the Asakusa neighborhood—symbolized by Sensōji—to understandings of Tokyo's Shitamachi is made clear in works such as Aoki and Nishizaka 2006.

23. Kitano knows Asakusa well, having moved there in his mid-twenties to embark on a career in comedy and show business.

24. In the main dream sequence, a demonic figure—played by butoh performer, director, and actor Akaji Maro (b. 1943)—dances threateningly around Masao and a young woman, who perhaps represents the boy's mother. While Masao desperately struggles to free himself from the ties that bind his hands, the young woman, who is unable to help him, can only shed tears. Akaji appeared earlier in the film in the role of a child molester who tried to prey on Masao before being stopped by Kikujirō.

25. While the journey originates in Masao's quest to find his mother, Kikujirō also seeks out his own mother—a woman who, like Masao's mother, left him when he was a boy. Just as Masao cannot approach the woman who now inhabits a world cut off from him, Kikujirō cannot approach his mother: living in a nursing home, she is portrayed as being physically, emotionally, and psychologically cut off from the world outside of the facility's doors.

WORKS CITED

Aoki Masami and Nishizaka Kazuyuki. 2006. *Tōkyō shitamachi 100-nen no ākaibusu: Meiji, Taishō, Shōwa no shashin kiroku* ("100 years of Tokyo *shitamachi* archives: A photographic record from the Meiji, Taishō, and Shōwa eras"). Tokyo: Seikatsu Jōhō Sentā.
Berra, John. 2011. "Café Lumière (2003): Location: Tomaru Bookstore." In *World Film Locations: Tokyo*, edited by Chris MaGee, 66–67. Chicago: Intellect Books, The University of Chicago Press.
Davis, Darrell William. 2001. "Reigniting Japanese Tradition with Hana-Bi." *Cinema Journal* 40 (4): 55–80.
Gerow, Aaron Andrew. 2007. *Kitano Takeshi*. London: British Film Institute.
Hou Hsiao-Hsien. 2003. *Kōhī jikō* (trans. *Café Lumière*). Tokyo: Shōchiku Co., Ltd. Distributed in the United States by Genius Entertainment and Wellspring Media, Inc.
Huyssen, Andreas. 2003. *Present Pasts: Urban Palimpsests and the Politics of Memory*. Stanford, CA: Stanford University Press.
Igarashi, Yoshikuni. 2000. *Bodies of Memory: Narratives of War in Postwar Japanese Culture, 1945–1970*. Princeton: Princeton University Press.
Kitano Takeshi. 1999. *Kikujirō no natsu* (trans. *Kikujiro*). Tokyo: Bandai Visual, et al. Distributed in the United States by Sony Pictures Classics.
Kritzman, Lawrence D. 1996. "Foreword: In Remembrance of Things French." In *Realms of Memory: Rethinking the French Past, Volume I: Conflicts and Divisions* (under the direction of Pierre Nora), edited by Lawrence D. Kritzman, ix–xiv. Translated by Arthur Goldhammer. New York: Columbia University Press.
Liu, Ching-chih. 2010. *A Critical History of New Music in China*. Translated by Caroline Mason. Hong Kong: The Chinese University Press.
Lu, Tonglin. 2011. "A Cinematic Parallax View: Taiwanese Identity and the Japanese Colonial Past." *positions: east asia cultures critique* 19 (3): 763–79.
Ma, Jean. 2010. *Melancholy Drift: Marking Time in Chinese Cinema*. Hong Kong: Hong Kong University Press.
Marubatsu Purodakushon, ed. January 2006. *Eiga de Tōkyō sanpo* ("A stroll through Tokyo in film"). Tokyo: Esquire Magazine Japan Co., Ltd.

Nora, Pierre. 1989 [1984]. "Between Memory and History: *Les Lieux de Mémoire*." Translated by Marc Roudebush. *Representations* 26: 7–24.

———. 1996 [1984]. "General Introduction: Between Memory and History." In *Realms of Memory: Rethinking the French Past, Volume I: Conflicts and Divisions* (*Les Lieux de Mémoire*), compiled under the direction of Pierre Nora and edited by Lawrence D. Kritzman, 1–20. Translated by Arthur Goldhammer. New York: Columbia University Press.

Robertson, Jennifer. 1991. *Native and Newcomer: Making and Remaking a Japanese City*. Berkeley: University of California Press.

Sand, Jordan. 2013. *Tokyo Vernacular: Common Spaces, Local Histories, Found Objects*. Berkeley: University of California Press.

Siegel, Allan. 2003. "After the Sixties: Changing Paradigms in the Representation of Urban Space." In *Screening the City*, edited by Mark Shiel and Tony Fitzmaurice, 137–59. New York: Verso.

Thornbury, Barbara E. 2010. "Re-imagining Ozu: Hou Hsiao-Hsien's *Café Lumière* and the Contemporary Tokyo Woman." *Proceedings of the Association for Japanese Literary Studies* 11: 365–76.

Waley, Paul. 1992. *Fragments of a City: A Tokyo Anthology*. Tokyo: The Japan Times, Ltd.

Wang, David Der-wei. 2015. *The Lyrical in Epic Time: Modern Chinese Intellectuals and Artists through the 1949 Crisis*. New York: Columbia University Press.

Yamamoto, Ichirō. 2014. "The *Jidaigeki* Film *Twilight Samurai*—A Salaryman-Producer's Point of View." Translated by Diane Wei Lewis. In *The Oxford Handbook of Japanese Cinema*, edited by Daisuke Miyao, 306–26. New York: Oxford University Press.

Zhu Tianwen and Hou Hsiao-hsien. 2016 [2004]. "Who Gets to Name Good Weather? A Conversation between Zhu Tianwen and Hou Hsiao-Hsien." Translated by Christopher Lupke. In *The Sinophone Cinema of Hou Hsiao-hsien: Culture, Style, Voice, and Motion*, by Christopher Lupke, 254–73. Amherst, N.Y.: Cambria Press.

Chapter Seven

Remaking Tayama Katai's *Futon* in Nakajima Kyōko's *FUTON*

Remembrance and Renewal of Urban Space through the Art of Rewriting

Angela Yiu

Nakajima Kyōko's (b. 1964) 2003 novel *FUTON*[1] does exactly what the title of this chapter suggests: it remakes Tayama Katai's (1872–1930) *Futon* (1907, trans. *The Quilt*, 1981) nearly a century after its publication. Even though literary history has always been singularly obsessed with tracing the models for Katai's[2] apparently sordid tale of confession about a teacher's infatuation with his live-in female pupil, Nakajima's *FUTON* redirects the focus of interpretation to Katai's delicate and perceptive depiction of Tokyo. *FUTON* adds an expanded cast of characters from multiple geographic, historical, social, cultural, and linguistic dimensions to reveal layers of Tokyo through time, space, memory, history, race, gender, and literary forms. Building a new text upon an old one is not unlike the forgotten art of remaking a quilt by recycling an old one: fluffing hardened cotton wadding for the stuffing, replacing the soiled velvet collar with new fabric, reusing useable materials after careful cleaning and trimming, and sewing the parts together with fresh, new threads. In evoking the past through an old text in a new language, Nakajima simultaneously summons and destroys the past in a process of remembering and renewal. This process serves as a metaphor for the constant remaking of an urban landscape that reflects and challenges vestiges of the past in human, spatial, and linguistic terms.

I will begin this chapter by situating Nakajima Kyōko and her works among selected women writers of urban literature in the past two decades, with an emphasis on *FUTON* and a comparison to its literary sources, namely

Katai's *Futon* and *Tōkyō no sanjūnen* (1917, trans. *Literary Life in Tokyo 1885–1915*, 1987),[3] and the postwar novella *Hakuchi* (1946, trans. "The Idiot," 1985) by Sakaguchi Ango (1906–1955). I will pay special attention to Nakajima's manipulation of space, characters, and language in her interpretation of a century of urban transformation. In particular, I will emphasize the way Nakajima draws upon literary allusions, adaptations, and the different manifestations of the Japanese language to capture the memory and reality of a linguistic Tokyo. Finally, in examining the mixture of old and new materials in Nakajima's text, I will identify the multiple narrative possibilities in contemporary urban literature in storytelling and the formation of collective memory.

WOMEN WRITERS AND THE CITY

Apart from a few memorable exceptions, such as works by Higuchi Ichiyō (1872–1896) and Tamura Toshiko (1884–1945) in the Meiji period (1868–1912),[4] Tokyo-based urban literature until the end of the Pacific War was predominantly male and largely associated with the flâneur, whether the writing falls under the rubrics of Yamanote literature or Shitamachi literature. The scholar Edward Seidensticker (1921–2007) famously coined the English terms High City to demarcate the Yamanote, and Low City to demarcate the Shitamachi in Tokyo. The Yamanote occupies the geographically elevated region of the city and has been the locus of government, bureaucracy, and academia since the Meiji period, while the Shitamachi, once the thriving center for plebeian culture, declined in glory and real estate value as power and policy-making became more centralized in the Yamanote.[5] The Yamanote features significantly in stories by Meiji writers Natsume Sōseki (1867–1916), Mori Ōgai (1862–1922), and Katai, and Taishō-period writers Mushakōji Saneatsu (1885–1976), Shiga Naoya (1883–1971), and Kajii Motojirō (1901–1932), while the Shitamachi features more prominently in stories by Nagai Kafū (1879–1959), Kubota Mantarō (1889–1963), and Tanizaki Jun'ichirō (1886–1965). Works by a number of women writers in the postwar years made an impact on urban literature, notably the Tokyo-based stories of Hayashi Fumiko (1903–1951), Sata Ineko (1904–1998), Miyamoto Yuriko (1899–1951), Kōda Aya (1904–1990), and Enchi Fumiko (1905–1986). Yet, literary history has a tendency to fall within the male gaze when it comes to war- and postwar-Tokyo narratives: one sees burnt-out Tokyo in writings by Ishikawa Jun (1899–1987), Dazai Osamu (1909–1948), and Ango. The surreal cityscape can be seen in the work of Abe Kōbō (1924–1993) and Ōe Kenzaburō (b. 1935), followed by the postmodern, "cool" metropolis of the two Murakamis—Haruki (b. 1949) and Ryū (b. 1952).

Beginning in the late 1970s, a steady stream of women writers produces urban literature that changes the way we see Tokyo. For instance, Tsushima Yūko's (1947–2016) *Chōji* (1978, trans. *Child of Fortune*, 1992) and "Danmari ichi" (1986, trans. "The Silent Traders," 1993) introduce the urban landscape from the perspectives of single, married, or divorced women coping with motherhood, work, desires, and entrapment. Yoshimoto Banana's (b. 1964) *Kitchin* (1988, trans. *Kitchen*, 1993) and "Mūnraito shadō" (1988, trans. "Moonlight Shadow," 1993) create a trend in *katakana*-titled urban stories that feature stylish modern Western décor in a cityscape of loss and detachment. These works pave the way for the profusion of urban literature by women writers in the 1990s and the twenty-first century. Selected representative works include Kirino Natsuo's (b. 1952) *OUT* (1997, trans. *OUT*, 2003) and *Yawarakai hoho* ("Soft Cheeks," 1999) and Miyabe Miyuki's (b. 1960) *Riyū* ("Reason," 1998) in the mystery and detective mode, Kakuta Mitsuyo's (b. 1967) *Mori ni nemuru sakana* ("Fish Sleeping in the Forest," 2008) and *Kūchū teien* ("Sky Garden," 2005) on social and family issues, Miura Shion's (b. 1976) *Mahoro eki bangaichi* ("Un-Numbered Plots near Mahoro Station," 2012) on life in suburban towns, and Yū Miri's (b. 1968) *Kazoku shinema* ("Family Cinema," 1997), Yang Yi's (b. 1964) *Kingyo seikatsu* ("Life of Goldfish," 2009), and *Suki · yaki* ("Sukiyaki," 2009) on the life of minority and immigrant women in Tokyo. These works and others provide a new guide to Tokyo filtered through the perception, mind, experience, and memories of women of all kinds—single, married, divorced, working inside or outside the house, daughters, wives, mothers, bisexual, lesbian, transgender, young, old, middle-aged, law-abiding, rule-breaking, rich, poor, middle-class, Japanese, non-Japanese, citizen of the world, citizen of nowhere—and together they create a steady flow of urban narratives that constitute what Jordan Sand calls Tokyo vernacular, "a language of form, space, sensation" (2013, 2).

It is within this context that Nakajima Kyōko made her debut with *FUTON*. Nakajima is without doubt a writer of the city, and nearly all her subsequent works are urban narratives. For instance, *Kankonsōsai* ("Coming of Age, Wedding, Funeral, Festival," 2010) captures the different milestones in the lives of the city dwellers. *Heisei daikazoku* ("The Big Heisei Family," 2010) resembles a comic and satirical variety show of urban social and family problems: a retiree couple living with a ninety-year-old mother and their thirty-year-old *hikikomori*[6] son suddenly finds the bankrupt family of their older daughter and their pregnant and unmarried younger daughter on the doorstep. *Chiisai o-uchi* ("The Little House," 2012), awarded the Naoki Prize[7] and made into a movie by Yamada Yōji (b. 1931) in 2014, shuttles between Tokyo in the 1930s and 2012 to suggest an alarming similarity between Tokyo preparing for war and the 1940 "phantom" Olympics then and an increasingly right-wing Tokyo in recent years. *Hanamomo mimomo*

("The Hanamomo Tenant Apartment Building," 2014) revisits with humor the familiar trope of the single woman in her forties battling social pressure and searching for a way to define herself and her place in society. *Tōkyō kankō* ("Tokyo Sightseeing," 2014) is an anthology of short stories that captures with comic and endearing touches vignettes of different Tokyo lives—an OL,[8] a Filipina immigrant, a crocodile in an urban botanical park—in their alternating moments of laughter and tears. True to the spirit of the Naoki Prize, Nakajima adheres to narrative strategies that entertain, move, and appeal to the reader, with a willingness to provide a firm closure for comfort. Her urban stories are thought-provoking but never, in the end, disturbing or pessimistic, a point that sets her apart from the dark urban tales of loss and despair in, say, Tsushima Yūko's or Murakami Haruki's literature.

TOKYO: THREE TIME FRAMES, THREE LOCI

A central concern in Nakajima's *FUTON* is the excavation of layers of the city embedded in multiple temporal and spatial dimensions. Nakajima anchors her excavation in three major time frames associated with three loci: the publication of Katai's *Futon* in 1907 (the Yamanote), the Tokyo air raids in 1945 and immediate postwar (the Shitamachi), and Tokyo in 2001 (the Shitamachi and the relatively new urban development on the Tokyo waterfront called Odaiba).[9] She explores the places, people, and language in each temporal dimension, and creates numerous links among them that crisscross time and space in Tokyo through nearly a century. A synopsis of the story is in order before I discuss layers of Tokyo in her story.

Dave Macqualie, a forty-six-year-old professor of Japanese literature in a small-town college in the United States, is writing an adaptation of Katai's *Futon*[10] from the narrative perspective of the teacher's wife. In his personal life, Dave is divorced and having a love affair with one of his students, a Japanese-American college sophomore named Emi, who, in the course of the story, has a fling with an exchange student from Kyoto, Kondo Yūki. This alludes to the triangular relationship in Katai's *Futon*, in which the thirty-five-year-old teacher Takenaka Tokio, married with three children, becomes infatuated with nineteen-year-old Yoshiko, who eventually becomes sexually involved with a student of religion at Dōshisha University in Kyoto. In Nakajima's *FUTON*, Emi's seventy-two-year-old grandfather Tatsuzō runs a sandwich joint (formerly a *soba* noodle shop) in a plebeian part of Tokyo. He inherited the place from his father Segawa Umekichi, who was born in 1906, a year before the publication of Katai's *Futon*.

After a falling out with Dave over Kondo Yūki, Emi leaves for Tokyo. Dave finds an excuse to pursue her and ends up waiting for days with no success in Tatsuzō's sandwich joint. While idling in Tatsuzō's shop, Dave becomes fascinated with thirty-one-year-old Izumi, an aspiring painter making a living as a caregiver for Umekichi. In a broken narrative set during the time of the Tokyo air raids, Umekichi recalls fragments of an intense love affair with a mentally challenged woman whom he believes he murdered out of jealousy after the war. Umekichi's story inspires Izumi to paint again, and encountering Dave serves as an impetus for her to leave Hanae (a.k.a. Ken-chan), a lesbian partner with whom she shares an apartment but not a physical relationship. Characteristic of a contemporary popular novel, *FUTON* keeps all of the threads of the story neatly trimmed and knotted at the end. Dave parts with Emi and Izumi on amicable terms, Hanae inherits Izumi's job taking care of Umekichi as she revives her dream of opening a nursing home, Tatsuzō continues to run his sandwich joint, and Miho, the teacher's wife in Dave's adaptation of Katai's *Futon*, dries her tears at the realization of her husband's infatuation and decides to air the futon as the piercing winter wind dies down and the sun begins to shine.

This cast of cross-border, cross-generation characters enables Nakajima to explore a multi-dimensional Tokyo in the text. First, Tokyo in 1907 is evoked in Dave's story-within-a-story, *Futon no uchinaoshi* ("Refluffing the Futon"),[11] a chapter-by-chapter adaption of Katai's *Futon*, set entirely within the confines of the Yamanote. Tokio lives in Yaraichō in Ushigome (now Shinjuku Ward), his sister-in-law, a military widow, resides in Sanbanchō in Kōjimachi (now Chiyoda Ward), where Yoshiko commutes to attend a girls' private school, and Tokio commutes to work as an editor for geography texts in Koishikawa (now Bunkyō Ward). Generations of scholars have emphasized a clear topographical and ideological divide between the Yamanote and Shitamachi since the rise of Tokyo as the capital of the modern nation state of Japan. In *Shisō to shite no Tōkyō* ("Tokyo as Modern Thought," 1978), Isoda Kōichi (b. 1931) points out that the "Complete Zoning Map of Tokyo Urban Planning" inserted in *The Latest Greater Tokyo Map* (1925)[12] demarcates western Tokyo as "residential," the area that corresponds to what is now Chiyoda and Chūō Wards as "commercial," and the Shitamachi and Kawasaki (a city in neighboring Kanagawa Prefecture) as "industrial" (1988, 14–15). Seidensticker's *Low City, High City* reflects this idea: "The High City gets higher and higher. The Low City is still the warmer and more approachable of the two, but the days of its cultural eminence are gone" (1983, 251).

The setting of Katai's *Futon*, however, often blurs the above-mentioned division between the Yamanote and the Shitamachi. Katai is less interested in a formidable High City of money and power, and more concerned with the lives of ordinary people still trudging the literally muddy paths that took them uphill and downhill within the Yamanote. Katai's *Futon* begins with Tokio's commute on foot "down the gentle slope of that road in Koishikawa that leads from the Kirishitansaka to Gokurakusui"[13] (Tayama 1981, 35).

Staggering in a drunken state from his home in Yaraichō to his sister-in-law's home in Sanbanchō, where Yoshiko was boarding, Tokio arrives covered with mud ("on the shoulder, knee, and hip of his plain white casual kimono [was] not merely a trace but a very large amount of mud" [Ibid., 57]). This echoes Katai's observation, recorded in *Literary Life in Tokyo*, that when he was an eleven-year-old errand boy in 1881,[14] "[i]n those days Tokyo was a muddy city" (Tayama 1983, 7).[15] Uchida Muneharu's three-dimensional mapping in *Mizu ga oshiete kureru Tōkyō no bichikei sanpo* ("Tokyo Detailed Topographical Walks—What Water Shows Us") links the topography to frequent flooding and muddy roads in the city (2013, 22).[16]

Katai's interest in the Yamanote is largely human-based. He translates the topography of the Yamanote into a metaphor for the ups and downs in the life of its residents. "The Yamanote swirls with the energy of first-timers in society, prone to setbacks but still filled with hope to make it in the world with the support of a cheerful wife at home" (Tayama 1983, 72). Furthermore, Katai's fondest memories of the Yamanote are associated with food. "Fish shops, noodle shops, wine shops, everything triggers my recollection. Flatfish, sea breams, the bright red of sea robins, mackerels, squids, shrimps—my mother, or a young woman like my wife, will be there waiting for the seafood to be dressed" (Ibid., 74). Muddy, energetic, and saturated with the smell of food, Katai's Yamanote rejects the association with power, status, and monumentalism, and appears to blend in comfortably with the Shitamachi.

The embedded story of "Refluffing the Futon" in Nakajima's text is faithful to Katai's setting except for a couple of deliberate twists. Told from the wife's perspective, the spatial emphasis is female-oriented and domestic rather than male-oriented and urban. Thus, most chapters take place in the house, in Yoshiko's room, Tokio's study, the wooden verandah around the house where Miho and Yoshiko hang persimmons to dry, and in the garden where Miho beats and airs the titular *futon*. Nakajima's female gaze turns Katai's male gaze on its head and marks the embedded story as a remake that is consciously and simultaneously linked to and separated from the original. As for the reference to Tokio's workplace in the printing district in Koishikawa, Nakajima clearly consulted *Literary Life in Tokyo*, where she also took Dave's last name Macqualie from the reference to the British historian Thomas Babington Macaulay (Ibid., 33).[17] In a chapter titled "Chiri no hensan" ("Editing Geography Texts"), Katai describes the industrial district in Koishikawa as follows: "Amidst the piercing sound of the siren in the factory, the rough manners of the workers, the unpleasant feeling that came from the industrial smoke and slipshod building, we would spend half a sleepy day or a cold night there" (Ibid., 243).[18]

Nakajima shifts the description of the printing industry in Koishikawa to the outer frame of the story in *FUTON* to create a link between Meiji and contemporary Tokyo. The valley behind Denzūin Temple[19] where Tokio worked remains a printing center even today. Nakajima situates that pocket of the printing industry in the otherwise bourgeois and scholarly Yamanote neighborhood where Yan's apartment is located. Yan is a Korean student of Japanese literature with whom Dave stays while in Tokyo.

> Yan's neighborhood, just as before, was filled with the rattling noise of printing from subcontractor factories. The alleys were crowded with the coming and goings of orange-colored forklifts. The freshly cut paper flapped in the wind. Cats wove in and out as though they owned the area. There wouldn't have been forklifts in Takenaka Tokio's time, but since the publisher of geography textbooks where he worked was located around here, he would have walked up these slopes listening to the incessant rattling noise of the machinery. (2014a, 174)

Nakajima describes the back alleys of Tokyo from Dave's perspective in order to emphasize the existence of working class and down-to-earth neighborhoods in the Yamanote. In fact, as huge stretches of land in the suburbs have been leveled to build American-style malls and outlet parks in recent decades, small-scale shopping streets can be found only in local communities in Tokyo.

> Dave had always loved to lose his way in these alleys. In the many little surprise encounters in these backstreets, he found the neighborhood and the gentle sounds of the Japanese language endearing. He sauntered in the neighborhood where he spent time in his youth and walked through the shopping street lined with cheap-looking artificial flowers found only in Japan. On the left was a shop that sold salted rice cake stuffed with sweet bean jam, on the right sugar sold by the weight, and further down, a shrine that housed the lord of the underworld who was rumored to pull your tongue out if you lied. Once you turned the corner, the sound of fish and vegetable vendors calling, "price down, price down!" would fill your ears. (Ibid., 175)

The description of the back alleys in the Koishikawa neighborhood serves as a bridge for Nakajima to cross over to the Shitamachi in two time frames, 1945 and 2001. She constructs an imaginary place called Uzura-chō (Quail Town) that combines the following coordinates and features. The reference to the Asakusa Rokku entertainment district[20] indicates that Uzura-chō lies in the part of the Shitamachi known for its temples and entertainment. But the hint that Uzura-chō lies north of Koishikawa (Ibid., 347) suggests that it could be a place in Arakawa Ward, somewhere around Nishi Nippori or Minami Senju, known for a mix of small- and medium-sized industrial firms, shopping streets, and residential areas, and a relatively high percentage of its residents both living and working in the ward.[21] The reference to Uzura-chō as what was once a "desert island on land" (*riku no kotō*) (Ibid., 191) indi-

A forklift outside a subcontractor factory in the Koishikawa printing district, September 2014. *Angela Yiu.*

cates a part of Tokyo that used to be far from any train station. One of the areas that fits the description of a desert island on land at the time of the publication of *FUTON* lies along the elevated tracks of the Nippori-Toneri Liner, a part of the Tokyo transit system that opened in 2008, running from Nippori in Arakawa Ward to Minumadai Shinsui Park in Adachi Ward.[22]

The subway routes that Dave takes to and from Uzura-chō are deliberately vague. To reach Uzura-chō, Dave travels deep underground by a new subway line with futuristic green stations (Ibid., 175 and 189). One possible place that fits the description is the greenish Iidabashi Station on the Ōedo line (opened in 1991, fully operational in 2000), with stops or easy connections to nearly all the major locales in Nakajima's story—Ushigome, Asakusa, Shiodome, and on to the Yurikamome monorail to Daiba. However, to go from Uzura-chō to Ginza, Dave has to transfer at Ōtemachi, which places Uzura-chō on any of the four subway lines (Marunouchi, Hanzōmon, Chiyoda, and Tōzai) that connect at Ōtemachi. The reference to an abundance of ethnic restaurants with signs in Hangul, Spanish, Portuguese, and Chinese, some indicating "Japanese menu available" (Ibid., 190), suggests a neighborhood resembling Korea Town near Shin Ōkubo Station on the Yamanote train line. Uzura-chō also boasts of a number of ateliers for crafts and shoes as well as picture galleries that attract young artists (Ibid., 255), reminiscent of the Yanesen area (Yanaka, Nezu, Sendagi).[23] Dave's observation of "violent graffiti in bad taste," "street art," and "remodeled buildings housing 1950-style cafés" evokes a "Tokyo style"[24] found in various parts of the city, including areas in Shinjuku, Shimokitazawa, Nippori, and some little towns along private railway lines. Finally, the mention of young men doing drugs during the daytime and bullying the elderly (Ibid., 304–5) suggests a seedy part of Shinjuku. Thus, Nakajima's Uzura-chō refers not to a single identifiable place but to a mixture of neighborhoods where a diversity of ordinary citizens live, work, or simply bide their time.

The depiction of Uzura-chō in 1945 alludes heavily to the burnt-out ruins of Tokyo in the works of Ango and Ishikawa Jun, both of whom are *apure geru* (après-guerre), Burai-ha writers[25] known for their bleak war and postwar landscapes. Nakajima's depiction of postwar Tokyo borrows from, for example, Ango's "The Idiot" and Ishikawa's *Yakeato no Iesu* (1946, trans. "The Jesus of the Ruins," 1998). Nakajima writes,

> In the earth-splitting sound of the roaring planes, everyone came dashing out of the factory. Swarming with B-29 bombers, the night sky shone with an eerie light. Firebombs rained from the sky like beans, and the familiar but disturbing clanging sound would not cease to ring. (Ibid., 221)

Alternately hiding in bomb shelters or running for their lives in the burning industrial area of the Shitamachi, then thirty-nine-year-old Umekichi and his feeble-minded lover, twenty-year-old Tsutako, are characters straight from the pages of Ango's "The Idiot."[26] The titular *futon*, where Umekichi had sex with Tsutako, ceases to be a telltale object of a man's confession in Katai's I-novel and becomes a symbol for the flesh or the body (*nikutai*) in defiance of the national polity (*kokutai*), a sustained theme in postwar literature of the flesh/the body (*nikutai bungaku*).[27] It also doubles as a safety covering and a second skin for Tsutako. "Grabbed by a strong gust of wind, [the *futon*] tore away from the woman's body and flew off" (Ibid., 224), preparing Tsutako to emerge as a different person in postwar Uzura-chō.

Postwar Uzura-chō was associated with black marketeering, prostitution, and cheap eateries. "Soon after the war, Uzura-chō set up 'comfort facilities'[28] catering to the needs of the occupational force. When these became off-limit, Uzura-chō thrived as a street of cafés" (Ibid., 225). When Umekichi opened his *soba* shop Sanshūya in Uzura-chō, Tsutako reappeared in a new hairstyle and clothes, reminiscent of the unforgettable Woman in Red in Ishikawa's "Ōgon densetsu" (1946, "The Legend of Gold," 1998), a "good wife"/war widow-turned-prostitute for survival in postwar Japan. Tsutako's sexual favors for the occupational forces earned her *Meriken* (American) wheat flour[29] and other goods that she promptly delivered to Sanshūya. She was also rumored to be involved with Umekichi's nineteen-year-old nephew, Kikuzō, who just returned from the war. In Umekichi's faulty memory as a ninety-five-year-old, he imagines killing Tsutako in a fit of jealousy. Thus, Uzura-chō in 1945 is the space of Burai-ha literature—dark, decadent, teeming with emotions, desire, sex, murder, and, above all, a strong will to live.[30]

Uzura-chō in 2001 departs from the traditional definition of the Shitamachi as a place associated with plebeian culture, entertainment, human warmth, and small shops and industry. It retains some of these features but it is more diverse and difficult to circumscribe. It is simultaneously multiethnic (*tajinshu*), multi-national (*takokuseki*), as well as "stateless" (*mukokuseki*), or, in the language of food culture, in a state of "fusion." This rich diversity is evident in the following features that mark the neighborhood: the numerous ethnic eateries in the neighborhood, Tatsuzō's recent conversion of Umekichi's Sanshūya *soba* shop to an American-franchised sandwich chain store "Rabuwei (Loveway) Uzura" (a pun on Subway), the appearance of Tatsuzō's Japanese-American granddaughter Emi in an ad for the store in the local free paper, the American professor's faithful patronage of the store, and old Tatsuzō's poker-face question to all customers, "Would you like *jalepeño*[31] on your sandwich?" (Ibid., 7).

Uzura-chō is also an aging neighborhood, populated with what the Ministry of Health, Labor, and Welfare has termed late-stage elderly[32]—people who, like Umekichi, have survived the destruction of a great part of Tokyo not only once, but twice, in 1923 (the Great Kantō Earthquake) and 1945 (the firebombing of Tokyo), and bore much of the personal and collective loss and trauma of twentieth-century Japan. Izumi's comment on the "disorder" in Tokyo (Ibid., 311) is a reference to the Post Traumatic Stress Disorder (PTSD) she observes in Umekichi's hallucination of murder and guilt.

Finally, Uzura-chō anticipates a more tolerant urban space for sexual minorities (LGBT),[33] a place where Hanae/Ken-chan can hide to lick her wounds from discrimination and harassment. She was a licensed nurse fired from her job because of her manifest sexual ambiguity and preference. Though a minor character, Hanae/Ken-chan strikes a memorable pose with her dyed-blonde spiky hair and a tough-guy vocabulary that consists of words such as *ore*, *teme~*, *kono yarō*, and *chikushō*.[34] But when she puts on a nurse's uniform to take care of Umekichi and dreams of opening a nursing home, she strikes a professional and motherly pose. "[Tatsuzō] was reminded of his reticent mother a long, long time ago, toiling from morning to night in the soba shop in the dead-end alley, filling orders from the American military during the Korean War" (Ibid., 360).[35]

For his official business in Tokyo, Dave stays in a hotel in Odaiba at the invitation of International Japan Tokyo Edogawa University (Nakajima's jab at attempts in higher education to package the traditional, national, and global in a single name). Originally built as a series of artificial islands serving as batteries along the shore in the 1850s, Odaiba expanded rapidly as a business and leisure area in the 1990s—part of the economic revitalization of the Tokyo waterfront. Beginning in 1985 with the opening of Tokyo Disneyland on land that used to be dilapidated fishing villages in the Urayasu area of Chiba Prefecture, the Tokyo waterfront has been transformed into futuristic and showtime TOKYO written in *katakana*, featuring a replica of the Statue of Liberty set against the background of Rainbow Bridge, the sci-fi-esque Fuji Television Building designed by Tange Kenzō (1913–2005), a 115-meter Ferris wheel in the shopping district Palette Town, and the Miraikan, Japan's National Museum of Emerging Science and Innovation, just to name an ostentatious few. Images of the Tokyo waterfront bring to mind those of other newly developed parts of old cities in the world: the Pudong skyline in Shanghai, the man-made Palm Jumeirah and World Islands off the coast of Dubai, and Astana, the capital of Kazakhstan. Preposterously futuristic and unapologetically new, flashy, monumental, and made for television- and online-imaging, these "visions of future" seem to thrive on the erasure of the past.

It is precisely this flat rejection of memory, both individual and collective, that compels Izumi to trace hidden wounds of the past. Gazing at the replica of the Statue of Liberty from Dave's hotel room window, she says, "This city is cheerful, noisy, and filled with new things. It always runs at super-full speed, and no one ever thinks that this place has a past. But it occurred to me, wasn't this city wounded in the past? Has it ever healed properly?" (Ibid., 313). Izumi's comments bring full circle the three time frames and three loci in Nakajima's narrative. Gazing at a twenty-first century cityscape that thrives on amnesia and erasure, Izumi is determined to find a way to literally depict on canvas the unhealed wounds of the city, drawing her inspiration from Umekichi's experience of Tokyo's devastation in 1923 and 1945. Since Umekichi was born in 1906, a year before the publication of Katai's *Futon*, Izumi's choice of subject for her art project and Dave's rewriting of Katai's story take the reader back to the beginning of the twentieth century in reflecting the changes embedded in layers of time in the city.

LANGUAGE AND THE CITY

Language in itself is a significant aspect of Katai's work that traces the transformation of the city, a feature that Nakajima inherits in her work. In *Literary Life in Tokyo*, Katai traces his linguistic exposure to various forms of Japanese, ranging from the language of *kanshibun* (poetry and prose in classical Chinese), Edo literature (works by Kyokutei Bakin [1767–1848], Tamenaga Shunzui [1790–1844]), *kokubun* (Japanese/national literature) in vernacular style (*genbun'itchi*), and translations of English and European works that filled the second floor of Maruzen bookstore.[36] In Katai's *Futon*, Yoshiko writes in vernacular Japanese when she is in Tokyo but reverts to the old-style *sōrōbun* used in letters and documents in the Edo period when she returns to her hometown in Bitchū (now Okayama Prefecture). As an homage to Katai, the layers of language that make up linguistic Tokyo come into play in Nakajima's *FUTON*.

FUTON opens with Emi lying in bed with Dave in the United States reading an email message in Japanese from Tatsuzō, in which he says, "We're in an age where people live a hundred years, so grandpa wants to *torai* something new" (Ibid., 9). Emi asks Dave, in English, "What's TORAI?"—to which he responds, in English "How do you spell it?" Emi then switches to Japanese, "TO as in *tora*, RA as in *tora*, and I as in *inu*." Dave says, again in English, "That's English. That means 'try.' T, R, Y, try." This comical opening scene places *FUTON* in the contemporary trend of cross-border literature in which multilingual authors, such as Mizumura Minae (b. 1951) and Hideo Levy (b. 1950), switch back and forth between Japanese and one or more foreign language(s) in the text. The textual appearance of the story in alternating lines of Japanese and English, as well as the reliance on online communication in the opening scene, suggest from the start the permeability of spatial and linguistic borders in twenty-first-century Tokyo. All names, except for names in the story-within-a-story, are presented in *katakana*, suggesting ubiquity, statelessness, and rootlessness in characters drifting in and out in the constantly changing city. In the Odaiba setting of the story, even Tokyo is written in *katakana* instead of the usual *kanji*, transforming Tokyo into a city with "multiple personality disorder" (Ibid., 311) that requires constant re-definition.[37] The visual impact of Tokyo in *katakana* in an otherwise conventional Japanese sentence produces a jolting and somewhat alienating effect, as though the city has been disconnected from its own past and history and has acquired a new personality that is foreign, devoid of familiar content, unrecognizable, and begging for an identity.

Within the story, Dave turns out to be one of the most eloquent and lucid writers and speakers of Japanese. In his adaptation of Katai's *Futon*, Dave attempts to use Meiji prose to cultivate a clear and rich modern language in order to capture the complexity of modernity. Dave is particularly mindful of the use of female speech among women in the Yamanote, as in the use of an incomplete sentence ending with an upward questioning lilt to soften the tone—for example, Yoshiko's "*otetsudai dekite?*" (May I help?) (Ibid., 81) and Miho's "*Tsuma taru watashi ni mukatte shitsurei dewa nakute?*" (You don't think what you said is rude to me as his wife?) (Ibid., 168). In contrast to that, Tokio's male speech is blunt and guttural, as in the expletives *omae ni wa wakaran* ("You don't know a thing!") (Ibid., 63, 130) and *baka!* ("Idiot!") (Ibid., 63). In endowing Dave with a mastery of Meiji prose and female speech, Nakajima allows him to cross borders on three fronts: ethnic/national, gender, and temporal. In doing so, she recreates and destroys Katai's male-orientated *Futon* by turning it on its head.

Dave is particularly sensitive to offenders of the Japanese language. For example, his resentment of Kondo Yūki is not limited to his presence as a rival for Emi's affection but also directed at his abhorrent Japanese, as in the following excerpt from Yūki's email response to Emi:[38] "ok, Tokyo's cool, plus there's a club i wanna take you to. my high school *senpai* works there as a DJ—a real cool place. and i wanna swing by Daiba or somethin'" (Ibid., 157).[39]

Equally befuddling, but in an entirely different way, is the excessive and arm-twisting use of *teineigo* (polite speech) delivered with a degree of impudence by Professor Morita from International Japan Tokyo Edogawa University in a lecture invitation to Dave by phone. "*You will allow us to* progress with the preparation, in the hope that the final answer from you will be an okay, but if for any reason if it doesn't work for you, *you will allow us* to think about it, and we would appreciate if you could move things around in a cooperative manner. Well then, that's about it" (Ibid., 104).[40] Dave turns the expression "you will allow us to"—*sashite morau*—in *katakana* in his head,[41] not knowing how to respond. Professor Morita ends the phone call with a linguistic acrobatic, "Well then, *you will allow us* to leave it at that, alright" (*sō sashite moraimassa~*) (Ibid., 105), a simultaneously humble, polite, pushy, brusque, and masculine expression that reverberates in *katakana* in Dave's head.

The real challenge for Dave is the write-up on Tatsuzō's sandwich joint in the free paper TOWN•BOM!

> WHAT'S COOL this week•real RESPECT for grampa Loveway's GUTS Gotta go after your dreams no matter how old you are, BABY!
> On WHAT'S COOL this week we've got 72-year-old TATSUZOU SEGAWA from LOVEWAY UZURACHO. No kidding! You don't mean 27? NO WAY, we've got you a real gutsy grampa! UZURACHO is a REAL *yabai* DISTRICT for you guys—right in the middle of a crappy building the USED SHOP "Nup" with a million RARE items shows up out of the blue, and Shop No. 2 for SILVER ACCESSORIES "@kEnEIE" just opened with a super COOL interior. But are you guys ready for a real surprise about a TOKYO that you never knew? . . .
> In the picture, see, on the left, is Tatsu's granddaughter. No kidding. This BEAUTIFUL, SEXY BABE who stole my HEART is his granddaughter Emi, OMG! isn't she super cute! Look at her kissing grampa! Are you serious? Hey, wait a minute. . . .
> GODDAM, I'm gonna be there no matter what. (Ibid., 187–188)[42]

Between Dave's mastery of Meiji prose and the youth- and street-language that puzzles and assaults him in twenty-first-century Japan lies a century of linguistic transformations that reveal the different faces of Tokyo. Nakajima borrows heavily from the postwar literature of the flesh (*nikutai bungaku*) to recreate the language that describes Umekichi and Tsutako in wartime Tokyo in 1945. "After the night shift, [Umekichi] lay down his exhausted body after a whole night at the turning mill and fell into a deathlike sleep. For a brief moment after that, he fondled the woman's dark and emaciated body, and pampered her like a baby when she cried and screamed" (Ibid., 196).

Tsutako's language brings to mind that of the woman in Ango's "The Idiot."[43] In the pitch-black bomb shelter amidst the sound of bombing, she repeats, "Mister, mister, I'm scared, we're going to die, we're going to die" (*dannasan, dannasan, kowai, shinde shimau yō, shinde shimau yō*) (Ibid.,195). Haunting, timeless, and repetitive, Tsutako's utterance, written entirely in *hiragana* except for the *kanji* for death,[44] embodies a deep physical horror of and a sense of repulsion toward the insanity and inhumanity of war.

When Umekichi narrates fragments of his wartime memory to Izumi, she finds his vocabulary difficult to understand. "In those days, white flour and buckwheat flour were all rationed (*tōsei*)," Umekichi says. "What's *tōsei*?" (Ibid., 133), Izumi asks, transforming the *kanji* used in Umekichi's script into *katakana*. Following that, Umekichi says, "We made *soba* and *udon* to get our wage (*kōchin*)," to which Izumi asks, "What's *kōchin*? You mean the Nagoya stuff?" (Ibid., 134), mistaking *kōchin* (wage) for Nagoya Kōchin, a brand of chicken bred for quality meat and eggs. In the comical linguistic gap between 1945- and 2001-Japanese, fragments of wartime Tokyo begin to emerge and seep into Izumi's twenty-first-century consciousness. That awareness awakens in her an aesthetic and intellectual desire to paint the multi-layered city—its history, people, space, language. It is a desire that no doubt echoes Nakajima's creation of *FUTON* as she unearths layers of Tokyo in writing a twenty-first century version of a 1907 novel.

CONCLUSION

In response to Izumi's uncertainty in finding a medium to capture the complexity of the city, Dave says,

> All works of art possess a meaning. The artist does not choose the subject; a work chooses the artist to manifest its form. The fact that similar works of art appear in the same age is a sign that different artists are able to interpret the meaning of an age. The time, the streets, history, nature, disasters, all of them embody a silent meaning in search of someone to express it in a visible form, in words, images, music, architecture, and many other things. TOKYO has chosen you. (Ibid., 315–16)

This passage reveals Nakajima's view of the artist's relationship to her urban literature. The artist is the medium through which the multiple meanings of the city take shape in a multitude of linguistic expressions and a host of voices. In *FUTON* and her subsequent works, Nakajima continues to create a polyphony for the multiple personalities of the city—simultaneously old and young, destroyed and reborn, Japanese and non-Japanese, male, female, and LGBT—to speak through her characters and the time and space they inhabit. She is a steady voice among the many voices of female and cross-border writers who re-evaluate the predominantly male-oriented and national narrative of the city and deliver a multi-layered Tokyo that is diverse and multicolor, constantly remade, re-stitched, and renewed, like the metaphor of the remaking of the futon in the title of Dave's story-within-a-story.

Particularly significant in Nakajima's narrative strategy in *FUTON* and many of her other works is the superimposition of different time frames to create a multi-dimensional cityscape. It is never only Tokyo in 1907, 1945, or 2001, but different time frames intersecting at different angles to allow the past to address the present and the future, and for the present and future to react to and learn from the past. In an article she published in the *Asahi Shinbun* on August 8, 2014, titled *Senzen to iu jidai* ("In an Age Called 'Prewar'"), Nakajima suggests an eerie similarity between the 1930s and contemporary Japan under the second Abe cabinet in the following respects: an overall indifference to politics in the public sphere, media self-censorship, and the forced passage of new laws as a means for the government to suppress civil liberty. Indeed, the record low percentage of voters,[45] the criticism of freedom of speech by fledgling Liberal Democratic Party lawmakers,[46] the hasty passage of the Special Secrecy Law on December 6, 2013,[47] and the forced passage of eleven security-related laws in the Lower House on July 16, 2015,[48] are all foreboding signs of our time that echo the past. Beginning with *FUTON*, Nakajima's urban stories continue to show a commitment to two fundamental ideas: first, it is crucial for memory of the past, especially wartime Japan, to exist as an organic part of the contemporary consciousness in order to illuminate the present and the future, and second, the stories that make up a great city stem not from heroes and authority but from the memory, hopes, and reflections of the ordinary citizens of and sojourners in Tokyo. *FUTON* is only the beginning of a series of urban narratives, including "The Little House" and "The Big Heisei Family," that continue to unearth and create layers of Tokyo in the multitudinous voices of the people, all of whom are connected to the destruction and rebirth of the city.

Finally, the most distinguishing feature of Nakajima's work is the construction of a polyphonic and linguistic Tokyo. Incorporating the rhetoric of the I-Novel, Burai-ha, postwar literature, and literature of the flesh, mixing that with the occasional appearance of bilingual text as well as the language of disembodied email messages and free papers, and tossing in the voices of Dave (an American professor of Japanese literature), Emi (a Japanese-American), Izumi (a frustrated woman artist), Hanae/Ken-chan (a transgender lesbian), Tatsuzō (a septuagenarian sandwich-joint shopkeeper in working class Tokyo), Umekichi (his ninety-five-year-old father), and Professor Morita at a so-called international university, Nakajima conjures a city of language(s) from different nationalities, genders, ages, and occupations from 1907 to 2001. The multi-dimensional spaces and memories of Tokyo, one realizes, are made up of a complex play of the words and sounds of those who inhabit the city, then and now.

NOTES

1. The title of Nakajima's *FUTON* appears in Romanization in the original, and is glossed as *fūton* in *katakana*, to approximate an Anglicized pronunciation of the word.

2. Tayama Katai is often referred to by his penname Katai rather than his full name.

3. Kenneth G. Henshall's translation of Katai's work contains a subtitle that reflects more accurately the content of the original title, "Thirty Years in Tokyo." The years included in Henshall's translated title are misleading. The actual record of events covers the years 1881 to 1916, a total of thirty-five years.

4. For examples of Ichiyō's urban literature, see "Takekurabe" (1896, trans. "Child's Play," 1981) and "Nigorie" (1895, trans. "Troubled Waters," 1981). For examples of Tamura's urban literature, see "Eiga" (1916, trans. "Glory," 1984) and "Miira no kuchibeni" ("The Lipstick of a Mummy," 1914).

5. For a full and anecdotal discussion of the Yamanote and Shitamachi, see Seidensticker 1983, 185–251.

6. *Hikikomori* refers to adolescents or adults who avoid social contact over a long period of time and retreat into their own rooms. The word has entered the Oxford English Dictionary as "In Japan, abnormal avoidance of social contact." See BBC News, "Hikikomori: Why are so many Japanese men refusing to leave their rooms, " July 3, 2013. Accessed 12 December 2016. http://www.bbc.com/news/magazine-23182523.

7. The Naoki Prize is a literary prize established in 1935 by the magazine *Bungei Shunjū*. It is awarded to new or experienced writers for newly published work of "popular" or "mass literature" (*taishū bungaku*), as opposed to the Akutagawa Prize, also established in the same year by *Bungei Shunjū*, awarded to writers of "pure literature" (*jun bungaku*). These categories of literature are debatable and no longer clearly distinguishable, though in general works awarded the Naoki Prize tend to have a wider appeal and are often made into popular movies. Recent recipients whose work became bestsellers include Kakuta Mitsuyo for *Taigan no kanojo* (2004, trans. *Woman on the Other Shore*, 2007), Higashino Keigo (b. 1958) for *Yōgisha X no kenshin* (2005, trans. *The Devotion of Suspect X*, 2011), and Miura Shion for *Mahoro ekimae Tada Benriken* ("The Tada Handyman Shop in Front of Mahoro Station," 2006).

8. OL is the abbreviation for "office lady," a term that refers to a female office worker typically assigned routine office duties that range from the preparation of paperwork to serving tea.

9. Odaiba is also known as the Tokyo Waterfront Secondary City Center (Tōkyō Rinkai Fukutoshin), that covers a largely reclaimed area encompassing Daiba in Minato Ward, the Ariake and Aomi districts in Kōtō Ward, and the Higashiyashio district of Shinagawa Ward. It is known for shopping and entertainment venues, the Venus Port mall, the Fuji Television Building, and a convention center known as Tokyo Big Site. It features eye-catching landmarks such as an outsized Ferris wheel and a replica of the Statue of Liberty.

10. Even though Katai's *Futon* is a work of fiction based loosely on Katai's personal experience, it was retroactively labeled in the 1920s as one of the earliest examples of the I-novel (*watakushi shōsetsu*) genre—to which Katai's name has become inextricably tied.

11. In a chapter titled "The Rise of Women Writers, the Heisei I-Novel, and the Contemporary *Bundan*," Kendall Heitzman translates the title of the story-within-a-story into "Futon Refluffed" (2016, esp. 293–97).

12. "The Complete Zoning Map of Tokyo Urban Planning" (*Tōkyō toshi keikaku chiiki sōranzu*) was originally an official notification from the prewar Department of the Interior issued in January 26, 1925, called "The Zoning Map of Tokyo Urban Planning" (*Tōkyō toshi keikaku chiikizu*). It was inserted in the 1925 *The Latest Map of Greater Tokyo* (*Saishin dai Tōkyō chizu*) to indicate the new zoning policy in Greater Tokyo (Isoda 1988, 14).

13. Kirishitansaka (Christian Slope) is a narrow slope going up from east to west in the Kobinata district of Bunkyō Ward, a short walk from Myōgadani Station on the elevated part of the Marunouchi subway line. In the seventeenth century, missionaries sent to Edo from Nagasaki were held as prisoners in the area, giving the slope its name. Gokurakusui ("Paradise Water") is a name of a well in the Koishikawa district of the Bunkyō Ward. It was part of Sōkeiji Temple and was known to have delicious water, though the well has dried up and is preserved only as a landmark.

14. Born in Tatebayashi-chō, Jōshū (now Gunma Prefecture), Katai first visited Tokyo in 1876 when he was six. His grandfather brought him to Tokyo again in 1881, and he began to work as an errand boy in a bookshop called Yūrindō in Kyōbashi. See Tayama 1983, 323.

15. Quotes from *Tōkyō no sanjūnen* are my translation.

16. Uchida points out that the flooding in the Edo Shitamachi was so horrendous that the Kanda River was redirected artificially to its current course through the neighborhood of Ochanomizu to flow into the Sumida River.

17. Katai mentions Thomas Macaulay's (1800–1859) works in the chapter titled "Atarashii bungaku no kyūsenpō" ("Frontline in New Literature"). Macaulay's name appears twice in English, and there is little doubt that Nakajima changes the spelling and adapts it for Dave's name, which she deliberately presents in English in *FUTON* (2014a, 154).

18. In *Low City, High City*, Seidensticker concurs with Katai's observation: "Koishikawa contained pockets of industry, one of them dear to chroniclers of the proletariat. The valley

behind the Denzūin, one of the two grand temples in the district, was a printing center" (1983, 246).

19. Denzūin is a temple of the Jōdo sect in the Koishikawa neighborhood in Bunkyō Ward. The writer Nagai Kafū (1879–1959) was born near the temple and had written essays about Denzūin, comparing it to Notre-Dame Cathedral in Paris. See Nagai Kafū, "Denzūin" (1910) in *Kafū zuihitsushū* jō ("Kafū's collected essays, Part One"), Iwanami shoten, 1986. Natsume Sōseki also boarded near Denzūin during his student days, and the temple featured in his fiction *Sorekara* (1909, trans. *And Then*, 1981) and *Kokoro* (1914, trans. *Kokoro*, 1957).

20. Asakusa Rokku, traditionally referred to as the Asakusa Kōen Rokku, acquired its name and reputation as an entertainment district located since 1884 in the vicinity of the Sensōji Temple. In the Meiji period, Rokku was known for its landmark twelve-story tower Ryōunkaku, as well as its vaudeville theaters and cinemas. In the late Taishō and early Shōwa period, it was famous for hosting operettas by the popular "Asakusa Opera" (1917–23) as well as light comedy by the Casino Follies (1929–33). For fiction set in the Asakusa Rokku in the 1920s and 1930s, see Kawabata Yasunari's *Asakusa kurenaidan* (1930, trans. *The Scarlet Gang of Asakusa*, 2005) and Hori Tatsuo's *Suizokukan* (1930, trans. *Aquarium*, 2013). In the 1960s, with the spread of television culture and the shift of popular and youth culture to Shinjuku, Shibuya, and Roppongi, Asakusa Rokku was consigned to the past and suffered a decline. In recent years, starting from 2013, the Rokku Broadway Shopping Street Revitalization Association (*Rokku burōdouei shōtengai fukkō kyōkai*) began a series of strategies to revive Rokku as a tourist attraction.

21. According the website of the Arakawa chapter of The Tokyo Chamber of Commerce and Industry, "75% of Arakawa Ward is semi-industrial area with many small and medium sized businesses, and there are numerous shopping streets that support the daily life of people who live and work there, creating what one would call a Shitamachi." See www.tokyo-cci.or.jp/arakawa/feature (accessed 3 September 2015).

22. See "Toneri rainā ensen, katsute no riku no kotō e" ("Along the Toneri Liner, Traveling to What Was Once a 'Desert Island on Land'") in *Nihon keizai shinbun* (digital), 13 July 2010. http://www.nikkei.com/article/DGXZZO10886730S0A710C1000000/ (accessed 3 September 2015).

23. Yanesen refers to the area from Bunkyō Ward to Kōtō Ward and include the districts of Yanaka, Nezu, and Sendagi. The temples and buildings that escaped destruction in both the 1923 Great Kantō Earthquake and the 1945 Tokyo firebombings retain vestiges of old Tokyo and attract a fair number of artisans and craftsmen. For a detailed discussion of the Yanesen area, see Sand 2013, 54–87.

24. "Tokyo" is written not in *kanji* but in *katakana*, usually used in loan words or non-Japanese names, to suggest, in the context of the description of the cafés in the 1950s, a style that departs from traditional Edo or Tokyo but embodies American influence during the Allied Occupation of Japan (1945–1952).

25. Burai-ha, loosely rendered as "libertines" or "ruffians," refers to the first wave of postwar writers—Sakaguchi Ango, Dazai Osamu, Ishikawa Jun, Oda Sakunosuke (1913–1947)—who wrote about denizens of the underbelly of society involved in black-marketeering, licentious relationships, alcoholism, drug abuse, and other anti-social activities as a form of resistance to the authoritarian and military rule during the war years.

26. Izumi remarks, when she heard the story from Umekichi, "it's just like 'The Idiot'!" (Nakajima 2014a, 216).

27. Literature of the flesh/the body (*nikutai bungaku*) is a movement that was started by Tamura Taijirō (1911–1983) and resonated in the postwar works of Sakaguchi Ango and Dazai Osamu. It redirects attention to the needs and suffering of the individual body (*nikutai*) as opposed to the notion of "national polity" or, literally, "the body of the state" (*kokutai*). In doing so, it stresses "individual freedom and aspirations as part of a political and moral backlash against the decades-long celebration of the concept of *kokutai*, which had been used to justify the authoritarian imperialist and militarist policies that resulted in catastrophic war and defeat" (Yiu 2013, 85).

28. The so-called comfort facilities (*ian shisetsu*), a term that shares the same euphemistic root as "comfort women" (*ianfu*), were brothels in disguise.

29. The term *Meriken-ko* dated back to the Meiji period, when Japan began to import wheat flour from the United States. Imported flour was commonly called *Meriken-ko* ("meriken" being an adulterated pronunciation of "American"), to distinguish it from flour produced at home, called *udon-ko*, literally udon noodle flour. In the immediate postwar years, Japan relied heavily on imported flour from the United States. The term is no longer in common use.

30. The word "decadent" here refers to Ango's *Darakuron* (1946, trans. *Discourse on Decadence*, 2010), a treatise that stresses the importance of a fall (*daraku*) from the lofty and abstract ideals of loyalty and patriotism to embrace fundamental human and physical needs in order to become human in postwar Japan.

31. *Jalepeño* refers to a hot green or red pepper grown in the southwestern part of the United States and in Mexico, commonly made into a sauce by the same name and used in Mexican cuisine.

32. This refers to *kōki kōreisha* in Japanese, seniors over seventy-five years old.

33. LGBT stands for lesbian, gay, bisexual, and transgender. Even though the term has been circulating in the United States and Europe since the 1990s, it is difficult to trace when it was first used in the media in Japan. NHK Online, the official website for NHK (Nippon Hōsō Kyōkai, or Japan Broadcasting Corporation), for instance, has a webpage called "*Nijiiro LGBT tokusetsu saito*" ("Rainbow Color LGBT Special Site") devoted to updates on news and events for sexual minorities (http://www.nhk.or.jp/heart-net/lgbt/). One of the early entries dates back to September 10, 2010, the date of the Seventh Pride Parade in Shibuya (http://www.nhk.or.jp/heart-net/lgbt/rensai/lgbtsenpai/senpai_003.html) (accessed 4 September 2015). Even though Nakajima does not use the term in the novel, the depiction of Hanae/Ken-chan precipitates the eventual awareness of LGBT in Japan.

34. *Ore* is a "tough guy" reference to the self, even though some school children, from elementary to high school, male and female, will use it to sound tough. *Teme~* is a slurred pronunciation of the familiar and often condescending way of addressing someone as *temae* (you). *Baka yarō* is a slang expression that means "you idiot." *Chikushō*, literally "beast," can mean "damn it," or a number of expletives that express anger, hurt, and frustration.

35. Nakajima uses the term *Chōsen tokuju*, special orders for goods and services from the U.S. military in Japan during the Korean War (1950–1955). These special orders contributed to an economic boom in Japan.

36. Maruzen opened its first store in Nihonbashi in 1870 and played an important role in introducing Western culture and literature to Japan. Literary works featuring the Maruzen bookstore include Kajii Motojirō's "Remon" (1925, trans. "Lemon," 1993) and Akutagawa Ryūnosuke's "Aru aho no isshō" (1927, trans. "A Fool's Life," 1999).

37. Izumi points out that Tokyo is like a person with MPD. "It has so many faces that it's hard to explain what's TOKYO" (Nakajima 2014a, 311). The MPD motif also appears in Okuizumi Hikara's *Tōkyō jijoden* ("An Autobiography of Tokyo," 2014), in which the mythical spirit that resides in the ground (*chirei*) of Tokyo appears in six different personalities from Edo to 2012 to tell its own story.

38. "[Dave] was incensed that his rival in love was an idiot who couldn't even write a proper sentence in Japanese (Nakajima 2014a, 158)."

39. In Japanese, "*ii yo, ore mo Tōkyō kekko~ suki da shi. Emi no koto turete ikitai kurabu mo arun da. kōkō no toki no senpai ga DJ yattete, ii kanji no toko dakara. Daiba tokamo ikite~shi*" (Nakajima 2014a,157).

40. In Japanese, "*Watakushidomo wa junbi o susume*sashitemoratte*, sorede saishūteki ni ookei o itadakuyō na hōkō de ikereba iin desu ga, mata sensei no hō ga dōshite mo dame na baai to iu nomo, watakushidomo no hō de kangae*sashitemoraimasunde*, sensei no hō demo dōnika tsugō o tsukeru yō na hōkō de ugoite itadaku, to iu koto de, hitotsu, ne*" (Nakajima 2014a, 104, my emphasis).

41. The conversion of this verbal ending to *katakana* serves two functions. First, it is for emphasis, since the visual impact of *katakana* in Japanese creates an estranging effect. Second, the use of *katakana* in Dave's head to contemplate the phrase suggests a cognitive, cultural, and linguistic dissonance between the speaker and listener, and that dissonance creates a comical and disturbing effect in the utterance.

42. The capitalized words in the translation appear in *katakana* in the original script. The place names Uzura-chō and Tokyo appear in capitalized Romanization in the original. OMG appears as *oomaiga* in *katakana*, the way "Oh my god!" is pronounced in street Japanese. The word *yabai*, which started as a youth expression and is now widely used by all age groups, can mean great or horrible depending on the context.

43. The woman in "The Idiot" is usually quiet, but on occasion she utters simple and barely intelligible phrases, mostly about bodily sensations experienced in a spectrum of time, such as "*Atashi, itai no, . . . ima mo itamu no, . . . sakki mo itakatta no*" ("It hurts, it's still hurting, it hurt just now, too") Sakaguchi 1989–1991, 24. My translation.

44. Tsutako's utterance transcribed in *hiragana* brings out three effects. First, it conveys her feeble-mindedness. Second, the phonocentric inscription emphasizes the overwhelming sonic reality of a dark enclosure that renders sight meaningless. Finally, it accentuates the one word, *shi* (death), in *kanji*, which lies at the core of her fear.

45. In the forty-seventh election for the Lower House in 2014, only 33% voters in their twenties and 42% in their thirties voted (compared to 67% and 78%, respectively, in 1967). In the twenty-third election for the Upper House in 2013, only 33% voters in their twenties and 44% voters in their thirties voted. See the website for the Ministry of Internal Affairs and Communications on elections, http://www.soumu.go.jp/senkyo/senkyo_s/news/sonota/nendaibetu/ (accessed 5 September 2015).

46. In a gathering of the so-called Culture and Art Discussion Group (*Bunka Geijutsu Konwakai*), organized by junior lawmakers in the LDP on 25 June 2015, the guest speaker and writer Hyakuta Naoki (b. 1956) said, in response to questions about criticism of the government in Okinawa, "Two newspaper agencies in Okinawa have to be destroyed." Following that, Ōnishi Hideo, a Lower House Representative, remarked, "The best way to punish the mass media is to strangle the income from commercials." See http://bylines.news.yahoo.co.jp/watanabeteruhito/20150630–00047120/ (accessed 5 September 2015).

47. The official name of the law is the Act on the Protection of Specially Designated Secrets. According to the *Japan Times* (January 9, 2015), "Under the law, 19 ministries and agencies can designate as state secrets information deemed to be sensitive in the areas of defense, diplomacy, counterterrorism and counterespionage." See http://www.japantimes.co.jp/news/2015/01/09/national/ministries-designated-382-secrets-last-year/#.VerheJ2qqko (accessed September 5. 2015). According to the *Asahi Shinbun* (December 7, 2013), the law "almost limitlessly widens the range of what can be considered confidential." See http://ajw.asahi.com/article/behind_news/politics/AJ201312070057 (accessed 5 September 2015).

48. According to the *Asahi Shinbun* (July 16, 2015), "The ruling coalition rammed its contentious package of security bills through the Lower House on July 16 as most opposition parties boycotted the vote in protest. . . . [T]he legislation is designed to greatly expand the range of overseas activities by the Self-Defense Forces." See http://ajw.asahi.com/article/behind_news/politics/AJ201507160050 (accessed 5 September 2015).

WORKS CITED

Heitzman, Kendall. 2016. "The Rise of Women Writers, the Heisei I-Novel, and the Contemporary *Bundan*." In *Routledge Handbook of Modern Japanese Literature*, edited by Rachael Hutchinson and Leith Morton, 285–98. New York: Routledge.

Isoda Kōichi. 1988 [1978]. *Shisō to shite no Tōkyō: Kindai bungakushiron nōto* ("Tokyo as Modern Thought: Notes on Modern Literary History"). Tokyo: Kokubunsha.

Nagai Kafū, 1986 [1910]. "Denzūin." In *Kafū zuihitsushū* jō ("Kafū's collected essays, Part One"). Tokyo: Iwanami Shoten.

Nakajima Kyōko. 2010. *Kankonsōsai* ("Coming of age, Wedding, Funeral, Festival"). Tokyo: Chikuma Shobō.

———. 2011 [2010]. *Heisei daikazoku* ("The Big Heisei Family"). Tokyo: Shūeisha.

———. 2014a [2003]. *FUTON*. Tokyo: Kōdansha.

———. 2014b [2012]. *Chiisai o-uchi* ("The Little House"). Tokyo: Bungei Shunjū.

———. 2014c. *Hanamomo mimomo* ("The Hanamomo Tenant Apartment Building"). Tokyo: Chūō Kōron Shinsha.
———. 2014d. *Tōkyō kankō* ("Tokyo Sightseeing"). Tokyo: Shūeisha.
———. 2014e. *"Senzen to iu jidai"* ("In an Age Called 'Prewar'"). *Asahi Shinbun*, August 8.
Okuizumi Hikari. 2014. *Tōkyō jijōden* ("An Autobiography of Tokyo"). Tokyo: Shūeisha.
Sakaguchi Ango. 1989–1991. *Hakuchi* ("The Idiot"). In *Sakaguchi Ango Zenshū* 4. Tokyo: Chikuma Shobō.
Sand, Jordan. 2013. *Tokyo Vernacular: Common Spaces, Local Histories, Found Objects*. Berkeley: University of California Press.
Seidensticker, Edward. 1983. *Low City, High City: Tokyo from Edo to the Earthquake*. New York: Knopf.
Tayama Katai. 1981. *The Quilt and Other Stories*. Translated by Kenneth G. Henshall. Tokyo: University of Tokyo Press.
———. 1983 [1981]. *Tōkyō no sanjūnen* ("Thirty Years in Tokyo"). Tokyo: Iwanami Shoten.
———. 1987 [1917]. *Literary Life in Tōkyō 1885–1915*. Translated by Kenneth G. Henshall. Leiden: E.J. Brill.
———. 2001 [1907]. *Futon* ("The Quilt"). In *Meiji no bungaku* vol. 23, edited by Tsubouchi Yūzō. Tokyo: Chikuma Shobō.
Uchida Muneharu. 2013. *Mizu ga oshiete kureru Tōkyō no bichikei sanpo* ("Tokyo Detailed Topographical Walks—What Water Shows Us"). Tokyo: Jitsugyō Nihonsha.
Yiu, Angela, ed. 2013. *Three-Dimensional Reading: Stories of Time and Space in Japanese Modernist Fiction, 1911–1932*. Honolulu: University of Hawai'i Press.

Chapter Eight

The Child of Memory

Cityscapes in Tsushima Yūko's Short Fiction of the 1980s

Eve Zimmerman

Yōko, the central character in Tsushima Yūko's story "Fusehime" ("Princess Fuse"), feels an eerie sensation when she visits a tailor's shop in her old neighborhood that looks exactly the way it did when she was a child.

> It was a neighborhood with many old houses, but if you compared it to the days when Yōko lived there with her mother, many of the shops along the main street had been renovated with exteriors of loud colors and she didn't recognize them. The area had more buildings than before, including some large condos that were under construction. The electric tram that had run through the street had disappeared when Yōko was in high school along with the wires and the rails, and a bus had taken its place. Although Yōko had a hard time recalling the electric tram, Akashi's shop looked so much the same that it gave her a creepy feeling, the exterior, the illegible tin sign with its flaking paint, all looked as if nothing had changed. (1984a, 24–25)

The description of the cityscape is puzzling. It is neither familiar nor has it been completely transformed, a neighborhood with many old houses but unrecognizable storefronts, where new buildings have risen but others are still under construction, where Yōko retains only a shred of memory of the old electric tram. Oddly, the one remaining shop that retains its role from the past, Akashi's tailor shop, does not provoke nostalgia in Yōko but rather a sense of unease. As she moves to the back of the shop and peers into the living quarters, Yōko's sense of unease turns to a feeling of resentment when she realizes that the interior also retains its original appearance. However, Yōko cannot access the origin of her own feelings: "she couldn't possibly put the past into words" (Ibid., 28). In story after story featuring a single mother told from the viewpoint of a character either in the first- or third-person in what is commonly called the *shishōsetsu* ("I-novel"), or semi-autobiographical narrative form, Tsushima creates passive subjects who seem at the mercy of a cityscape that proves subtly disorienting; cut off from the recourse of nostalgia, they also seem unable to access memory in concrete, reliable form.[1] At the same time, Tsushima harnesses the very passivity of her subjects, turning their dreams and visions into a mode of alterity that challenges the pragmatism of Japan's "bubble era."

Yōko's reaction to her old neighborhood seems commensurate with the rate of change that was occurring in Tokyo in the 1980s. Urban historians writing about Tokyo in that decade emphasize the breakneck speed of urban development.[2] Machimura Takashi, for example, traces the speed of change in the 1980s to the policies of Prime Minister Nakasone (b. 1918) who, pressed by trade conflicts with the United States, turned to urban redevelopment to stimulate domestic demand and attract transnational investors. The city would be turned into a "frontier for economic development" as Nakasone opened the door to "coalitions" or loosely organized bodies comprised of public institutions and private corporations (1993, 122). Through provisions such as reduced taxes and subsidies, corporations invested private capital in government land, old estates, and unused manufacturing sites to expand floor space upwards and outwards. Government emphasis on the development of "multi-core" centers within Tokyo also led to a wide dispersion of radical redevelopment that affected more residents than development confined to the city center. As a result, social tensions broke out between coalitions and residents when land prices skyrocketed and many could no longer afford to live in the neighborhoods where they were born. Writing in 1993, a decade after Tsushima published "Fusehime," Machimura lamented the lack of resistance at the grassroots level, asking plaintively, "Will Tokyo continue to take a course to becoming a giant growth machine solely for processing global capital and information?" (Ibid., 127).

MAPPING TOKYO: AN APPROACH TO TSUSHIMA

Japanese critics who were contemporaries of Tsushima tend to locate her oeuvre within the domestic sphere of home and family, creatively parsing Tsushima's methods for subverting Japan's patriarchal family system or emptying out notions of maternal instinct.[3] Others read in a more biologically reductive fashion. In an essay on Tsushima's collection of stories, *Hikari no ryōbun* ("The Domain of Light," 1979), Kawamura Minato, for example, asserts that the first-person narrator is "like a girl (*shōjo*) learning about sex" and that her apartment is a womb within which she floats (1993, 248). Even Yonoha Keiko, an avowedly feminist critic, focuses on the "human relationships" in Tsushima's fiction, pointing to examples of how the writer subtly assigns power to women within those relationships (1989, 341). Miura Masashi, a critic who has been aligned with postmodern circles, strives to avoid the pitfalls of thematic reading, but he too writes that "there is no reality in Tsushima's fiction beyond psychological reality," and that by focusing on family relationships, Tsushima exposes the Japanese family system to be nothing but a mental construct (1988, 440–44).

By limiting our reading to the interiorized realm of the womb/apartment, we do Tsushima's fiction a disservice. As Livia Monnet suggests, a truly feminist reading demands that attention be paid to the broader historical and cultural context of Tsushima's fiction and to her particular epistemological stance (1996, 383–84). Given the transformations that were occurring in the built environment in Japan in the late 1970s and 1980s, we might better read Tsushima for the ways that she mapped the world outside the realm of the womb-like apartment. Tsushima's depiction of space makes for a productive contrast with another intellectual working in the mid-1980s, the "spatial anthropologist" Jinnai Hidenobu. In 1985, Jinnai published an influential book titled *Tōkyō no kūkan jinruigaku* (1985, trans. *Tokyo: A Spatial Anthropology*, 1995). To Jinnai, modern city planners were in the process of destroying the vestiges of the old Edo, a city that had been built on water and hilly terrain and still lay sometimes hidden, sometimes visible, beneath the structures of contemporary Tokyo. In the same way that Tsushima's characters view the city on foot, Jinnai suggests that one must walk through Tokyo in order to glimpse the still vibrant remnants of the old city, which testify to the environmental sensitivity of the early urban developers.

> Now look at Tokyo. From the standpoint of modern rationalism, with its reverence for clarity, it is truly difficult to form an overall picture of Tokyo's urban space. Increasingly, there are few tasteful old buildings, and the streets and neighborhoods are losing their character. And yet, walking the streets of the city, one is treated to repeated changes in the cityscape. There is unexpected variety in the topography, with the high city's hills and cliffs, widening roads, shrine groves, and large, verdant estates; and the low city's canals and bridges, alleyways and storefront planter pots, and crowded entertainment centers. For the walker in Tokyo, the unexpected is always waiting. Tokyo may not have the old buildings of New York, but each place evokes a distinctive atmosphere nurtured over a long history: this makes Tokyo what it is. (1995, 2)

Jinnai makes an appeal to save the distinctive atmosphere of Tokyo by recognizing the city's many layers, protecting the integrity of old neighborhoods, and practicing a localized form of city planning that honors Tokyo's geographical and cultural idiosyncrasies. His goal in *Tokyo: A Spatial Anthropology* is to educate the reader before it is too late.

In contrast to Jinnai, Tsushima does not overtly assert a preservationist stance nor express cultural nostalgia. Rather, she records detailed observations in order to make a record of loss. As she writes about her own neighborhood of Hon-komagome, a place filled with old people, cats, and funerals, "Something ended long ago, now you wait for it to vanish entirely. . . . it's a town with that kind of atmosphere" (1982, 160). In order to explore Tsushima's interest in spaces and things that have ended but leave a vestige behind, I turn to Pierre Nora's concept of the "memory site." As Nora suggests in *Les Lieux de Mémoire* (1984–92, trans. *Realms of Memory: Rethinking the French Past*, 1996–98), "memory sites" are symbolic locations where a society seeks out continuity with a vanishing past:

> Our curiosity about the places in which memory is crystallized, in which it finds refuge, is associated with this specific moment in French history, a turning point in which a sense of rupture with the past is inextricably bound up with a sense that a rift has occurred in memory. But that rift has stirred memory sufficiently to raise the question of its embodiment: there are sites, *lieux de mémoire*, in which a residual sense of continuity remains. *Lieux de mémoire* exist because there are no longer any *milieux de mémoire*, settings in which memory is a real part of everyday experience. (1996 [1992], 1)

To Nora, the emergence of a memory site requires two pre-conditions: first, a dislocation in history, and second, the perception that a rift in memory has occurred. By requiring these distinct conditions, Nora, too, shows a fascination with endings that leave traces behind. More importantly, he provides a route out of reflexive cultural nostalgia, stressing the social functions of memory. Building on Nora's work, Andreas Huyssen also stresses the social aspects of memory when he coins the phrase "lived memory," which he defines in the following terms: "Lived memory is active, alive, embodied in the social—that is, in individuals, groups, nations and regions. These are the memories that are needed to construct different local futures in a global world" (2003, 28).

Through her privileging of spaces populated by cats and old people, Tsushima creates a local topography that is rooted in urban reality but also suggests a shadow realm. Indeed, Tsushima's work navigates a path through Japan's explosive growth of the 1980s, on the one hand, and, on the other, what Jordan Sand describes in *Tokyo Vernacular* as informal grass-roots movements that sought to retain a sense of belonging within existing or imagined local neighborhoods and alternative spaces (2013, 54–87). The resulting dissonance between these poles results in the mild vertigo that Tsushima's characters experience as they wander the city, wondering at the state of their environment. In the following pages, I turn to three of Tsushima's stories written in the early 1980s in order to test the link between Tsushima's private vision and the collective experience of city dwellers in the decade of high growth.[4] But before turning to Tsushima's fiction, I touch on a few salient facts of her life and her writing, situating her within the context of the literary world of the 1970s and 1980s, decades that seemed to be immeasurably quieter than the decade that had preceded them.

TRACING A LIFE, A DEATH

In Japan and abroad, obituaries of Tsushima Yūko (1947–2016) did not fail to mention her father, the writer Dazai Osamu (1909–1948), who became famous in the postwar period for advocating a philosophy of "decadence" and who committed suicide with a lover in the Tamagawa River in Tokyo when Tsushima was barely a year old ("Fuhō sakka no Tsushima Yūko-san" 2016). Ironically, Tsushima measured her own accomplishments in terms of the distance she achieved from her tortured father, once stating, "I wasn't the child of a criminal but I felt that way and I couldn't bear it. . . . Through writing, I intended to turn the secrets that clung to me into things that belonged to no one in particular" (1989, 344–45). That Tsushima was discussing her own unique set of family circumstances is clear, but in a subsequent piece she ascribed her interest in criminality to the state of early postwar Japan, remembering adults warning children of dangerous veterans who wandered the city like ghosts, committing horrendous crimes (Ibid., 13). The question of whether Tsushima wrote semi-autobiographical fiction to exorcise the hauntings of a war that had shaken Japan to its very foundations is beyond the scope of this chapter, but she was nevertheless prolific, publishing at least one volume of fiction or non-fiction every year between 1971 and 2016. More importantly, Tsushima added a distinctive and original voice to postwar Japanese literary culture and paved the way for the explosion in the publication of writing by women in the last two decades.

Born in Mitaka, a suburb to the west of central Tokyo, Tsushima moved at age one with her mother and her older brother and sister to the Mukōgaoka area of Hon-komagome in Tokyo's Bunkyō Ward, a hilly northern area of the city that remains rather isolated due to its lack of a train station. Although it is the site of one of the University of Tokyo campuses, according to Tsushima "it is a boring neighborhood so quiet that it puts young people to sleep" (1982, 160). For much of her life, Tsushima lived within a short distance of the "old house" in Mukōgaoka, which her uncle had lent to her family in 1949 after Dazai's suicide. Tsushima's family life continued to be marked by loss. In 1958 the family moved to a newly built house that was adjacent to Rikugien, an Edo-period estate in Hon-komagome that had been turned into a strolling garden. Within two years, Tsushima's sixteen-year-old brother, who had Down's syndrome, died of pneumonia. During her primary and secondary school years, Tsushima attended Shirayuri Girls' School in

Tokyo, later matriculating at and graduating from Shirayuri College in 1969. From there she enrolled in Meiji University with the intention of pursuing a Master's degree in English literature. However, classes were often cancelled because of student protests and she withdrew from school in 1971. Over the next five years, Tsushima married and had two children, a daughter with her husband and, when her marriage fell apart in 1976, a son with a married lover. Like her mother, she raised her children alone, only to be visited by tragedy again in 1985 when her son, Daimu, died suddenly from an asthma attack, an event that Tsushima later made reference to in fiction. In February 2016, still engaged in her long and productive career, Tsushima herself succumbed to lung cancer at the relatively young age of 68.[5]

THE POWER OF WORDS

Tsushima experienced success as a writer early in her career. In 1967, before she graduated from college, she published her first story in *Bungei Shuto* ("Literary Metropolis"), a literary journal with its own coterie of writers. In subsequent years, Tsushima received many of the top literary prizes in Japan, including ones named after Japan's most famous writers: the Kawabata Yasunari Prize for "Dannmari-ichi" (trans. "Silent Traders," 1988) in 1982 and the Tanizaki Jun'ichirō Prize for *Hi no yama—yamazaru ki* ("Mountain of Fire: The Wild Monkey's Account") in 1998.[6] In addition to fiction, Tsushima also published literary criticism as well as essays on social and cultural issues of the day. English-language translations of Tsushima's work include *The Shooting Gallery*, a volume of short stories, and three novels–*Chōji* (1978, trans. *Child of Fortune*, 1983), *Yama o hashiru onna* (1980, trans. *Woman Running in the Mountains*, 1991) and *Warai ōkami* (2000, trans. *Laughing Wolf*, 2011).

A highly successful writer who moved about freely in Tokyo literary circles, Tsushima nevertheless identified with cultures that originated on the margins of Japanese society, whether construed in linguistic, geographic, or even culinary terms. Less often mentioned in the obituaries is Tsushima's mother, Michiko, who raised Tsushima and her two siblings in Tokyo, but who Tsushima once described as "a woman from the mountains."[7] That Tsushima would describe her mother's origins in terms of a rural place is not surprising given the fact that many Japanese trace their origins to a *kokyō* or ancestral home, but her mother's habit of "taking honeycomb directly from the hive and sautéing it in butter" falls outside the rubric of everyday Tokyo cuisine. Rather, it suggests remnants of Japanese cultural practices of the northern countryside where historically life had been a struggle for survival. Tsushima also traces her interest in folk culture back to stories that her mother told her, stories of marriages between human beings and animals, and of mysterious women who raised children alone in the mountains.

Instead of arising from nostalgia for a simple countryside home, however, Tsushima's interest in folk culture needs to be put within the context of her generation of Japanese writers who came of age at the end of the idealistic and highly politicized 1960s and who experienced the first decades of Japan's high growth. In reaction to both the failure of the leftist movement against re-ratification of the U.S.-Japan Security Pact in 1960 and the rise of what historians label "Japan Inc.," Tsushima espoused an interest in marginalized forms that seeped into mainstream Japanese life and made their presence felt (Gordon 2009). The critic Kawamura Jirō identifies in Tsushima's work an underlying current of dreams and images that distorts realism, transforming the reader's perception of the "common sense everyday" (1991, 220). In an essay written in 1982 anticipating what kind of fiction would be written in the 1980s, Tsushima focuses on her writing method in a discussion of the "identity" of writers in her cohort. Having read Freud, she suggests that she—and, by extension, her generation—values "not the flow of conscious ideas," but rather the power of the unconscious. Consequently, she and others attempt to express that value in their work. Implying a sharp contrast with the cerebral (and politically engaged) writers of the immediate postwar period, Tsushima states her preference for "fictions that don't think" (*kangaenai shōsetsu*) (1982, 31–32).

Moving further into the 1980s, Tsushima expanded her interest in the unconscious to include Japanese pre-modern literary genres such as *setsuwa* (didactic Buddhist tales) and *fudoki* (gazetteers that told in maps and words the stories of famous travel destinations), the Ainu song cycles or *yukar*, and, in later years, ethnic Taiwanese folk culture. In pursuit of such marginalized forms, Tsushima identified an uncanny otherness that haunts modern life and reasserts its presence in spite of the predominance of a market-driven capitalist system.[8] At the same time, she suggested that such vanishing forms of culture could be reinvested with meaning and potentially transform modern paradigms of gender and sexual identity.[9]

THE HOUSE ON THE CUL-DE-SAC

The extent to which Tsushima viewed writing as an expression of the unconscious directly informs her treatment of urban space in three stories that date to the early 1980s. "Maboroshi" ("Phantom," 1984), a story told from the perspective of a grown daughter, revolves around the childhood memory of an "old house" at the end of a cul-de-sac, where the grown daughter's single mother had once fled with her three children after the death of her husband—whether in an accident or by his own hand, we do not learn.[10] In this story, the memory site is imbricated with the woman's nine-year-old self, a being who retains a ferocious hold on the grown woman's memory. The plot of "Maboroshi" is mapped out through the device of three dwellings where the daughter, now a young single mother herself, has lived or currently lives: the apartment, the mother's house, and the "old house" on the cul-de-sac. The first of these is the rickety apartment building where the grown daughter lives with her two children by different men. Set in a dank alleyway in the city, the apartment, as the grown woman notes, receives direct sunlight for no more than an hour each day. The air is stagnant, an appropriate metaphor for her relationship with the father of her second child, a married man who will never leave his wife and is in the process of abandoning her. The children suffer from ill health brought on by their cramped, unhealthy living conditions.

During the New Year's holiday, the grown daughter visits the second dwelling in the story, the house where the mother still lives. Built in a newly created residential area of Tokyo in the 1950s, when the daughter was a girl of ten, the house contains many rooms and it reflects the family's hopes for upward mobility at the time. After years of domestic misery, which had begun when the father died, the mother had had high hopes for the family in the new house. Instead of marking the end of the family's troubles, however, the mother's new house merely increased their misery. In the beautiful new house, the family's only son was diagnosed with an intellectual disability and his sisters were told that they should never have children. A year later the brother died of pneumonia, the mother sank into a long period of mourning, and, finally, the elder sister left home for good. In subsequent years, the mother's "new house" falls into neglect and disrepair.

The third dwelling, the old house on the cul-de-sac, can only be accessed in memory and in visions, as we shall soon see. However, even before the grown daughter has visions of the old house, we learn that she has had a recurring dream about the mother's house. In the dream, the daughter passes by her mother's house only to see that it has been razed to the ground, leaving a gaping hole. The destruction of the mother's house unfolds in different scenarios in the dream that share two constant elements: the daughter never approaches the mother's house and, as the men work around her, the mother stands in the garden staring mournfully into a broken-down, old washing machine. The daughter realizes that she feels resentment toward the house and she wonders if she perhaps is sharing one of her mother's dreams. But she concludes that she is the sole dreamer and she asks herself, "shouldn't it be my mother wondering, 'why, oh why is this house the only thing left?'" (Tsushima 1984b, 45).

The key to the dream about the mother's house is soon revealed: once the mother's house disappears, the old house on the cul-de-sac returns. The grown daughter recounts a detailed description of the old house:

> Until they built the new house, they had lived in a small house in an old neighborhood close to central Tokyo, which lay at the very end of a cul-de-sac. . . it had a four-and-a-half-mat tearoom, a six-mat room, and a small Western-style room with a bay window. We lived there from the time I was a baby of one until I grew into a girl of ten who had gotten taller than my own mother. (Ibid., 43)[11]

In the house on the cul-de-sac, the family had eked out a living, trying to cope with the intellectually disabled brother who would often get lost on his way home at night. But to the young woman, the house served as a refuge where the mother and her children had "rolled like animals on fire into the first puddle of water that they spied" (Ibid.).

The vision of the old house on the cul-de-sac appears to the daughter on New Year's Day after she and her children have spent the holiday with her mother. On the way home, the daughter is suddenly visited by a *maboroshi*, a vivid phantom of the past, and she can see herself again as a girl, aged nine, standing in the city street at night, near the old house on the cul-de-sac:

> I coughed and stopped in my tracks. I noticed that I was standing in a place that looked identical to the cul-de-sac where the old house had once stood. I opened my mouth and looked around. A branch extending from a tree behind a wall cast a dark shadow on the ground, and a cat stood on the lid of a large plastic bucket left outside a nearby apartment, staring in our direction. Windows on either side of us cast a faint light. And then I saw my mother, my brother and me from behind, walking toward our old house at the end of the cul-de-sac in the gloom. How many times, in the dead of night, had we walked home this way? All three of us were exhausted, looking down, as if we were submerged in deep water. (Ibid., 58)

As past and present collapse into one another, and all three of the family members look down in exhaustion, feeling as if they are in deep water, the vision moves inside the house:

> My mother had forgotten her hunger and my own, and sat glaring at a point on the tatami by her knees. Neither my sister nor I could say a word to her. We couldn't get up and we couldn't go to sleep. My mother wasn't grieving; she was confronting her searing feelings of anger at her own loneliness. The house was dark inside and out, and I stared down at the tatami just like my mother. (Ibid., 60)

Far from generating nostalgia, the vision is stark in its outlines. The grown woman shares her mother's anger toward a society that has forced them onto its margins and where, under a broken patriarchal family system, women alone provide shelter and food for their children. Certainly, the grown daughter identifies with the mother's suffering because she, too, is in the process of being abandoned by a man. In sum, the return of the nine-year-old girl in the vision tells the grown woman that her own visions of the happy family had always been an illusion or *maboroshi*. So, too, were her dreams of having a life with a man who will not leave his wife. Standing at the bottom of the rickety staircase of her apartment, at the urging of her daughter, the woman turns to watch a comedy show on television through her neighbors' curtains. Peering from across the way, the two can just see a family (mother, father and two children) gathered around a flickering television screen. The first "phantom" of the story, the grown daughter's vision of the cul-de-sac, has been replaced by another *maboroshi*: the nuclear family clustered around the television screen, a mediator of dreams. Given that the nuclear family—with the father at work and the mother at home raising children—was seen as the ideal unit for rebuilding the nation in the aftermath of the war, it is no surprise that the single mother and daughter stand outside in the night. The woman laughs at the *maboroshi* in the lighted room and turns to enter the door of her own apartment where she now seems to better comprehend the coordinates of her own life.

The grown daughter has neither a memory nor a dream about the cul-de-sac. Rather, Tsushima uses the word *maboroshi*, which might be translated as a "vision" or a "phantom." In quite literal terms, *maboroshi* occurs when "[t]he form of something that doesn't exist seems to appear in reality."[12] The vision of the cul-de-sac represents simultaneity at work, a sign that, just beyond the delineations of the visible, another kind of time still flows—and the traces of Jinnai's "distinctive atmosphere" linger. The vividness of the image reflects the importance of retaining the house, both the refuge where the mother and children had fled and the site of the girl's trauma when she felt the mother's rage. Rather than stand for any idealized Japanese family system, it is a site where the affective bonds of family are forged through visceral experience and burned into the psyche. The configuration of an intimate space (the house itself is remembered in loving detail) darkly echoes Jordan Sand's discussion of preservation movements in Tokyo in the 1980s when homeowners in Yanesen—three distinct neighborhoods that coalesced into an imagined "Shitamachi" (downtown) neighborhood—realized that the value of their old houses in the neighborhoods surpassed sheer monetary value (2013, 54–60). Sand explains: "The negative real estate value of Yanesen's old houses was counterbalanced by their value in terms of what legal scholar Carol Rose has called 'un-real real estate' or 'illusory property': a right claimed by virtue of the fact that the site can be seen" (2013, 78). Through her vision in the city street, the grown daughter, too, stumbles across the value of the old house, revisiting the sense of painful connection that she had once experienced there.

"Maboroshi" taps into the collective experience of the city dweller in the decades of high growth. Through the destruction of the mother's "new house" in the grown daughter's dream, Tsushima makes a larger historical point about her mother's willful optimism, which blinded the mother to the fact that dreams of upward mobility and prosperity are essentially triangulated, restlessly moving from one object to the next, and thus unresolved. The mother had imagined that the new house would allow the family to forget the past, but in fact the move to the new house hastened—even caused—the brother's death. Now, in the grown daughter's dream, the mother stands in the garden, seeming to suffer from amnesia as she stares blankly into the old washing machine, a symbol of domestic productivity and efficiency in the 1950s. In the same way that the mother clings to her illusions, Tsushima suggests, so too did an entire generation believe in the myth of economic development, in building houses "with many rooms." To Tsushima, a belief in economic prosperity simply served as a means to sublimate personal (and collective) dislocation in a myth of material success. And it is the grown daughter who must carry the psychic burden of the dream that the mother's generation has blocked.

Tsushima first published "Maboroshi" in 1980 in the literary journal *Sakuhin* ("Work") as Japan began to ride a wave of economic development and urban restructuring in the aftermath of the financial crises of the late 1970s. Her work, rooted in observation of a disjunction between generations, reflects what the bubble economy presaged for the built environment in 1980s Tokyo. As we have seen, Machimura Takashi, writing in 1993, describes how the accumulation of capital wrought significant changes in the lives of city residents. Those with fewer financial resources, for example, were driven out of the city as private-public coalitions prepared the ground for huge urban-redevelopment projects. Tsushima records the other side of the story: what was lost in affective and psychological terms as the well-to-do bought into a national agenda that was geared toward the relentless pursuit of prosperity.

As the 1980s progress, Tsushima widens her focus from the old neighborhood to identify other liminal spaces in the city that offer inhabitants intangible forms of belonging. Like the neighborhood of Mukōgaoka, Tsushima accords these liminal spaces different ontological weight and posits a ghostly interface between the shiny new cityscape and a realm that can best be described as a "memory site"—a layer of myths and cultural memory, or what Nora calls "Möbius strips, endless rounds of the collective and the individual, the prosaic and the sacred, the immutable and the fleeting" (1996 [1992], 15). Although Tsushima's single mothers live in generic apartment buildings, they are fascinated and repelled by shadowy spaces, an alleyway, a park or a thicket behind a house. In "Kikumushi" (1983, trans. "Chrysanthemum Beetle," 1988), for example, the main character visits a friend who lives by a park and she notes the prevalence of desiccated insect bodies that collect in the light fixtures. These spark memories of her adolescence, her fascination with the insect world, and the recounting of a traditional folk tale.

In "Yokushitsu" (1984, trans. "The Bath," 1993), the woman returns to her mother's house only to be startled by the sight of a lizard clinging to the outside of the bathroom window, which revives a series of dreams she once had about her dead brother pressing his pale face against the glass. Cats and dogs populate these stories, serving as avatars that carry news between this world and the next. Like an ethnographer, Tsushima sketches in the shadowy spaces of the city where the remnants of old tales and superstitions at once give shape to and provoke wonder in her characters' lives.

THE WOOD

Perhaps Tsushima's most productive vision of a *lieu de mémoire* appears in the short story "Danmari-ichi" (1984, trans. "Silent Traders," 1988). Within this story, personal memories spread out like ripples over the surface of a pond, coming to represent the memory of the collective. As in "Maboroshi," the protagonist of the story is a single mother struggling to make a life in the city. The father of the younger child, a boy, has left her to return to his wife and his legitimate children. The central locus of the story is Rikugien, the Edo-period garden in northern Tokyo. In a series of memories from her childhood, during which she lived with her mother in the shadow of Rikugien, and in her experiences in the present, the young woman contemplates her long relationship with the park.

"Danmari-ichi" opens with the line, "There was a cat in the wood" (1988b [1984], 35). However, the next few lines of the story qualify this seemingly commonplace observation. First, the narrator attempts to justify her agitated reaction at the sight of a house cat by embedding "cat" in a broader taxonomy of wild cats that would naturally provoke fear: "Not such an odd thing, really: wildcats, pumas and lions all come from the same family and even a tabby shouldn't be out of place" (Ibid.). And, second, the narrator attempts to compensate for the use of the word "woods" to describe the sedate geography of the strolling garden:

> When I say "wood," I'm talking about Rikugien, an Edo-period landscape garden in my neighborhood. Perhaps "wood" isn't quite the right word, but the old park's trees—relics of the past amid the city's modern buildings—are so overgrown that the pathways skirting its walls are dark and forbidding even by day. It does give one the impression of a wood, there's no other word for it. (Ibid.)

The narrator's fears of the park are heightened by her intuition that she and the park exist in an antagonistic relation to each other: when the kitten "bristles and glares" in her direction, she feels it as a direct slight.

When the narrator visits the park one day with her own children, memories of the park begin to return to her in a limited form. Soon after her brother died of pneumonia, she returned home one day to find that the family's rambunctious dog had disappeared. Her mother finally confessed that she had thrown the noisy puppy over the walls of Rikugien. From that moment on, the young woman began to nurse a fantasy that the puppy had transformed into another being inside the park and the place filled her with fear: "it was the domain of the dog abandoned by my mother" (Ibid., 39). In the opening of the story, the woman's young son crawls into the bushes in pursuit of a wild kitten and he cannot extricate himself. Although the woman realizes that she should brush off fears of a mere kitten and retrieve her son, she sends her daughter in after the boy. It seems that her fears of the park have transformed her, too, into a mother who would abandon her own children to the darkness. As the park repels and attracts the young woman, it seems to emanate a malevolent power that influences events in the young woman's life.

One final memory further suggests the central role that the park plays in the woman's consciousness. When she was a ten-year-old girl, the woman and her friends buried a time capsule with handwritten notes under a knoll by the tallest pine tree in the garden. Now, she cannot find the pine tree or the knoll and she is not even certain if the memory of the time capsule is accurate. Within the park, her memory becomes skewed and unreliable. Through this incident, the narrator dismisses a nostalgic view of her past. Rather than serve as a map to her own personal history, the park destabilizes the authority of the narrator, transforming her into an adolescent girl seeking to make sense of her own personal coordinates.

By disrupting the park as the source of personal memory, Tsushima creates a *lieu de mémoire*, thereby linking the park to the collective memory of an entire community of city dwellers. On that first visit to Rikugien, when the woman and her children spy a number of stray cats in the bushes, the woman imagines that at night the cats find food on one of the verandas of the apartments that encircle the park. There, in return for food, the cats serve as fathers to any child that needs one. Such fantasies jog her memory of an old story about "silent traders" who would come down from the mountains to exchange goods with the inhabitants of farming villages in the deep north.[13] The woman imagines that she, too, will enter into an exchange with the cats for the sake of her children.

After her realization, the woman's psychic transformation proceeds apace and she openly identifies more and more with the abandoned animals that dwell within the forest. Rather than fear the forest, the woman has crossed to the other side, to the space where "discarded things"—the puppy, her children, herself—start a new life and enter into a transactional relationship with human society. By doing so, she fills up the terrifying space of the forest, and makes up for the absence of father figures in the lives of her children. She also suspects that her children are ahead of her. "Perhaps my children really have begun dealings with a cat who lives in the wood" (Ibid., 44). By turning the cats into fathers who will claim any child as their own, Tsushima transcends the central role that a patriarchal system has played in modern Japanese culture, a system in which children born outside of marriage are denigrated and ignored. The longing for "father," a fixed term in the national imaginary, is simply another *maboroshi*: any being will do.

Tsushima extends the metaphor of silent trading, expanding upon the story of one mother and her children to represent the city dwellers of the 1980s, poised on the edge of dramatic change, but still gazing at the liminal spaces of the culture. By living next to the park, the woman's family creates new life for itself:

> I am coming to understand that there was nothing extraordinary in striking such a silent bargain for survival. People trying to survive—myself, my mother, and my children, for example—can take some comfort in living beside a wood. We toss various things in there and tell ourselves that we haven't thrown them away, we've set them free in another world, and then we picture the unknown woodland to ourselves and shudder with fear or sigh fondly. Meanwhile the creatures multiplying there gaze stealthily at the human world outside; at least I've yet to hear of anything attacking from the wood. (1988b [1984], 44)

At first, we may be tempted to read this dream as a nostalgic recycling of early modern rural myths in which the city stands as the source of corruption and the rural setting as home. But how does one "sigh fondly" for a place one does not know (here Tsushima uses the word "natsukashii" in Japanese)? Instead of nostalgia for the past, Tsushima suggests a model for what Andreas Huyssen describes as nostalgia for the future: "memories that are needed to construct different local futures in a global world" (2003, 28). The existence of the wood within the city reflects the fact that apartment dwellers, too, need to actively resist the social institutions, practices and places that have failed them. The narrator notes that even in the new buildings, the verandas face the wood, thus becoming conduits between this world and that world. The silence between the trading partners arises from their recognition of their mutual dependence, a compact that can only be made within the shadows.

THE TAILOR'S SHOP

In the last story, "Fusehime," quoted at the beginning of this chapter, Tsushima generalizes from the memory site of the old neighborhood to encompass an entire city that seems intent on erasing its past. "Fusehime" tells the story of Yōko, a single mother with two children, who has recently taken up with Akashi, an older man whom she has known since childhood. The story opens in the present outside a bar in a narrow alleyway alongside the Yamanote line railroad tracks where Yōko and Akashi have met for a drink.[14] Although Yōko and Akashi's location is not identified, the story takes place in a neighborhood that resembles Hon-komagome with a few large houses and inns untouched by development. Emerging from the bar, Yōko, a single mother with two children, pauses to pet a puppy, remembering her daughter's requests for a dog. As in "Danmari-ichi," the animal seems to stare back resentfully at Yōko, startling her, as if she had done something wrong. Eventually she and Akashi emerge from the alleyway and find themselves on the embankment that runs along the tracks. There Yōko notes how much colder the wind has become since the construction of a tall building nearby. Finally, the two duck into an inn where they will spend a few hours making love. From that point on, the action of the story unfolds in conversations with Akashi and in memories of the couple's long and tangled relationship.

In "Fusehime" Tsushima sets up a contrast between the vestiges of old Tokyo with its networks of alleyways, bars and inns—where one can rent a room by the hour—and the new Tokyo of towering, isolated structures. In Akashi and Yōko's first meandering walk through the city, Tsushima equates their exploration of the city's streets with a form of free-floating eroticism that appears in pockets of the city's past. In her non-fiction study of her own neighborhood, she writes in similar terms about Shinmeichō, or Hon-komagome go-chōme, the area which once served in the pre-modern period as a red-light district:

> Since the birth of my children, I've long felt a connection to Hon-komagome go-chōme, or the area that's called Shinmeichō, a densely packed area at the bottom of the hill, which was once a commercial hub. Even today you can hear the sound of a shamisen reverberating in the afternoon, and the area is full of cheap rooms and small bars. For seven years, I took my children to a nursery school there. (1982, 160)[15]

While I do not mean to suggest that Tsushima's fiction and her non-fiction are interchangeable, it is nevertheless striking that Yōko and Akashi's love affair, a relationship that is resurrected from the past, unfolds in the older corners of the contemporary city. Indeed, we might read Yōko's renewed affair with Akashi as a metaphor for the city dweller's deep sense of connection to places of the past, a hedge against life in an era of accelerated change.

Consisting of interwoven past and present narrative threads, "Fusehime" reveals that what draws Yōko and Akashi back together in the present is the old neighborhood where they grew up. At the same time, Tsushima scrupulously avoids a nostalgic vision of the past in "Fusehime." When Yōko's daughter turned nine, Yōko had been struck by an urge to see what had happened to Akashi, her first love. Yōko and Akashi had first met when she was a ten-year-old girl and when Akashi, fifteen years her senior, was striking out on his own as a freelance photographer. Growing obsessed with Akashi, Yōko began to trail him around the old neighborhood where they both lived. Eventually, Akashi's mother barred Yōko from the house and she haunted the alleyway behind the tailor's shop. One day, growing frustrated by the girl's persistence, Akashi knocked Yōko down in the street, giving her a bloody nose. Shocked by the rejection, Yōko went to her mother and reported that Akashi had sexually assaulted her. The police took him in for questioning and, although Akashi was not charged with a crime, from that moment on he refused to see Yōko again. Much later, after his own marriage failed, he reappeared in Yōko's life, asking her if she would begin a relationship with him, but at that point she refused him. Now, after more than a decade apart, they have reunited.

Yōko and Akashi's early relationship unfolded against the backdrop of the city streets of the old neighborhood: the alleyway behind the shop where Yōko watched Akashi enter and leave, the street where he knocked her down, and even the streetcar stop where he would lose Yōko because she could not afford the car fare. The grown Yōko searches for the reason that she was obsessed with Akashi and she concludes that this too was atmospheric; outside her own family, she could "breathe more easily with him" (1984a, 54). Akashi had rejected the usual path of the university graduate; instead, he set up his own photography studio, and roamed the city with his camera on assignments. However, Tsushima's refusal to idealize the past is made clear when the relationship between the adolescent Yōko and the adult Akashi turns violent. As if to reinforce the lack of sentimentality between them, their adult conversations reflect tense negotiation. At the beginning of the story, Yōko complains that her female relatives have accused her of being like an animal for having a child out of wedlock. Akashi, in turn, accuses her:

> "You're the same as you were when you were a kid. Shameless, selfish.... So that's why you're always doing the same thing. Anyone would want to run away."
> "You, too?" Yōko asked. (Ibid., 19–20)

Yōko's question hangs in the air without a response. In his silence, Akashi reveals why he feels ineluctably drawn toward her: she retains her ability to carry through on her desires much in the same manner as she did in the past.

Through Yōko's relatives' description of her as an animal, Tsushima further taps into plebian forms of culture that the old city once produced. The title of the story refers to Takizawa Bakin's (1767–1848) 106-volume chronicle, *Nansō Satomi Hakkenden,* some of which has been translated into English (1814–1842, trans. *The Eight Dogs Chronicles*, 2002). It tells the story of Princess Fuse, a virgin who was forced to marry a dog because of a promise made by her father. After living an unblemished life immersed in the chanting of sutras in a cave, Fusehime commits suicide and in a miraculous act of spontaneous asexual reproduction produces eight dog-princes out of her own dying body. Through Yōko's references to the seemingly endless profusion of animals in the city—her children's pets include a kitten, a hamster, two guinea pigs, a turtle, a hermit crab, a loach, a newt and an earthworm—Tsushima links Yōko with Fusehime, a being who could spontaneously produce life.

"Fusehime," like "Danmari-ichi," uses the trope of the animal to question social practices under a patriarchal family system that was rigidly codified in the early Meiji period (1868–1912). At the end of the story, Yōko remembers a recurring dream in which she becomes Fusehime, the mother of the dog princes, and gives birth to six puppies. Examined more closely, the dream of six babies, two with puppy faces, two with Akashi's features, and two that resemble her own, reveals that Yōko has finally attained a balance between her human and animal selves, her girlhood and adult selves. Notable, too, is the fact that Yōko can reproduce herself. Rather than give sexual agency to the older male, Tsushima explores female desire through the matrix of the city—the streetcar, the tailor's shop, and the surrounding neighborhood. By returning to the tailor's shop and claiming Akashi as her own, Yōko pulls together fragments of herself while still embracing a multiplicity of identities and forms. "Her dream from the old days had finally become reality. Yōko's heart overflowed. Akashi's large hand continued to stroke her head and at his touch, her ecstasy radiated outwards" (Ibid., 69).

Through "fictions that don't think," Tsushima negates a confident belief in narratives of national progress in favor of a collective unconscious that is embodied in the spaces we inhabit and in memory sites that are "no longer quite alive but not yet entirely dead, like shells left on the shore when memory has receded" (Nora 1996 [1992], 7). In the three stories above, Tsushima demonstrates how spaces from the past live on in the psyche, although the visible environment seems irreversibly transformed. In stressing forgotten or repressed spaces, Tsushima suggests a hedge against the excesses of capitalism that were pitching the country into the decade of unparalleled high growth. It should come as no surprise that the grown woman cannot find the time capsule in the woods of Rikugien or that Yōko, when first encountering Akashi, cannot put the past into words. "What had she wanted to talk to him about now that they had met? . . . she couldn't possibly put the past into words" (Ibid., 28). By keeping meaning at bay, Tsushima subsumes the destiny of the city-dweller in the magnitude of the "forest," the large dark space in Tokyo where fluidity enables the modern subject to move beyond the constrictions of gender, family, social class, and even historical era.

Tsushima's strengths as a writer lie in her archaeological instincts. Rather than create fantasy or utopianism, she turns to the world that we know and begins to excavate down layer by layer. Her project is indeed linked with personal memory but cannot be contained by personal memory alone or even by the constraints that pen in the gendered modern subject. The dreamscapes of Tsushima's adult characters—and the circuitous routes they take into the past—represent the city dweller's search for what Jinnai Hidenobu calls "topoi replete with expressions of memory and meaning tied to human life" (1995, 18). Perhaps the best example of how Tsushima's poetics illuminate memory can be seen in her masterpiece "Danmari-ichi." The main character's past is forever obscured in a time capsule under a pine tree in a park that is enclosed by shiny new towers. The grown woman may not be able to access her past in any reliable form, but her long history with the park tethers her to the dark, teeming space in which eventually the psychic tensions of her own life and of her generation can be unleashed, recalibrated, and, to some degree, made legible.

NOTES

1. For a discussion of the semi-autobiographical narrative form that is told from the viewpoint of a single character, whether in the first- or third-person, see Suzuki 1996.
2. For a concise overview of the speed of change in the 1970s, see Waley 2007.
3. Takahashi 1990 is a characteristic essay. Also see Koyama 1994.
4. Although I use the book publication dates in this essay, the three stories were first published in the early 1980s. "Fusehime" first appeared in the literary journal *Gunzō* ("Collective Voices") in 1983; "Maboroshi" in *Sakuhin* ("Work") in 1980; and "Danmari-ichi" in 1982 in *Umi* ("The Sea").
5. See Fuse 2005 for a complete chronology of Tsushima's life and works.
6. In addition, her literary prizes include the Izumi Kyōka Prize for *Kusa no fusedokoro* ("Bed of Grass") in 1977; the Women's Literary Prize for *Chōji* (trans. *Child of Fortune*, 1983) in 1978; the Noma Hiroshi Prize for New Writers for *Hikari no ryōbun* ("Domain of Light") in 1979; the Yomiuri Prize for *Yoru no hikari ni owarete* ("Pursued by the Light of Night") in 1986; and the Osaragi Jirō Prize for *Warai ōkami* (trans. *Laughing Wolf*, 2011) in 2000. Such prizes indicate the sustained success of Tsushima's literary career.
7. This material here—and in the remainder of this paragraph—derives from personal notes taken during a lecture at Columbia University in 1992.
8. One of Tsushima's best known contemporaries is Nakagami Kenji (1946–1992), a writer from Shingū, Wakayama Prefecture. Nakagami belonged to the *buraku* or outcaste group, a class of people who were stigmatized for the supposedly unclean jobs they performed. Early in their respective careers, Tsushima and Nakagami met in the *Bungei Shuto* circle. Like Tsushima, Nakagami demonstrated an interest in marginalized cultural forms—those with roots in the oral forms of his community—as central ingredients of his fiction. Both writers also shared a belief in the power of literature to provide an alternate path to the growing materialism of Japan in the 1970s.
9. As Charlotte Eubanks (2013) illustrates in a convincing article, Tsushima recasts elements of the *setsuwa* and *fudoki* traditions in which encounters between humans (male) and non-human beings (female) enact the pacification of untamed places. According to Eubanks, Tsushima reverses this paradigm, placing her single mothers in the position of the untamed other. Through such retellings, Tsushima provides an antidote to the ways that a culture continually restages acts of sexual violence.

10. "Maboroshi" has not been translated into English. All translations that follow are my own.
11. The old house is not located in what is traditionally viewed as Shitamachi, the districts that are typically viewed as belonging to the working classes of Tokyo.
12. *Kōjien* 1983, s.v. "maboroshi."
13. Kawamura 1991 proposes that Tsushima had tales of a "ghost market" from Chinese fiction in mind.
14. The Yamanote Line is the circular train line that runs around the center of Tokyo.
15. http://tokyodeep.info/post_935/. See this site for the history of Shinmeichō.

WORKS CITED

Eubanks, Charlotte. 2013. "Envisioning the Invisible: Sex, Species and Anomaly in Contemporary Japanese Women's Fiction." *Marvels and Tales* 27: 205–17.
"Fuhō sakka no Tsushima Yūko-san shikyo 68-sai, Dazai Osamu no jijo" ("The Death of Writer Tsushima Yūko, Age 68, Second Daughter of Dazai Osamu"). 2016. *Mainichi Shinbun* (*Mainichi Newspaper*). 18 February.
Fuse Kaoru. 2005. "Tsushima Yūko nenpu ("Tsushima Yūko Chronology"). In *Gendai josei sakka dokuhon Tsushima Yūko* ("Critical Readers on Japanese Women Writers: Tsushima Yūko"), edited by Kawamura Minato, 151–57. Tokyo: Kanae Shobō.
Gordon, Andrew. 2009. *A Modern History of Japan: From Tokugawa Times to the Present*. New York: Oxford University Press.
Huyssen, Andreas. 2003. *Present Pasts: Urban Palimpsests and the Politics of Memory*. Stanford: Stanford University Press.
Jinnai, Hidenobu. 1995. *Tokyo: A Spatial Anthropology* (*Tōkyō no kūkan jinruigaku*, 1985). Translated by Kimiko Nishimura. Berkeley: University of California Press.
Kawamura Jirō. 1991. "Kaisetsu" ("Afterword"). In *Danmari-ichi* ("The Silent Traders" [1984]), by Tsushima Yūko, 218–24. Tokyo: Shinchōsha.
Kawamura Minato. 1993. "Hikari, oto, yume ("Light, Sound, Dream"). In *Hikari no ryōbun*. ("In the Domain of Light" [1979]), by Tsushima Yūko, 246–55. Tokyo: Kōdansha.
Kōjien, 3rd ed. 1983. Tōkyō: Iwanami Shoten.
Koyama Tetsurō. 1994. "Tsushima Yūko intabyū: haha to iu monogatari" ("Interview with Tsushima Yūko: The Fiction of 'Mother'"). *Bungakukai* ("Literary World") 49: 188–203.
Machimura, Takashi. 1993. "The Urban Restructuring Process in Tokyo in the 1980s: Transforming Tokyo into a World City." *International Journal of Urban and Regional Research* 16: 114–28.
Miura Masashi. 1988. "Shinriteki jijitsu ni tsuite" ("On Psychological Truth"). In *Hi no kawa no hotori de* ("On the Banks of the River of Fire" [1983]), by Tsushima Yūko, 439–49. Tokyo: Kōdansha.
Monnet, Livia. 1996. "*Connaisssance délicieuse*, or the Science of Jealousy: Tsushima Yūko's 'The Chrysanthemum Beetle.'" In *The Woman's Hand: Gender and Theory in Japanese Women's Writing*, edited by Paul Schalow and Janet Walker, 383–423. Stanford: Stanford University Press.
Nora, Pierre (under the direction of). 1996–1998 [1984–1992]. *Realms of Memory: Rethinking the French Past* (*Les Lieux de Mémoire*). Translated by Arthur Goldhammer. Edited by Lawrence D. Kritzman. 3 volumes. New York: Columbia University Press.
Sand, Jordan. 2013. *Tokyo Vernacular: Common Spaces, Local Histories, Found Objects*. Berkeley: University of California Press.
Suzuki, Tomi. 1996. *Narrating the Self: Fictions of Japanese Modernity*. Stanford: Stanford University Press.
Takahashi Isao. 1990. "Sabotāju no shisō" ("The Idea of Sabotage"). *Gunzō* ("Collective Voices") 45: 222–34.
Takizawa Bakin. 2002 [1814–1842]. "The Eight Dogs Chronicles" ("Nansō Satomi Hakkenden"). Translated by Chris Drake. In *Translations from the Asian Classics: Early Modern*

Japanese Literature: An Anthology, 1600–1900, edited by Haruo Shirane, 886–901. New York: Columbia University Press.

Tsushima Yūko. 1982. *Shōsetsu no naka no fūkei* ("The Landscape of Fiction"). Tokyo: Chūō Kōronsha.

———. 1983 [1978]. *Child of Fortune (Chōji)*. Translated by Geraldine Harcourt. New York: Kōdansha.

———. 1984a. "Fusehime" ("Princess Fuse"). In *Ōma monogatari* ("Creepy Tales"), 8–69. Tokyo: Kōdansha.

———. 1984b. "Maboroshi" ("Phantom"). In *Danmari-ichi* ("Silent Traders"), 41–61. Tokyo: Kōdansha.

———. 1984c. "Yokushitsu" ("The Bath"). In *Danmari-ichi* ("Silent Traders"), 198–217. Tokyo: Kōdansha.

———. 1988a [1984]. "Chrysanthemum Beetle" ("Kikumushi"). In *The Shooting Gallery and Other Stories*. Translated by Geraldine Harcourt, 45–79. New York: New Directions.

———. 1988b [1984]. "Silent Traders" ("Danmari-ichi"). In *The Shooting Gallery and Other Stories*. Translated by Geraldine Harcourt, 35–44. New York: New Directions.

———. 1989. *Hon no naka no shōjo-tachi* ("Girls in Books"). Tokyo: Chūō Kōronsha.

———. 1991 [1980]. *Woman Running in the Mountains (Yama o hashiru onna)*. Translated by Geraldine Harcourt. New York: Pantheon.

Waley, Paul. 2007. "Tokyo-as-World-City: Reassessing the Role of Capital and the State in Urban Restructuring." *Urban Studies* 44: 1465–90.

Yonaha Keiko. 1989. "Sakka annai Tsushima Yūko" ("Guide to the Author—Tsushima Yūko"). In *Ōma Monogatari* ("Creepy Tales," 1984), by Tsushima Yūko, 341–52. Tokyo: Kōdansha.

Index

Abe Kōbō, 138
Abe Shinzō, Prime Minister, 151
Adachi Ward, 145
Adriasola, Ignacio, 52, 58
Ainu song cycles, 165
Akaji Maro, 135n24
Akasaka, xii, 81, 91; Prince Hotel, 104
Akihabara, xii
Akihito, Crown Prince, 110
Akutagawa Ryūnosuke, xxin8, 28, 80, 155n36; Prize, xix, 28, 50, 153n7
Ankersmit, Frank, 77
Anpo (Treaty of Mutual Cooperation and Security between the United States and Japan), 87, 165
Aoyama, 82, 104; Avenue, 104–105, 114n13, 114n14
Arai Takako, 4, 22n3
Arakawa River, 55
Arakawa Ward, xvii, 117, 143, 145, 154n21
Araki Nobuyoshi, 75, 80, 89–90, 93n3
Arts Award, xix, 45, 65n3
Asagaya, xiv, 31, 35
Asakusa, xii, xvi–xvii, 72, 81–82, 91, 121, 130–133, 134n22, 135n23, 145; Kannon Temple, 134n22; Rokku, 143, 154n20
Asano Tadanobu, 117

Bakhtin, Mikhail, 71

Barthes, Roland, 46
Baudelaire, Charles, 78
Benjamin, Walter, 26, 74–75, 77–78
bubble era, ix–x, xv, 47, 50–51, 59, 62, 70, 81, 88, 160, 169; post-bubble era, ix, xiv–xv, 27, 47, 75, 79–81, 88
bullet train, 103, 114n9, 114n14
Bunkyō Ward, xix, xxin6, 100, 141, 153n13, 154n19, 154n23, 163
Burai-ha, 145–146, 152, 154n25
Byōbu-zaka, 7

Cannes Film Festival, xix, 133n6, 134n14
Chiyoda line, 145
Chiyoda Ward, xvii, 118, 141
chronotope, 71
Chūō-Sōbu line, 31, 35, 39
Chūō Ward, xvii, xxin6, 88, 118, 141
Cohen, Harold, 1, 5–6
Cole, Teju, 71
Cooper Marcus, Clare, 76
cosplay, xiv, 35, 38, 57
counterfactual scholarship, 97–98
counter-history, 108–110, 112
Crinson, Mark, viii

Daiba. *See* Odaiba
Dazai Osamu, 31, 87, 138, 154n25, 154n27, 163
Denzūin Temple, 143, 153n18, 154n19
documentary literature, 76–77

Dodd, Stephen, 47
Dore, Ronald P., xxin6

earthquake, 1923, viii–x, 33, 70, 80, 88, 90, 93n4, 146, 154n23
Eckersall, Peter, viii–ix
Edo, vii–ix, xii–xiii, 15–16, 46, 78–79, 84, 89–90, 92, 153n13, 153n16, 154n24, 161; Bay, 50; castle, xii; literature, 148; period, x, xii, 16, 78–79, 81, 84, 148, 155n37, 163, 170
Edogawa Ranpo, 88
Edogawa Ward, 100
Egawa Hidetatsu Tarōzaemon, 50
Enchi Fumiko, 138
environmental autobiography, 76
Etō Jun, 86
Eubanks, Charlotte, 176n9

Fantasia International Film Festival, xix, 26
Fedman, David, 48
firebombing, 1945, ix–x, xiii–xiv, xviii, 7, 48, 70, 82, 134n22, 141, 145–146
flâneur, 26, 78, 138
fudoki, 165, 176n9
Fujita Yoshinaga, xiv, xix–xx, 25, 27–29, 39
Fukagawa, 101
Fukuda Kazuya, xvi, xix–xx, 71, 78, 83–86
furusato, x, 47, 124–125

Gerow, Aaron, 131
geta-haki apartments, 104–105, 114n12
Ginza, xii, xv, xvii, 29, 57, 63, 81, 86, 114n11, 118, 120, 127–130, 132, 134n19, 145
Gokurakusui, 141, 153n13
Goldhammer, Arthur, 134n10
Gōruden Gai, 42

Hachiōji, 46
Hagiwara Sakutarō, xxin8, 2, 4; Prize, xix, 2
Hamamatsuchō, 58
Haneda, 100; Airport, 105
Hanzōmon line, 145
Harajuku, xii, xvi, 3, 81; "for grannies", 3

Harumi, xv, 57, 59; Island Triton Square, 91
Hattori Bushō, 79
Hayashi Fumiko, 80, 138
Hein, Carola, viii
Higashino Keigo, 153n7
Higuchi Ichiyō, 138, 152n4
Hijiya-Kirschnereit, Irmela, 54
hikikomori, 139, 153n6
Hino Keizō, xv, xix, 45–50, 53–58, 60, 63–65, 103
Hirabayashi Taiko, xxin8; Literature Prize, xix, 50
Hitoto Yō, 117, 119, 129–130, 133n5
Hongō, 100
Hon-komagome, xix, 162–163, 173
Hori Tatsuo, 154n20
Hotel New Otani, 103, 113n7
Hou Hsiao-Hsien, xvii, xix, 117–122, 124–130, 132, 133n4, 133n6, 133n8, 133n9, 134n13, 134n14
Hutcheon, Linda, 29
Huyssen, Andreas, 132, 162, 172
Hyakuta Naoki, 156n46

Ibuse Masuji, 31
Igarashi, Yoshikuni, 130
Igusa Hachiman Shrine, 29, 33–34, 38
Iidabashi Station, 145
Ikebukuro, xii, xiv, 34, 36–37; Station, 36
Imperial: Family, 57, 110; Household, 111; Japanese Army, 82; Palace, xiv, 26, 41, 46, 55, 110
Inarichō, xii
Inokashira: *dango*, 31; Park, xiv, 26, 30, 34, 40
I novel, 1, 54, 152, 160
Ishida Ira, 36
Ishihara Shintarō, Governor, 83
Ishikawa Jun, 138, 145–146, 154n25
Ishikawa Kōyō, 48
Ishizeki Zenjirō, xvi, xx, 71, 75, 83, 87–90, 92
Isoda Kōichi, 141
Itabashi Ward, 3
Itō Hiromi, xiii, xix, 1–6, 11–12, 15, 18–21, 22n1, 22n4
Iwanosaka, 3, 12, 16–18
Izu and Ogasawara island chains, xi

Index

Izumi Kyōka, xxin8, 80; Prize, xix, 176n6

Japan Railways, 6, 33, 36
Jiang Wenye, xvii, 118–122, 127–130, 133n2, 133n3
Jinbōchō, xvii, 118, 120, 125–126, 132
Jinnai Hidenobu, xiii, 25, 51, 90, 161–162, 168, 176
Jizō, xiii, 2–3, 6–21

Kadokawa Haruki, 86
Kajii Motojirō, 138, 155n36
Kakuta Mitsuyo, 139, 153n7
Kami-Chiba, 88
Kaminarimon, 134n22
Kanaseki Hisao, 5
Kanda, xiv, 7; River, 153n16
Kannon, 15–18, 134n22; "Washing Kannon", 15–16, 17
Karacas, Cary, 48
Kasai, 51
Kasumigaseki, 26, 33–35
Kataoka Yoshio, 85
Katsushika Ward, 88
Kawabata Yasunari, xxin8, 154n20; Prize, xix, 164
Kawamura Jirō, 165, 177n13
Kawamura Minato, 160
Keiō University, 28, 83
Kiarostami, Abbas, 133n4
Kichijōji, 26, 29–31, 33–34; Station, 30–31, 33
Kido Shuri, 4
Kikuchi Kan, 28
Kimura Shōhachi, 77, 80, 85
Kinema Junpō Award, 26
Kirino Natsuo, 31, 139
Kirishitansaka, 141, 153n13
Kishibojin, 120–125, 130, 132; Temple, 118, 121, 122, 125, 134n15
Kishibojin-mae Station, 121, 123
Kishida Ryūsei, 80
Kishimoto Kayoko, 131
Kitahara Hakushū, 80
Kitano Takeshi, xvii, xix, 121, 130–132, 134n14, 135n23
Kita Ward, 83, 88
Kobayashi Hideo, 87
Kobayashi Nenji, 124

Kobayashi Nobuhiko, xv–xvi, xx, 69, 71, 75, 77–83, 86, 93n3
Kobinata, 153n13
Kōda Aya, 138
Kōenji, xvii, 118, 120, 127–130, 132
Kōganji Temple, xiii–xiv, 2, 7, 9, 10, 14–19, 17
Koishikawa, 141–145, 153n13, 153n18, 154n19
Kōjimachi, 141
Komagome, 88
Komi Michio, 2
Kōrakuen, xiv, 39
Korean War, 147, 155n35
Kōtō Ward, 153n9, 154n23
Kritzman, Lawrence D., 134n11
Kubota Mantarō, 138
Kuhn, Annette, 46, 64
Kumamoto, 3, 5, 11–13, 18; University, 3, 5, 12
Kunikida Doppo, 31
Kyōbashi, 46, 153n14
Kyokutei Bakin, 148, 174

Lee Ping-Bing, Mark, 126
Levy, Hideo, 148
lieux/lieu de mémoire, viii, xvii, 64–65, 72, 117, 119–121, 124, 131, 133, 134n10, 134n11, 162, 170–171
lost decade, x, 50
Lucky Dragon incident, 52
Lu, Tonglin, 119, 130, 133n7

Machimura Takashi, 160, 169
Mackie, Vera, 54
Marunouchi, xii, 46; line, 145, 153n13
Maruzen, 148, 155n36
Matsumoto Ken'ichi, 124, 134n17
Meiji: period, xiv, 46–47, 61, 83, 138, 142, 149–150, 154n20, 155n29, 175; reforms, 79; Restoration, vii, xiii, 79, 81; University, 164
Meireki fire, 15–16
meisho, 83–84
memory studies, 64
Miki Satoshi, xiv, xix, 25–30, 39–40
milieux de mémoire, 120, 124, 134n12, 162
Minami Senju, 143
Minashita Kiriu, 4, 22n3

Minato Ward, xxin6, 60, 82, 113n6, 153n9
Minobe Ryōkichi, Governor, 52
Minowabashi Station, xvii, 117
Minumadai Shinsui Park, 145
Mishima Yukio, xxin8, 83; Prize, xix, 83
Mitaka, 26, 31, 163
Miura Masashi, 161
Miura Shion, 139, 153n7
Miura Tomokazu, 26
Miyabe Miyuki, 139
Miyamoto Yuriko, 138
Miyuki-zoku, 103, 114n11
Mizumura Minae, 148
Monnet, Livia, 161
Mori Ōgai, 82–83, 138
Mori Tower. *See* Roppongi Hills
Motohasunuma, 3
Mukōgaoka, 163, 169
Murakami Haruki, xxn2, 31, 47, 138, 140
Murakami Ryū, 138
Murasaki Shikibu, xxin8, 2; Prize, xix, 2
Musashino, 26, 31; Art University, 33
Museum of Maritime Science, 59
Mushakōji Saneatsu, 138
Myōgadani Station, 153n13

Nagai Kafū, 78, 84–85, 89, 118, 138, 154n19
Nagatachō, 26
nagaya, 88
Nakagami Kenji, 176n8
Nakajima Kyōko, xviii–xx, 137–143, 145, 147–152, 152n1, 153n17, 155n33, 155n35
nakamise, 134n22
Nakano, 37; Broadway, 35; Station, xiv, 35; Ward, xxin6
Nakasendō, 16
Nakasone Yasuhiro, Prime Minister, 160
Naoki Sanjūgo, xxin8; Prize, xix, 28, 98, 139–140, 153n7
National Diet, xi, 26
National Museum of Emerging Science and Innovation, 147
National Stadium, xvi, 98–100
Natsume Sōseki, 88–89, 118, 138, 154n19
NEET, 35
New Historicism, 110
Nezu, xii, 91, 145, 154n23

NHK (Nippon Hōsō Kyōkai), 104, 155n33
Nihonbashi, xvi, 46, 81, 86, 155n36; Bridge, 81
Nihon University, 33
nikutai bungaku, 146, 150, 152, 154n27
Nippon Budōkan Hall, 113n8
Nippori, 145; Station, 33
Nippori-Toneri Liner, 145
Nishi Ginza, 63
Nishikata, 100
Nishi Masahiko, 5, 12
Nishi Nippori, 143
Nishi Ogikubo, xiv, 29, 31, 34–36
Noguchi Fujio, 77
Noma Hiroshi, xxin8; Prize, xix, 176n6
Nora, Pierre, viii, 64–65, 72, 117, 119–120, 124, 134n10, 134n11, 134n12, 162, 169

Obon, 124–125, 134n16
Occupation, Allied, ix, 53, 146, 154n24
Ochanomizu, 153n16
Odagiri Joe, 26
Odaiba, xii, xviii, xxin7, 51, 59, 140, 145, 147–149, 153n9
Oda Sakunosuke, 154n25
Ōedo line, 145
Ōe Kenzaburō, 111, 114n18, 138
Ōi, 59, 101
Okawabata River City 21, 91
Okuda Hideo, ix, xvi–xvii, xix–xx, 98–99, 106–107, 112
Okuno Takeo, 50
Olympics: 1936 (Berlin), 127; 1940 (Tokyo, proposed), 57, 139; 1964 (Tokyo), viii–ix, xvi, 69–70, 81, 97, 99, 101, 103–105, 108, 112, 113n7, 113n8, 114n10, 114n11, 114n14; 2020 (Tokyo), ix, 99, 101, 113n1
omiyage, 125
Ōmori, 58
Omotesandō, xii, 29, 82
Ōoka Makoto, 49
Ōsaki Sayaka, 4, 22n3
Osaragi Jirō, xxin8; Prize, xix, 176n6
Ōta Ward, xvii, 118
Ōtemachi, 145
Ozu Yasujirō, 74, 118–122, 129, 133n4, 133n9

Pacific War, 81, 138
Palette Town, 147
Pamuk, Orhan, 71
Perry, Commodore Matthew, 50, 61

Radstone, Susannah, 64
Rainbow Bridge, 147
Ravel, Maurice, 33
Remarque, Erich Maria, 53–54
Ricoeur, Paul, 112
Rikkyō University, 36
Rikugien, 163, 170–171, 175
Robertson, Jennifer, 124, 134n17
roji, 73, 85–86
Roppongi, xii, xvi, 72, 81–82, 154n20; Hills, x
Rose, Carol, 168
Rosenbaum, Roman, 49
Rothenberg, Jerome, 5
Roudebush, Marc, 134n10
Russell, Catherine, 41–42
Ryōgoku Bridge, 8

Saitō Shigeta, 114n13
Sakaguchi Ango, xviii, 138, 145–146, 150, 154n25, 154n27, 155n30
sakariba, 84–86
Sakazaki Shigemori, 76
Sakuradamon, 27, 35, 41
Sanbanchō, 141–142
Sand, Jordan, 106, 108, 112, 128, 139, 162, 168
Sano Yō, 49
San'ya, xii, xvi
Sata Ineko, 77, 81, 138
Satō Hachirō, 77, 81
Satō Izumi, 54–55
Self-Defense Forces, 102, 156n48
Seibu: department store, 36; railway system, 36
Seidensticker, Edward, xii, 46, 102, 138, 141, 153n18
seikatsushi, 89
Seishindō, 126
Sekiguchi Yūsuke, 130
sekkyō-bushi, 6
Sendagi, xii, 88, 91, 145, 154n23
Sendak, Maurice, 126
Sensōji Temple, 131, 134n22, 154n20

Senzoku-ike Park, xvii, 118, 120, 127–130, 132
setsuwa, 165, 176n9
shamisen, 173
Shiba Park, 113n6
Shibaura, 60
Shibuya, xii, 46, 72, 86, 104–105, 122, 154n20, 155n33; Station, xii; Ward, xi–xii, 82
Shiga Naoya, 138
Shimazaki Tōson, 133n2
Shimokitazawa, 145
Shimo-Ochiai, 37
Shinagawa, 57–59, 101; Ward, xxin6, 153n9
Shinjuku, xii, xvi, 36, 42, 46, 55, 72, 81–82, 86, 122, 145, 154n20; Station, xii, xiv; Ward, xi–xii, xvii, xxin6, 81, 117, 141
Shinmeichō, 173, 177n15
Shiodome, 145
Shiomi, 51
shishōsetsu. *See* I novel
Shitamachi, xii–xiii, xvi–xviii, 2, 13, 18, 31, 41, 46, 72, 74–75, 82–83, 121, 131, 134n22, 138, 140–143, 145–146, 152n5, 153n16, 154n21, 168, 177n11; literature, 138; Museum, xiii
Shōchiku Company, Ltd., 118–119, 133n4, 133n8
Shōda Michiko, 110
Shōwa: Emperor, 54; period, vii, x, 99, 106, 112, 154n20
Siegel, Allan, 120
Sino-Japanese War (1937), 57
Skytree, x, xii, xxin3
Sōkeiji Temple, 153n13
Sugamo, xiv, 2–4, 6–7, 9–10, 12–16, 18–21; Jizō, 11, 13, 15, 18–19; Jizō Shopping Street, 6, 8; Station, 6
Suginami Ward, xiv, xvii, 118
Suidōbashi Station, xiv, 39
Sukiyabashi, 57
Sumida River, 8, 57–58, 63, 84, 90, 102, 131, 134n22, 153n16

Tabata, 83, 88
Taishō period, 31, 47, 138, 154n20

Taiwan, 38, 118–119, 121, 124–126, 129–130, 132, 133n5, 133n7; colonial occupation of, ix, xvii, 118–119, 129–130, 133n7; folk culture, 165; New Cinema movement, 119
Tajima Kayo, xxin6
Takabe Uichi, 75
Takadanobaba, 30, 37
Takayama Akira, viii
Takizawa Bakin. *See* Kyokutei Bakin
Tama, xi, 46
Tamagawa, 55, 163
Tamanoi, 84
Tamenaga Shunzui, 148
Tamura Taijirō, 154n27
Tamura Toshiko, 138, 152n4
Tanaka Chōtoku, 86
Tange Kenzō, xi, xxin7, 52–53, 90–91, 104, 147
Tanizaki Jun'ichirō, xxin8, 88, 93n4, 138; Prize, xix, 47, 164
Tatsumi, 51
Tayama Katai, xviii, xx, 76, 93n2, 137–138, 140–142, 146, 148–149, 152n2, 152n3, 153n10, 153n14, 153n17, 153n18
Terakado Seiken, 79
Tetsugakudō Park, 37
Tōbu: department store, 36; railway system, 36
Toden Arakawa line, xvii, 117, 121–123, 133n1
Tokugawa shoguns, vii, xii, 50
Tokugawa period. *See* Edo period
Tokyo: Bay, xiii, xv–xvi, xviii, xxin6, xxin7, 45–48, 50–53, 55–57, 63, 65, 90, 101; Disneyland, 147; Dome City Attractions, 39; elevated highways, xiii, xvii, 103–105, 113, 114n10; Megalopolis Region, xi; Metro (rapid transit system), 36; Metropolis, xi; Metropolitan Government, xi, 52, 59, 133n1; Metropolitan Police Department, xiv, 26, 32, 35; Metropolitan Theatre, 36; reclaimed land, xv, xviii, xxin6, 45, 47–48, 50–51, 57–61, 90–91, 101, 153n9; Station, xii; tourism, xii, 113n6, 133n1, 154n20; Tower, 58, 74, 102–103, 113n6;
University of Fisheries, 52; University of the Arts, 118; wards, xi–xiii, xxin6, 81, 102; World Trade Center Building, 58
Tomaru Shoten, 128, 134n20
Toshima Ward, xiv, xxin6, 2, 36, 88
Toyosu, 58
Tōzai line, 35, 145
Tsuchida Mitsufumi, 76
Tsukiji, xii, 101; market, xii, xv, 57
Tsukishima, xii, xv–xvi, 57, 59, 88–92, 101
Tsukudajima, xvi, 82, 90–91
Tsushima Yūko, xviii–xx, 139–140, 159–176, 176n5, 176n6, 176n8, 176n9, 177n13
Tuan, Yi-fu, 14, 21

Uchida Muneharu, 142, 153n16
Ueno, xii, xvi, 72, 75, 88; Park, xiv, 7; Station, xiii; Zoo, 39
University of Tokyo, xvi, 49, 100, 163
Ushigome, 141, 145

van Gennep, Arnold, 32
Venice Film Festival, xix, 119, 133n6, 134n14

Waley, Paul, x, xii–xiii, xx, 134n15
Waseda: Station, xvii, 117; University, 27
Wenders, Wim, 133n4
White, James, viii, x
Women's Literary Prize, 176n6

yakeato, 49, 53–54, 57, 65
Yamada Yōji, 139
Yamaguchi Hitomi, 50
Yamaguchi Koken, 79
Yamamoto Ichirō, 133n8
Yamamoto Kanae, 80
Yamanote, xii–xiii, xviii, 31, 46, 82, 138, 140–143, 149, 152n5; Avenue, xiii, 104; line, xiii, 6, 33, 46, 60, 145, 173, 177n14; literature, 138
Yamazaki Takashi, 74, 106
Yanaka, x, xii, 33, 42n3, 72, 82, 88, 91, 145, 154n23; Cemetery, 33–34; Ginza, 73
Yanesen, xii, 145, 154n23, 168

Yang Yi, 139
Yaraichō, 141–142
Yasuoka Shōtarō, 77
Yiu, Angela, 31
Yo Kimiko, 119, 124, 133n5
Yomiuri: newspaper, 50, 63; Prize, xix, 176n6
Yomota Inuhiko, 92
Yoneyama, Lisa, 64–65
Yonoha Keiko, 160
Yosano Akiko, 31
Yoshimi Shun'ya, 84, 111, 114n17
Yoshimoto Banana, 139
Yoshimoto Takaaki, xvi, 50, 87–90, 92

Yoshiyuki Kazuko, 131
Yoyogi, xvi, 104; National Gymnasium, 104; Park, 104
Yumenoshima, xv–xvi, 45, 51–53, 55, 60–61, 65n1, 99, 101–103, 106–107; Park, 51, 102
Yū Miri, 139
Yūrakuchō, 134n19; Station, 57
Yurikamome, 145
Yushima, 7

Zenpukuji Park, 33
Zhu Tianwen, 133n4
Zōshigaya Cemetery, 118, 122

About the Editors and Contributors

Barbara E. Thornbury is professor of Japanese studies in the Department of Asian and Middle Eastern Languages and Studies at Temple University. Her research and teaching interests include Tokyo in literature and film, Japan's performing arts, Japanese mystery and crime fiction, and cinematic adaptations of Japanese literature. Her recent publications include "Cultural References in the Novels of Fuminori Nakamura: A Case Study in Current Japanese-to-English Literary Translation Practices and Challenges," *Asia Pacific Translation and Intercultural Studies* (2017); "Tokyo, Gender, and Mobility: Tracking Fictional Characters on Real Monorails, Trains, Subways, and Trams," *Journal of Urban Cultural Studies* (2014); and *America's Japan and Japan's Performing Arts: Cultural Mobility and Exchange in New York, 1952–2011* (University of Michigan Press, 2013).

Evelyn Schulz is professor of Japanology in the Department of Asian Studies at Ludwig Maximilians University Munich, where she teaches modern Japanese literature and culture. She has published on the novelist Nagai Kafū, Tokyo/Edo discourses, images of the urban in Japanese literature and culture, and the revitalization of Tokyo's *roji* ("alleyway") areas and waterways from a cultural studies perspective. Recent books include *Urban Spaces in Japan: Cultural and Social Perspectives* (Routledge, 2012), co-edited with Christoph Brumann, and *Neue Konzepte japanischer Literatur? Nationalliteratur, literarischer Kanon und die Literaturtheorie* (*New Concepts of Japanese Literature? National Literature, the Literary Canon and Literary Theory*) (EB-Verlag, 2014), co-edited with Lisette Gebhardt. Most recently she has addressed cultural and literary exchange within a global context, and deceleration phenomena and discourses in modern Japanese society.

About the Editors and Contributors

* * *

Jeffrey Angles is professor of Japanese literature at Western Michigan University. He is the author of *Writing the Love of Boys* (University of Minnesota Press, 2011) and *These Things Here and Now: Poetic Responses to the March 11, 2011 Disasters* (Josai University, 2016). He is also the award-winning translator of dozens of Japan's most important modern authors and poets. His most recent translation is an annotated, critical edition of the modernist classic *The Book of the Dead* by Orikuchi Shinobu (University of Minnesota Press, 2017). Angles is also a poet. His collection of Japanese-language poetry *Watashi no hizukehenkōsen* (*My International Date Line*), published by Shichōsha in 2016, won the Yomiuri Prize for Literature.

Kristina Iwata-Weickgenannt is associate professor of Japanese modern literature at Nagoya University. Her Ph.D. research at Trier University, Germany, was on performative constructions of gender and ethnicity in the work of *zainichi* writer Yū Miri. She received the university's Best Dissertation Award and was awarded the European Association for Japanese Studies Book Prize in 2008. Before coming to Nagoya, Kristina spent six years as a senior research fellow at the German Institute for Japanese Studies (DIJ) in Tokyo, a city that she spent much time exploring on foot. She has widely published on *zainichi* minority literature, precarity culture, and cultural responses to Japan's 3.11 disaster. Her recent publications include *Visions of Precarity in Japanese Popular Culture and Literature* (Routledge, 2015), co-edited with Roman Rosenbaum, and *Fukushima and the Arts—Negotiating Nuclear Disaster* (Routledge, 2017), co-edited with Barbara Geilhorn.

Mark Pendleton is lecturer (assistant professor) in Japanese Studies in the School of East Asian Studies at the University of Sheffield, where he teaches East Asian history, memory studies, gender studies, and Japanese language. He has published widely on topics related to modern and contemporary Japan, including "Memory, Justice and Post-terror Futures," in *Historical Justice & Memory* (University of Wisconsin Press, 2015), edited by Klaus Neumann and Janna Thompson, and, with Deborah Dixon and Carina Fearnley, "Engaging Hashima: Memory Work, Site-Based Affects, and the Possibilities of Interruption," *GeoHumanities* (2016). He is also co-editor, with Jamie Coates, of a forthcoming special issue of the journal *Japan Forum* (2018) entitled "Thinking from the Yamanote: Space, Place and Mobility in Tokyo's Past and Present." The research for the chapter on Hino Keizō's novel *Yume no shima* in this volume was supported by the Arts and Humanities Research Council (UK), which funded a three-month fellowship at the

International Research Centre for Japanese Studies (Nichibunken) in Kyoto in 2015.

Bruce Suttmeier is associate professor of Japanese and interim dean of the College of Arts and Sciences at Lewis & Clark College. He has published on several postwar writers, including Kaikō Takeshi and Ōe Kenzaburō, as well as on travel writing in the 1960s and on war memory in the postwar period. His recent work includes "On the Road in Olympic-Era Tokyo," in *Cartographic Japan: A History in Maps* (University of Chicago Press, 2016), edited by Kären Wigen, Sugimoto Fumiko, and Cary Karacas. His current research examines Tokyo in its frenetic preparations for the 1964 Olympic Games. He hopes to expand this research to encompass Tokyo's current, newly frenetic, preparations for the 2020 Olympiad.

Angela Yiu is professor of Japanese literature in the Faculty of Liberal Arts at Sophia University. Areas of research include modern and contemporary Japanese literature, modernism, urban literature, Sino-Japanese comparative literature, war and postwar literature, and utopian studies. Recent edited volumes include *Three-Dimensional Reading: Stories of Time and Space in Modernist Japanese Literature, 1911–1932* (University of Hawai'i Press, 2013) and, with Kobayashi Sachio and Nagao Naoshige, *Sekai kara yomu Sōseki* Kokoro (*Reading Sōseki's* Kokoro *from a Global Perspective*) (Bensei Shuppan, 2016). Recent book chapters include "Mizumura Minae and Hideo Levy: National Literature and Beyond," in *Routledge Handbook of Japanese Literature* (Routledge, 2016), edited by Rachael Hutchinson and Leith Morton, and "Delivering Lu Xun to the Empire: The Afterlife of Lu Xun in the Works of Takeuchi Yoshimi, Dazai Osamu, and Inoue Hisashi," in *The Affect of Difference: Representation of Race in East Asian Empire* (University of Hawai'i Press, 2016), edited by Christopher Hanscom and Dennis Washburn.

Eve Zimmerman, associate professor of Japanese, is chair of the Department of East Asian Languages and Cultures at Wellesley College. Her main research focus is postwar Japanese literature and material culture, but she teaches a range of Japanese culture courses and a comparative literature course on East Asia. She is currently writing a book on the trope of the girl in postwar Japanese women's literature. Her publications include *Out of the Alleyway: Nakagami Kenji and the Poetics of Outcaste Fiction (*Harvard University Asia Center, 2007); "Ethnographic Architectural Photography: Futagawa Yukio and *Nihon no minka*," *Journal of Architecture* (2015), co-authored with Claire Zimmerman; and "Angels and Elephants: Historical Allegories in Ogawa Yōko's 2006 *Mīna no kōshin* ('Mena's Procession')," *U.S.-Japan Women's Journal* (2016).

CPSIA information can be obtained
at www.ICGtesting.com
Printed in the USA
BVOW06*0147061017
496362BV00006B/9/P